Mendelssohn Remembered

in the same series

TCHAIKOVSKY REMEMBERED
edited by David Brown

GERSHWIN REMEMBERED
edited by Edward Jablonski

PURCELL REMEMBERED
edited by Michael Burden

SATIE REMEMBERED
edited by Robert Orledge

BRUCKNER REMEMBERED
edited by Stephen Johnson

MENDELSSOHN REMEMBERED

ROGER NICHOLS

faber and faber

LONDON · BOSTON

This paperback edition first published in 1997
by Faber and Faber Limited
3 Queen Square London WCIN 3AU

Photoset by RefineCatch Limited, Bungay, Suffolk
Printed in England by Clays Ltd, St Ives plc

A CIP record for this book
is available from the British Library

ISBN 0-571-17861-8

2 4 6 8 10 9 7 5 3 1

CONTENTS

List of illustrations, vii
Introduction, ix
Acknowledgements, xi
Chronology, xiii

    I   Early years; Goethe; *St Matthew Passion*, 1

   II   Family perspectives and marriage, 23

  III   As conductor, 59

  IV   As teacher, 69

   V   As performer and improviser, 79

  VI   Musical tastes and attitudes – and struggles with opera, 97

 VII   In Britain, 1829–1844, 121

VIII   The Schumanns, 155

  IX   Berlioz and other composers, 169

   X   Manners, appearance, character, 183

  XI   *St Paul* and *Elijah*, 221

 XII   Last years, 235

Index, 255

ILLUSTRATIONS

1 Mendelssohn's mother, Lea. Sketch by Wilhelm Hensel, 1823. *Staatsbibliothek Preussischer Kulturbesitz, Mendelssohn Archives, Berlin.*

2 Mendelssohn's father, Abraham. Sketch by Wilhelm Hensel, 1823. *Staatsbibliothek Preussischer Kulturbesitz, Mendelssohn Archives, Berlin.*

3 Mendelssohn at thirteen. Sketch by Wilhelm Hensel, c. 1822. *Staatsbibliothek Preussischer Kulturbesitz, Mendelssohn Archives, Berlin.*

4 Fanny Mendelssohn Bartholdy. Sketch by Wilhelm Hensel, 1829. *Staatsbibliothek Preussischer Kulturbesitz, Mendelssohn Archives, Berlin.*

5 First page of Mendelssohn's autograph of a fugue in E flat, c. 1826. *The Bodleian Library, Oxford, M. Deneke Mendelssohn Collection, c. 8, fol. 19r.*

6 Residence of the Moscheles family, 3 Chester Place, drawn by Mendelssohn, 1835. *Staatsbibliothek Preussischer Kulturbesitz, Mendelssohn Archives, Berlin.*

7 Portrait of Mendelssohn by Joseph Schmeller, 1830. *Photo AKG London.*

8 Oak tree at Interlaken drawn by Mendelssohn, 1842. *Staatsbibliothek Preussischer Kulturbesitz, Mendelssohn Archives, Berlin.*

9 Portrait of Cecile Jeanrenaud by Eduard Magnus; Mendelssohn married her in 1837. *Staatsbibliothek Preussischer Kulturbesitz, Mendelssohn Archives, Berlin.*

10 Ignaz Moscheles. *Lebrecht Collection.*

11 Karl Klingemann. Sketch by Wilhelm Hensel. *Staatsbibliothek Preussischer Kulturbesitz, Mendelssohn Archives, Berlin.*

12 Eduard Devrient.

13 A *Punch* cartoon of an 1845 London performance of Sophocles's *Antigone* with choruses by Mendelssohn. 'The

choir leader,' he wrote, 'with his tartan trews showing, is a masterpiece.'

14   Leipzig Gewandhaus Orchestra, with first violins Ferdinand David, Klengel and Joachim, rehearsing presto passage in Beethoven's *Leonora Overture no. 3*. After sketches by violoncellist Riemers, *c.* 1850. *Lebrecht Collection*.

15   Portrait of Mendelssohn by Eduard Magnus, 1845/6. *Photo AKG London*.

INTRODUCTION

The fact that Felix Mendelssohn was a boy genius already offered opportunity enough to later hagiographers; that he should also have died young was more than they could reasonably resist. As early as 1858, only eleven years after his death, his friend and pupil William Sterndale Bennett was pleading for a biography of him that told the unvarnished facts, and it is fair to say that much of what was written about him and his music in the latter part of the nineteenth century did his cause more harm than good. Even intelligent critics such as Friedrich Niecks felt that 'the serene beauty of Mendelssohn's music has to most of us not the same charm as the rugged energy, the subtle thoughtfulness and morbid world-weariness of other composers'. Myself, not only do I find Mendelssohn's music as subtly thoughtful as any ever written, but as a late twentieth-century music lover I confess to feeling at times rather ground down by the 'rugged energy' and 'morbid world-weariness' of much so-called serious music written over the last hundred years or so. It seems to me that Niecks's comment tells us more about Niecks than about Mendelssohn and that, like many other critics, he quite failed to appreciate the profundity without pomposity that marks Mendelssohn at his best.

The present volume tries specifically to describe Mendelssohn the man rather than the composer. Such divisions are always hazardous, but in this case I freely confess to problems in compartmentalizing Mendelssohn in any way whatever. If the testimonies of his contemporaries (Wagner always excepted) concur upon one thing, it is that Mendelssohn was an indivisible entity: talk of his personal charm led naturally to descriptions of his beautiful manuscript, the economy and decisiveness of his conducting, the finish and expressivity of his piano playing and so forth. For this reason, although I have divided the book into twelve sections, there is a certain amount of material which has claims to be included in two or even more of them. Uncredited translations are my own.

Hagiography aside, there was far more material available than

could possibly be included in a single volume of this series. But I
hope to have presented enough evidence of Mendelssohn's extraordinary standing among his contemporaries (and, dare I say, of his
existence on a plane some way below sainthood) to encourage new
interest in him on the 150th anniversary of his death, and to
strengthen those who already love his music in the courage of their
convictions.

ACKNOWLEDGEMENTS

I am grateful to the Registrar of The Royal Archives at Windsor Castle and to her staff for providing me with transcripts of hitherto unpublished excerpts from Queen Victoria's *Journal*; also to Roger Judd for his help in this matter. These excerpts are published here by the gracious permission of Her Majesty The Queen.

I also owe a debt of gratitude to two leading authorities on Mendelssohn: to Dr Peter Ward Jones, Music Librarian of the Bodleian Library, Oxford, for his help in making available material for the book and for his patience in answering my questions, and to Professor R. Larry Todd, Professor and Chair of the Department of Music at Duke University, North Carolina, for finding time in his busy schedule to suggest material unknown to me, including the Reinecke memoir and the corrected text of Schumann's reminiscences; and to Dr Kevin Hilliard of St Peter's College, Oxford, for his expert assistance over the translations from German sources.

Roger Nichols
Kington, Herefordshire
October 1996

CHRONOLOGY

MENDELSSOHN'S LIFE AND WORKS
CONTEMPORARY FIGURES AND EVENTS

1805 *14 November* Fanny Cäcilie Mendelssohn born, Hamburg

1809 *3 February* Jakob Ludwig Felix Mendelssohn born, Hamburg

> Tennyson born
> Haydn dies
> First performances of *Fernand Cortez* (Spontini)

> 1810 Chopin, Nicolai, Schumann, S.S. Wesley born
> First performance of *Silvana* (Weber), *La cambiale di matrimonio* (Rossini)

> 1811 Hiller, Liszt, Ambroise Thomas born
> First performances of *Abu Hassan* (Weber)

1812 Family move to Berlin

> Browning, Dickens, Flotow, Thalberg born
> Dussek dies
> First performances of *L'inganno felice*, *La scala di seta* (Rossini)

> 1813 Alkan, Dargomizhsky, Verdi, Wagner born
> Grétry dies
> First performances of *Il signor Bruschino*, *Tancredi*, *L'italiana in Algeri* (Rossini), *Les abencérages* (Cherubini)

> 1814 Henselt born
> First performances of *Il turco in Italia* (Rossini)

> 1815 Bismarck, Heller, Trollope born
> First performances of *Elisabetta regina d'Inghilterra* (Rossini)
> Battle of Waterloo

1816 Felix's first visit to Paris

> Sterndale Bennett, Charlotte Brontë born
> Paisiello dies
> First performances of *Il barbiere di Siviglia*, *Otello* (Rossini), *Faust* (Spohr)

1817 First lessons with Carl Zelter

> Gade born

Méhul dies
First performances of *La cenerentola*, *La gazza ladra* (Rossini)

1818   *28 October* First public appearance

Emily Brontë, Gounod, Karl Marx, Turgenev born
First performances of *Mosè in Egitto* (Rossini)
Die Welt als Wille und Vorstellung (Schopenhauer)

1819   Albert of Saxe-Coburg-Gothe, Charles Hallé, Offenbach,
Clara Schumann, Queen Victoria born
First performances of *La donna del lago* (Rossini)
Atlantic first crossed by a steamship

1820   *September Die Soldatenliebschaft*
Piano Sonata in G minor

Engels, Jenny Lind, Vieuxtemps born
First performances of *Die Zwillingsbrüder* (Schubert)
George III is succeeded by George IV

1821   *November* First visit to Goethe in Weimar
Piano Quartet in C minor

Baudelaire, Dostoievsky, Flaubert, Pauline Viardot born
Napoleon dies
First performances of *Preciosa*, *Der Freischütz* (Weber)
Philosophie des Rechts (Hegel)

1822   The family visit Switzerland
Concerto in A minor for piano and strings

Franck, Raff born
Shelley dies

1823   His grandmother gives him a score of the *St Matthew
Passion* as a Christmas present
Piano Quartet in F minor; Concerto in D minor for violin
and strings; Concerto in D minor for piano, violin and
strings; Concerto in E for two pianos and orchestra

Lalo, Renan born
First performances of *Semiramide* (Rossini), *Jessonda* (Spohr),
Euryanthe (Weber)
Diabelli asks fifty-one composers for variations on his waltz
theme
The Monroe doctrine

1824   First lessons from Moscheles
First Symphony in C minor; Concerto in A flat for two
pianos and orchestra

Bruckner, Cornelius, Puvis de Chavannes, Smetana born
Byron, Louis XVIII die
First performances of *Il crociato in Egitto* (Meyerbeer)

1825   *March–April* Second visit to Paris. Meets Cherubini,
Halévy, Hummel, Kalkbrenner, Meyerbeer, Rossini
20 May Second visit to Goethe; dedicates B minor Piano
Quartet to him
2 November Trumpet Overture performed
Piano Sonata in E, op. 6; String Octet; opera, *Die Hochzeit
des Camacho*

Hanslick, Johann Strauss II born
First performances of *Il viaggio a Reims* (Rossini), *La dame
blanche* (Boieldieu)

1826   String Quintet in A; *A Midsummer Night's Dream* overture

Moreau born
Weber dies
First performances of *Oberon* (Weber)

1827   *20 February A Midsummer Night's Dream* overture first
performed, Szcecin
29 April Die Hochzeit des Camacho premiered, Berlin
Municipal Theatre, with scant success
October Enters Friedrich Wilhelm University, where he
attends Hegel's course on aesthetics
Friendships with Karl Klingemann, A.B. Marx, Eduard
Devrient and Ferdinand David
String Quartet in A minor; Piano Sonata in B flat

Beethoven, Blake die
First performances of *Il pirata* (Bellini)
Cromwell (Hugo)
Treaty of London lays foundations of Greek independence

1828   *February* Cantata for 300th anniversary of the death of
Dürer performed
During latter part of year, studies *St Matthew Passion*

Taine, Tolstoy born
Schubert dies
First performances of *La muette de Portici* (Auber), *Der Vampyr*
(Marschner), *Le comte Ory* (Rossini)

1829   *11 and 21 March* Conducts *St Matthew Passion*

April First visit to England
25 *May* Conducts First Symphony
July Goes on to Scotland with Klingemann
August On his own to Wales, to Mr Taylor, for whose
daughters he writes *Fantaisies* op. 16
String Quartet in E flat; operetta, *Die Heimkehr aus der
Fremde*
Sketches for *Hebrides* overture

> Anton Rubinstein born
> Gossec, Friedrich von Schlegel die
> First performances of *Guillaume Tell* (Rossini)
> Chopin gives first public recital

1830   20 *May* Third visit to Goethe
6 *June* To Munich
September Vienna
9 *October* Venice
1 *November* Rome
Fifth Symphony in D (Reformation); first book of *Songs
without Words*
16 *December* First version of *Hebrides* overture

> Von Bülow, Goldmark born
> First performances of *Fra diavolo* (Auber), *I capuletti e i
> montecchi* (Bellini), *Anna Bolena* (Donizetti), *Symphonie
> fantastique* (Berlioz)
> *Hernani* (Hugo)
> The July Monarchy
> George IV is succeeded by William IV

1831   *March* Meets Berlioz in Rome
Travels through Switzerland back to Germany, reaching
Munich, (17 September), where he gives first performance of
G minor Piano Concerto
December Third visit to Paris
First Walpurgis Night
Scottish and Italian Symphonies begun

> Joachim born
> Hegel dies
> First performances of *La sonnambula* (Bellini), *Zampa* (Hérold),
> *Robert le diable* (Meyerbeer), *Norma* (Bellini)

1832   *January* Friendship with Chopin

April Second visit to England
14 May First performance of revised version of *Hebrides* overture
First volume of *Songs without Words*; *Capriccio brillant* for piano and orchestra

> Doré, Manet born
> Clementi, Goethe, Sir Walter Scott, Zelter die
> First performances of *L'elisir d'amore* (Donizetti), *Le pré aux clercs* (Hérold)
> Reform Act passed in Britain

1833 *January* Fails to be appointed director of the Berlin Singakademie in succession to Zelter
13 March Italian Symphony finished
16 March Appointed director of Lower Rhine Festival
April–May, June–August Third and fourth visits to England
25 September To Düsseldorf
Overture, *The Fair Melusine*
Revisions to *Calm Sea and Prosperous Voyage*

> Brahms, Burne-Jones born
> Hérold dies
> First performances of *Beatrice di Tenda* (Bellini), *Hans Heiling* (Marschner), *Ali Baba* (Cherubini), *Lucrezia Borgia* (Donizetti), *Rob Roy* overture (Berlioz)

1834 *8 March* Conducts *Messiah*
August Conducts *Dettingen Te Deum*
October Returns to Düsseldorf
Rondo brillant for piano and orchestra
St Paul begun

> Borodin, Ponchielli, Whistler born
> Boieldieu, Coleridge die
> First performances of *Harold in Italy* (Berlioz)
> *Le père Goriot* (Balzac)

1835 *July* Resigns from Lower Rhine Festival
August Takes up post as director of Leipzig Gewandhaus
3 October Meets Schumann
19 November Father dies suddenly
Further work on *St Paul*

> Saint-Saëns born
> Bellini dies

First performances of *I puritani* (Bellini), *La juive* (Halévy), *Lucia di Lammermoor* (Donizetti)

1836 *8 March* Receives honorary doctorate from Leipzig University
April Meets Wagner
22 May St Paul performed in Düsseldorf
Summer In Frankfurt meets Cécile Jeanrenaud; becomes engaged to her in September

> Balakirev born
> Maria Malibran dies
> First performances of *Les huguenots* (Meyerbeer), *Das Liebesverbot* (Wagner), *Le postillon de Longjumeau* (Adam), *A Life for the Tsar* (Glinka)

1837 *28 March* Marries Cécile Jeanrenaud
August Fifth visit to England
12 September First English performance of *St Paul*, London
19 October Gives first performance of D minor Piano Concerto, Leipzig
Psalm 42; String Quartet in E minor, op. 44/2
Preludes and Fugues, and second and third books of *Songs without Words* published
Begins to plan *Elijah*

> Guilmant born
> Field, Hummel, Leopardi, Pushkin, S. Wesley die
> First performances of *Roberto d'Evereux* (Donizetti), *Le domino noir* (Auber), *Zar und Zimmermann* (Lortzing), Requiem (Berlioz)
> William IV is succeeded by Queen Victoria

1838 *January* Suffers from headaches and temporary deafness
7 February First child, Karl Wolfgang Paul, born
June Conducts in Lower Rhine Festival, Cologne
String Quartets in D and E flat; Cello Sonata in B flat; Psalm 95
Violin Concerto begun

> Bizet, Bruch born
> Talleyrand dies
> First performances of *Benvenuto Cellini* (Berlioz)
> *Ruy Blas* (Hugo)

1839 *22 March* Conducts first performance of Schubert's C

major Symphony (newly discovered by Schumann), Leipzig
May Conducts in Lower Rhine Festival, Düsseldorf
September Conducts in Brunswick
12 October Second child, Marie, born
Ruy Blas overture; Psalm 114; Piano Trio in D minor
  Musorgsky, Rheinberger born
  First performances of *Oberto* (Verdi), *Roméo et Juliette*
  (Berlioz)
  'Fighting Temeraire' (Turner)
  La chartreuse de Parme (Stendhal)
  Invention of photography

1840 *April* First moves towards founding of Leipzig Conservatory
6 August Gives all-Bach organ recital; Thomaskirche, Leipzig
September Sixth visit to England
23 September Conducts *Hymn of Praise*, Birmingham
November King Frederick William IV of Prussia begins negotiations to bring M. to Berlin
  Redon, Tchaikovsky, Zola born
  Caspar Friedrich, Paganini die
  First performances of *La fille de régiment*, *La favorite*
  (Donizetti), *Un giorno di regno* (Verdi), *Grande symphonie funèbre et triomphale* (Berlioz)
  Frederick William IV ascends Prussian throne

1841 *18 January* Third child, Paul, born
31 March Conducts first performance of Schumann's First Symphony, Leipzig
4 April Conducts another performance of the *St Matthew Passion*, Leipzig
Is appointed director of the music section of the Academy of Arts in Berlin and moves there (May)
28 October Incidental music to Sophocles' *Antigone* performed, Potsdam
Fourth book of *Songs without Words* published
Variations sérieuses
  Chabrier, Dvořák born
  First performances of *La guitarrero*, *La reine de Chypre* (Halévy)

1842   *3 March* Conducts first performance of Scottish
Symphony, Leipzig
May Conducts in Lower Rhine Festival for the last time,
Düsseldorf
late May Seventh visit to England
13 June Conducts Scottish Symphony, London
20 June Received by Queen Victoria and Prince Albert at
Buckingham Palace
King Frederick William commissions music for Sophocles'
Oedipus at Colonus, Racine's *Athalie* and Shakespeare's *A
Midsummer Night's Dream*
November Returns to Leipzig and founds Conservatory
12 December Mother dies
> Mallarmé, Massenet, Sullivan born
> Cherubini dies
> First performances of *Nabucco* (Verdi), *Linda di Chamounix*
> (Donizetti), *Rienzi* (Wagner), *Ruslan and Ludmila* (Glinka), *Der
> Wildschütz* (Lortzing)

1843   *4 February* Berlioz conducts in Leipzig at M's invitation
3 April Leipzig Conservatory opens
4 May Fourth child, Felix, born
18 October Music for *A Midsummer Night's Dream*
performed, Potsdam
Psalm 2; Psalm 98; Cello Sonata in D
> Grieg born
> First performances of *Der fliegende Holländer* (Wagner), *Don
> Pasquale* (Donizetti), *I lombardi* (Verdi), *The Bohemian Girl*
> (Balfe)

1844   *May–June* Eighth visit to England
16 September Violin Concerto finished, Soden
December Leaves Berlin and settles in Frankfurt, in
doubtful health
Fifth book of *Songs without Words* finished
> Sarah Bernhardt, Nietzsche, Rimsky-Korsakov, Verlaine born
> First performances of *Ernani*, *I due Foscari* (Verdi), *Carnaval
> romain* overture (Berlioz)

1845   *13 March* Ferdinand David gives first performance of
Violin Concerto, Leipzig

September Returns to his post in Leipzig; teaches piano and composition at Leipzig Conservatory

19 September Fifth child, Lilli, born

String Quintet in B flat; Piano Trio in C minor

Sixth and eighth books of *Songs without Words* finished

> Fauré, Widor born
> August von Schlegel dies
> First performances of *Giovanna d'Arco*, *Alzira* (Verdi), *Undine* (Lortzing), *Tannhäuser* (Wagner)

1846 *14 February* Conducts Wagner's *Tannhaüser* overture

August Ninth visit to England

26 August Conducts *Elijah*, Birmingham

5 November Conducts first performance of Schumann's Second Symphony, Leipzig

> First performances of *Attila* (Verdi), *La damnation de Faust* (Berlioz)
> *La cousine Bette* (Balzac)

1847 *April* Tenth and last visit to England; conducts *Elijah* six times in the month

14 May Sister Fanny dies

Summer Visits Switzerland

August Quartet in F minor finished

4 November Mendelssohn dies, Leipzig, leaving unfinished opera, *Loreley*, and oratorio, *Christus*

> Edison born
> First performances of *Macbeth*, *I masnadieri* (Verdi)
> *Martha* (Flotow), *Haydée* (Auber)

I

EARLY YEARS; GOETHE; *ST MATTHEW PASSION*

EDUARD DEVRIENT

(1801–1877)

German theatre historian, librettist and baritone. He
sang the part of Christus in Mendelssohn's performances
of the *St Matthew Passion* in 1829, but lost his voice
some years later through overwork. He was a noted
theatrical historian and reformer and was Director of
the Karlsruhe Court Theatre from 1852 to 1870.

He first met Mendelssohn in January 1822:

I had seen the boy occasionally, – his long brown curls had attracted
my notice as he trudged sturdily through the streets in his big shoes,
holding his father's hand. Of late years I had often noticed him,
when on my accustomed way to my betrothed, busily playing at
marbles or touchwood with other boys before the door of his
grandmother's house on the new Promenade. I had heard in musical
circles of the extraordinary talents of the boy, had seen him at the
Singakademie, at Zelter's Friday practices, and had met him at a
musical party, where he took his place amongst the grown-up
people, in his child's dress – a tight-fitting jacket, cut very low at the
neck, and over which the wide trousers were buttoned; into the
slanting pockets of these the little fellow liked to thrust his hands,
rocking his curly head from side to side, and shifting restlessly from
one foot to the other. With half-closed eyelids, beneath which
flashed his bright brown eyes, he would almost defiantly, and with a
slight lisp, jerk out his answers to the inquisitive and searching
questions that people usually address to young prodigies. His technical command of the pianoforte, and musicianly way of playing,
struck me then as surprising, but still inferior to that of his elder
sister Fanny, and compositions, even little operas of the child, were
talked of.

Considering the wealth ascribed to Felix's father, the house gave
an impression of studied plainness: the walls and furniture were of
extreme simplicity, but the drawing-room was decorated with
engravings of the Loggie of Raphael. The singers sat round the large
dining-table, and close to the grand piano, raised on a high cushion,

sat Felix, grave and unembarrassed, leading and directing us with an ardour as if it had been a game he was playing with his comrades.

That so many grown people should be troubling themselves about compositions of his, seemed to impress him much less than that this was his second operetta, and that he was actually engaged upon a third. He was there for the sole purpose of hearing and performing the music, and he took for granted that it was the same with us. It struck us the very first evening how weak selfconsciousness and vanity were in his nature, in comparison with emulation, and the determination of thoroughly mastering whatever he undertook. When the little work had been tried through, his first thought was carefully to collect the parts and place them in order; this he did before he would take any notice of our admiring comments on the work. These he received pleasantly enough, but preferred to lead off the conversation to questions or explanations on the details of performance.

The mother, a highly-cultivated and intelligent woman as well as an active housewife, ever occupied either in reading or some domestic duty, kept the children to their work with inflexible energy. The unceasing activity of Felix, which became a necessity of life with him, is no doubt to be ascribed to early habit. He must have often wearied of his tasks at the mother's feet, by Rebecka's little table. If I called in the forenoon upon the mother, and he came with his lunch into the front room, during which he was allowed to quit his work, and we happened to chat longer than the bread-and-butter rendered necessary, the mother's curt exclamation, 'Felix, are you doing nothing?' quickly drove him away into the back room.

But it was easy to perceive that the most important influence upon the son's development was the father. Abraham Mendelssohn was a remarkable man, in whose mental and spiritual being life was reflected with singular clearness. His thoughts and feelings led him to find the highest satisfactions in the intellect. This was natural in the Jewish-born son of the philosopher Moses Mendelssohn, but to me, then in the age of religious effervescence, this did not become clear till later in life, and by degrees; his sound and certain judgment, however, impressed me even then. The conviction that our life is given us for work, for usefulness, and constant striving – this conviction Felix inherited from his father.

> Towards the end of the summer of 1825, the Mendelssohn family moved into a larger house in the Leipziger Strasse in Berlin:

In the new house Felix entered upon his young manhood, with freshly awakened powers and inclinations. With his usual energy and ardour he now devoted himself to gymnastic exercises. The father had a small gymnasium fitted up for his sons in the large and beautiful garden of the house. Felix attained the greatest perfection in these exercises, and was able to keep them up for a long time. He took great pleasure, too, in his riding-lessons, and used to have much to tell about the horses, and of the jokes of the old royal riding-master, which I already knew. Swimming was practised during the ensuing summer with intense enjoyment. A small swimming society had been formed; Klingemann, who lived at the Hanoverian Embassy, which was in an upper story of the Mendelssohns' house, belonged to this society; he wrote the words of swimming-songs, to which Felix composed the music, and these the members tried to sing as they were swimming about.

Eduard Devrient: *Meine Erinnerungen an Felix Mendelssohn-Bartholdy* (Leipzig, 1869; Eng. tr. Natalia Macfarren, London, 1869), pp. 1–5, 8–9, 20–21 (with cuts)

SIR JULIUS BENEDICT
(1804–1885)

> Benedict was an English composer and conductor of German birth and a pupil of Hummel and Weber. From 1835 he lived in London and in 1848 conducted *Elijah* there, with Jenny Lind making her first oratorio appearance. He was knighted in 1871.

My first meeting with Felix took place under such peculiar circumstances, that I may, perhaps, be permitted to enter into some particulars about it.

It was in the beginning of May, 1821, when, walking in the

streets of Berlin with my master and friend, Carl Maria Von Weber, he directed my attention to a boy, apparently about eleven or twelve years old, who, on perceiving the author of Freischütz, ran towards him, giving him a most hearty and friendly greeting.

''Tis Felix Mendelssohn,' said Weber; introducing me at once to the prodigious child, of whose marvellous talent and execution I had already heard so much at Dresden. I shall never forget the impression of that day on beholding that beautiful youth, with his auburn hair clustering in ringlets round his shoulders, the look of his brilliant clear eyes, and the smile of innocence and candour on his lips. He would have it that we should go with him at once to his father's house; but as Weber had to attend a rehearsal, he took me by the hand, and made me run a race till we reached his home. Up he went briskly to the drawing-room, where, finding his mother, he exclaimed, 'Here is a pupil of Weber's, who knows a great deal of his music of the new opera. Pray, mamma, ask him to play it for us;' and so, with an irresistible impetuosity, he pushed me to the piano-forte, and made me remain there until I had exhausted all the store of my recollections. When I then begged of him to let me hear some of his own compositions, he refused, but played from MEMORY such of Bach's fugues or Cramer's exercises as I could name. At last we parted – not without a promise to meet again. On my very next visit I found him seated on a footstool, before a small table, writing with great earnestness some music. On my asking what he was about, he replied, gravely, 'I am finishing my new Quartet for piano and stringed instruments.'

I could not resist my own boyish curiosity to examine this com-position, and, looking over his shoulder, saw as beautiful a score as if it had been written by the most skilful copyist. It was his first Quartet in C minor, published afterwards as Opus 1.

But whilst I was lost in admiration and astonishment at behold-ing the work of a master written by the hand of a boy, all at once he sprang up from his seat, and, in his playful manner, ran to the pianoforte, performing note for note all the music from Freischütz, which three or four days previously he had heard me play, and asking, 'How do you like this chorus?' 'What do you think of this air?' 'Do you not admire this overture?' and so on. Then, forgetting quartets and Weber, down we went into the garden, he clearing high hedges with a leap, running, singing, or climbing up the trees like a squirrel – the very image of health and happiness.

Sir Julius Benedict: *A Sketch of the Life and Works of the Late Felix Mendelssohn-Bartholdy* (London, 1850), pp. 7–9

JULIUS SCHUBRING
(1806–1889)

Schubring came to Berlin in 1825 to study theology at the University. In 1832 Mendelssohn engaged his help in preparing the libretto of his first oratorio, *St Paul*; Schubring also collaborated on *Elijah*.

That the boy Felix should not go to school, but be taught, partly with his sisters and partly alone, was quite in keeping with his peculiarly reserved and gentle nature, and advanced him the more quickly, because it enabled him to enter more deeply into the subject taught, and developed uninterruptedly his character. On the other hand, however, I think I perceive in this fact the reason of his feeling easily offended and out of sorts, and of his never being altogether at home in general society. The softness of his disposition, never having been hardened, could not easily overcome disagreeable impressions. Perhaps this susceptibility might have been lessened had he, when young, gone through something of the rough training to be obtained among a number of schoolfellows.

Julius Schubring: 'Reminiscences of Felix Mendelssohn-Bartholdy', *Musical World*, 31 (12 and 19 May 1866); reprinted in *Mendelssohn and his World*, ed. R. Larry Todd (Princeton, 1991), p. 223

LEA MENDELSSOHN
(1777–1842)

Born Lea Salomon, she married Abraham Mendelssohn in December 1804. They made their home in Hamburg, moving to Berlin in 1812.

Letter to her sister-in-law, Henrietta Mendelssohn, Berlin, 1821
'Just fancy that the little wretch is to have the good luck of going to

Weimar with Zelter for a short time. He wants to show him to Goethe, and is to take him there next week after they have been to the exhibition of Schadow's picture of Luther at Wittenberg. You can imagine what it costs me to part from the dear child, even for a few weeks. But I consider it such an advantage for him to be introduced to Goethe; to live under the same roof with him, and enjoy the blessing of so great a man. I am also glad of this little journey as a change for him; for his impulsiveness sometimes makes him work harder than he ought to at his age.'

Lea Mendelssohn, quoted in Carl Mendelssohn-Bartholdy: *Goethe und Felix Mendelssohn-Bartholdy* (Leipzig, 1871; Eng. tr. M.E. von Glehn, London, 1872), pp. 4–5

RUDOLF VON BEYER

> Rudolf von Beyer, a very young pupil of Zelter's, tells in his memoirs of a rehearsal of Handel's *Athalia* at the Singakademie in which he was to play the viola solos together with the even younger Mendelssohn. 'You can rely on Felix,' the old virtuoso Casper had reassured him, 'he'll come to your aid if anything goes awry.'

Through the hall strode a large, broad-shouldered man with carelessly powdered hair. He gave a very dignified, rather unapproachable impression in his blue tail-coat with shiny buttons, dazzling white cravat and perfect flowery piqué waistcoat, which only half concealed a soberly pleated ruffle. With a somewhat shuffling gait and dispensing easy greetings right and left to the members of the Akadamie, he went to the fortepiano and struck a chord of A with his gout-twisted fingers: it was Karl Friedrich Zelter. All the instruments seemed to be in haste to get in tune.

A boy, as pretty as a picture, with a noble, unforgettable face, dark, flowing locks and the large, deep eyes of genius into which a benevolent Creator had laid the heaven of his grace, made his way nimbly towards his viola. All eyes turned to him. There was no posing, nothing of the 'boy prodigy' about him: the modesty of his behaviour only emphasized his radiant appearance. Even the solemn man at the keyboard allowed an expression of satisfaction to play over his features. And in his heart he must have felt pride in his pupil. The boy quickly picked up his instrument and in a moment was ready; the director gave the signal to begin and the wonderful overture sounded forth.

My bowing was uncertain. My eyes were glued to the note-heads, which soon began to dance. 'You there, on the viola, you must have more spirit,' Zelter shouted at me. The finely modelled, expressive mouth of my partner smiled, and he gave me an encouraging look.

Rudolf von Beyer, quoted in Hans Gerhard Weiss: *Felix Mendelssohn-Bartholdy: ein Lebensbild* . . . (Berlin, 1947), pp. 30–31

KARL AUGUST VARNHAGEN VON ENSE
(1785–1858)

In one middle-sized town, I can't remember which, there suddenly started up, for no good reason, a wild anti-Jewish clamour. With the wild yell of 'Hep, Hep!', individuals were assaulted and followed in the streets, their homes attacked and partly plundered, and abuse and violence of all kinds used on them. But no blood was shed – that was where the courage or the ill-nature of the malefactors ended. As fast as the rumour spread of this extreme behaviour, so did the behaviour itself, like a burning flame or an infectious Saint Vitus' dance. The violence was accompanied by a heedless mockery and pleasure in making mischief; one royal prince jovially shouted 'Hep, hep!' after the boy Felix Mendelssohn in the street. Not all of this was done with malicious intent, and some of those who shouted like that would, if necessary, have come to the Jews' assistance if things had gone any further.

Karl August Varnhagen von Ense: *Denkwürdigkeiten und vermischte Schriften*, (Leipzig, 1859), IX, pp. 614–15

CARL FRIEDRICH ZELTER
(1758–1832)

After training as a mason, he turned to music and became Director of the Berlin Singakademie in 1800. He also founded a training orchestra and the *Liedertafel*,

the prototype of the nineteenth-century male voice choir.
As well as Mendelssohn, Loewe and Meyerbeer were
among his pupils.

Letter to Goethe, Berlin, 11 March 1823
My Felix has entered upon his fifteenth year. He grows under my
very eyes. His wonderful pianoforte playing I may consider as quite
a thing apart. He might also become a great violin player. The second act of his fourth opera is finished. In everything he gains, and
even force and power are now hardly wanting; everything comes
from within him, and the external things of the day only affect him
externally. Imagine my joy, if we survive, to see the boy living in the
fulfilment of all that his childhood gives promise of!

Letter to Goethe, Berlin, 8 February 1824
Yesterday we gave a complete performance, with dialogue, of
Felix's fourth opera.* There are three acts and two ballets, filling up
about an hour and a half. The work met with a very favourable
reception. I cannot get over my astonishment at the enormous
strides which this boy of fifteen makes. Novelty, beauty, individual-
ity, originality, all alike are to be found in him, – genius, fluency,
repose, harmony, completeness, dramatic power, and the solidity of
an experienced hand. His instrumentation is interesting; not over-
powering or fatiguing, and yet not mere accompaniment. The musicians like playing his music, and yet it is not exactly easy. Now and
then a familiar idea comes and passes on again, not as if borrowed,
but, on the contrary, fit and proper for its place. Gaiety, spirit without flurry, tenderness, finish, love, passion, and innocence. – The
Overture is a singular thing. Imagine a painter flinging a dab of
colour on his canvas and then working it about with fingers and
brushes till at last a group emerges, and you look at it with fresh
wonder, and only see that it must be true because there it is. No
doubt I am talking like an old grandfather bent on spoiling his
grandchild. But I know what I say, and say nothing which I can't
prove. And my first proof is public approval, especially that of the
players and singers; because it is easy to discover whether their

---

* The fourth opera was 'Die beiden Neffen, oder Der Onkel aus Boston. Oper in 3
Acten' [*The Two Nephews*, or *The Uncle from Boston*] – still in manuscript.

fingers and throats are set in motion by coldness and ill-will, or love and pleasure. You must surely understand this. Just as a writer who speaks to the heart is sure to please, so is a composer who gives the player something which he can not only play and enjoy himself, but make others enjoy too. This speaks for itself. – I may hope that you will take my account of Felix's progress as grist to my own mill.

Letter to Goethe, Berlin, 6 November 1825
He takes his time by the ears, and has his own way with it. A few weeks ago he gave his excellent tutor Heyse a most pleasant birthday present – namely, Terence's 'Andria' translated entirely by himself in metre; and it seems that there are some very good lines in it, but I have not yet seen it. He plays the piano like fury, and isn't backward at stringed instruments; and with all that he is strong and healthy, and can swim against the stream like anything.

They have reviewed his quartetts and symphonies somewhat coldly in the musical paper, but it won't hurt him; for these reviewers are themselves but young fellows looking for the very hat they hold in their hands.

If one did not remember how Gluck and Mozart were criticised forty years ago, one might lose heart. Things that are completely above the heads of these gentlemen, they cut up as coolly as possible, and fancy they can judge the whole house by one brick. And what I especially give him credit for, is the way in which he works at everything as a whole and with his whole might; and finishes whatever he begins, let it turn out as it will; and he therefore seldom shows any special affection for the finished things. Of course one now and then finds a little heterogeneous material, but it gets carried away by the stream, and ordinary faults and weaknesses are rare.

Letter to Goethe, Berlin, 20 February 1827
My Felix has accepted an engagement at Stettin to perform his latest works there, and set off on the 16th. The dear boy attained his nineteenth year on the 3rd of this month, and his productions gain in ripeness and originality. His last opera, which occupies a whole evening, has been promised at the Theatre Royal for more than a

year, but has not yet managed to see the light; whereas all manner of French trash and rubbish gets put on the boards, and hardly survives a second representation. As we are young and able to stand against all the prejudices which embitter the best part of the lives of so many other people, it cannot do us much harm; but I do wish that with all his industry he may as quickly as possible grow out of this time of ours, for one has to be civil to it, whether one likes it or not; and in this I could still be of use to him, by making him lean more and more on himself.

> In the summer of 1827, Felix matriculated at the Berlin university, and attended the lectures of Gans, Ritter, Lichtenstein and Hegel.

Letter to Goethe, Berlin, summer 1827
Hegel is just giving a course of lectures on music; Felix writes them out thoroughly well, but, like a rogue, manages to introduce all Hegel's personal peculiarities in the most naïve manner.

Carl Friedrich Zelter, quoted in Carl Mendelssohn-Bartholdy: *Goethe und Felix Mendelssohn-Bartholdy* (Leipzig, 1871; Eng. tr. M.E. von Glehn, London, 1872), pp. 39–41, 56–9 (with cuts)

EDUARD DEVRIENT

Even the parents of Felix, who were nothing loth to see so important an event as the revival of the 'Passion' inaugurated by their son, felt doubtful as to the result. Marx hesitated, and the old ladies of the Academy shook their heads. Felix so utterly disbelieved that it could be done that he replied to my entreaties, and those of the still more zealous enthusiasts, Baur, Schubring, and Kugler, only with jest and irony. He offered to give a public performance on a rattle and penny-trumpet, described the different phases through which the undertaking would have to pass, in the most ludicrous way, and absurdly pictured the temerity it would be in him to attempt to move Berlin out of its time-honoured groove, without credentials and the insignia of office. So hopeless seemed the chance of reviving this wondrous work, after having lain buried for a century, even amongst its truest worshippers.

*

I could not let the matter rest. One evening in January, 1829, after
we had gone through the first part, Baur singing the 'Evangelist' and
Kugler the principal bass, and we had all gone home profoundly
impressed, a sleepless night brought me counsel as to how a performance might be brought about. I waited impatiently for the late
day to dawn; Theresa encouraged me, and so I set forth to see Felix.
He was still asleep. I was going away, when Paul suggested that it
was quite time to wake him; so we went up, and Paul commenced
the operation. I found, on this occasion, that Felix had not exaggerated what he told me about his death-like sleep. Paul took hold of
him under the arms and raised him, calling out, 'Wake, Felix, it is
eight o'clock.' He shook him, but it was some time before Felix said,
dreamily, 'Oh! leave off – I always said so – it is all nonsense——;'
but his brother continued to shake him and call out to him until he
knew that Felix was roused, when he let him fall back on the pillow.
At last Felix opened his eyes wide, and, perceiving me, said in his
usual pleasant way, 'Why, *Edeward*, where do you come from?' I
now told him that I had something to say to him. Paul took me to
Felix's little workroom, where, on the large white writing-table, his
breakfast was waiting, while his coffee stood on the stove.

When he came in I told him to make a good breakfast, and not to
interrupt me too often. With excellent humour and capital appetite
he went at it, and I now roundly told him that during the night I had
determined to have the 'Passion' publicly given, and that in the
course of the next few months, before his intended journey to
England.

He laughed. 'And who is going to conduct?'

'You.'

'The d—— I am!' My contribution is going to be——'

'Leave me alone with your penny trumpets! I am not jesting now,
and have thoroughly considered the matter.'

'Upon my word, you are growing solemn. Well, let us hear.'

My argument was, that having all of us the conviction that the
'Matthew Passion' was the grandest and most important of German
musical works, it was our duty to revive it to the world for general
edification. As Felix made no rejoinder to this, I was free to draw
the conclusion: 'No living man but you can conduct its performance, and on this account you are bound to do it.'

'If I were sure I could carry it through, I would!'

I now urged that in case he had any apprehensions about organizing the scheme by himself, both Zelter and the Singakademie owed me some return for my eight years' co-operation at all their concerts; this return I would now claim. Zelter should give the use of the room for the concert, and should lend his influence to persuade the society to sing in the choruses. Felix thought they would not refuse me. I went on to say that if he would not despise me for a partner, and share the responsibility with me – he being sole musical director – the credit of the whole transaction would be sure; and finally, that if we devoted the proceeds to some charitable object, all cavillers would be silenced. So I concluded my proposal, promising to take upon myself all the business cares, and to sing the part of Christ, he to conduct and revive the old buried treasure. Felix still looked thoughtful; he said: 'What pleases me about the affair is that we are to do this together; that is nice, but Zelter will never give us his countenance. He has not been able to bring about a performance of the 'Passion,' and therefore believes it cannot be done.'

I had more faith in Zelter's excellent sense and underlying kindness. The father was doubtful about Zelter's opposition, but we were of good cheer.

Thus prepared, we set out at once for Zelter's room, on the ground-floor of the Academy. At the very door Felix said to me: 'If he grows abusive, I shall go. I cannot squabble with him.'   'He is sure to be abusive,' said I, 'but I will take the squabbling in hand myself.'

We knocked. A loud, rough voice bid us come in. We found the old giant in a thick cloud of smoke, a long pipe in his mouth, sitting at his old instrument with double row of keys. The quill-pen he used in writing was in his hand, a sheet of music-paper before him; he wore drab-coloured knee-breeches, thick woollen stockings, and embroidered slippers. He raised his head, with its white hair combed back, his coarse, plebeian but manly features turned towards us, and recognizing us through his spectacles, he said kindly in his broad accent: 'Why, how is this? what do two such fine young fellows want with me at this early hour? Here, sit down.' He led us to a corner of the room, and sat down on a plain sofa; we took chairs.

Now I began my well-studied speech about our admiration of

Bach, whom we had first learnt to prize under his guidance, and further studied at Mendelssohn's; that we felt irresistibly impelled to make a trial of the work in public, and that we desired, by his leave, to ask the Academy to co-operate with us. 'Oh, yes,' he said, tardily, putting up his chin as he generally did when he was particularly emphatic, 'that is all very well, but now-a-days these things cannot be done quite so easily.'

He had become excited, rose, put aside his pipe, and began walking about the room.

At last the old gentleman broke out: 'That one should have the patience to listen to all this! I can tell you that very different people have had to give up doing this very thing, and do you think that a couple of young donkeys like you will be able to accomplish it?'

This rough sally he fired off with immense energy. I could scarcely help laughing. Zelter was in the habit of saying what he liked, and no one was offended: we were ready to put up with more than this for the sake of Bach, and our dear old master. I looked round at Felix, who was at the door holding the handle; he beckoned me to come away, and looked pale and hurt. I motioned to him that we must stay, and recommended my argument. I then pleaded that youth was the time to grapple with difficulties, and that it would reflect as much honour on him as on ourselves if two of his pupils could bring about this great result. My argument now began to take visible effect; the crisis was passed. He made yet some demurs, and speaking of the help we hoped to get from the Academy choir, said, 'You will have nothing but misery with them! To-day ten will come to rehearsal, and to-morrow twenty will stop away.' We laughed, and knew that we had gained our point. Felix explained how he intended to manage the rehearsals, at first in the small room, and place the orchestra under the leadership of Eduard Rietz. Zelter objected nothing more; at parting he said: 'Well, I will say a good word for you when the time comes. Good luck go with you; we shall see what will come of it all.' So we left our capital old bear with thankful and friendly feelings. 'We have won!' I cried, when we were in the hall. 'But listen,' replied Felix. 'Do you know that you are a regular rascal, an arch-jesuit?' 'Anything you like for the honour of Sebastian Bach!' and triumphantly I stepped out into the keen winter air.

*

It was now time to invite the solo-singers, and we settled to make the round together. Felix was child enough to insist on our being dressed exactly alike on the occasion. We wore blue coats, white waistcoats, black neckties, black trousers, and yellow chamois-leather gloves that were then fashionable.* In this 'Bach' uniform we started off gaily, after partaking of some of Felix's favourite chocolate provided by Theresa, to whom this was a solemn occasion. We were speaking of the strange chance that, just a hundred years after the work could have been last heard, it should now again see the light. 'And to think,' said Felix triumphantly, standing still in the middle of the Opern Platz, 'that it should be an actor and a Jew that gives back to the people the greatest of Christian works.'

Felix was quite carried away by his joyful mood; on other occasions he avoided all reference to his Jewish descent.

Eduard Devrient: *Meine Erinnerungen an Felix Mendelssohn-Bartholdy* (Leipzig, 1869; Eng. tr. Natalia Macfarren, London, 1869), pp. 46–61 (with cuts)

FANNY MENDELSSOHN
(1805–1847)

Fanny was the eldest of Abraham and Lea's four children. She married the artist Wilhelm Hensel in 1829. Her compositions are at last beginning to receive the credit they deserve.

Felix's performances of Bach's *St Matthew Passion*, put on partly to prove to his friend Julius Schubring that Bach was not merely mathematics, were almost certainly the first anywhere since the composer's death in 1750.

Letter to Karl Klingemann, Berlin, 22 March 1829
We are soon going to send you Felix. He has left himself a beautiful memorial here by two crowded representations of the 'Passion' for

---

* On this occasion I became aware under what strict control the young man of twenty yet stood. His pocket-money being run out, I lent him a thaler for the purchase of the gloves. His mother was displeased with me for this, saying, 'One ought not to assist young people in their extravagances.'

the benefit of the poor. What used to appear to us a dream, to be realised in far-off future times, has now become real: the 'Passion' has been given to the public, and is everybody's property.

Felix and Devrient had been talking for a long time of the possibility of a representation, but the plan had neither form nor shape until one evening at our house they settled the affair, and walked off the next morning in bran-new yellow kid gloves (very important in their eyes) to the managers of the academy. They very carefully minced the matter, and in all possible discreetness put the question whether they might be allowed the use of the concert-hall for a charitable purpose. In that case, and as the music they were going to perform was likely to be very successful, they offered to give a second performance for the benefit of the academy. This the gentlemen declined with thanks, and preferred to insist on a fixed payment of fifty thalers, leaving the profits to the disposal of the concert-givers. By-the-by, they are still ruminating over that reply of theirs! Zelter made no objections, and the rehearsals began on the Friday following. Felix went over the whole score, made a few judicious cuts, and only instrumented the recitative, 'And the veil of the temple was rent in twain.' Everything else was left untouched. The people were astonished, stared, admired; and when, after a few weeks, the rehearsals in the academy itself commenced, their faces became *very* long with surprise at the existence of such a work, about which they, the members of the Berlin Academy, knew nothing. After having got over their astonishment, they began to study with true, warm interest. The thing itself, the novelty and originality of the form, took hold of them, the subject was universally comprehensible and engaging, and Devrient sang the recitatives most beautifully. The genial spirit and enthusiasm evinced by all the singers during the very first rehearsals, and which each new rehearsal kindled to ever-increasing love and ardour; the delight and surprise created by each new element – the solos, the orchestra, Felix's splendid interpretation and his accompanying the first rehearsals at the piano from beginning to end *by heart*, all these were moments never to be forgotten. Zelter, who had lent his help at the first rehearsals, gradually retreated, and during the later rehearsals, as well as at the concerts, with praiseworthy resignation took his seat among the audience. And now the members of the academy

themselves spread such a favourable report about the music, and
such a general and vivid interest was created in all classes, that on
the very day after the first advertisement of the concert all the tickets
were taken, and during the latter days upwards of a thousand
people applied in vain. On Wednesday, March 10,* the first representation took place, and excepting a few slight mistakes of the solo-
singers it may be called a perfect success. We were the first in the
orchestra. As soon as the doors were opened, the people, who
already had been long waiting outside, rushed into the hall, which
was quite full in less than a quarter of an hour. I sat at the corner,
where I could see Felix very well, and had gathered the strongest
alto-voices around me. The choruses were sung with a fire, a striking power, and also with a touching delicacy and softness the like of
which I have never heard, except at the second concert, when they
surpassed themselves. The room was crowded, and had all the air of
a church: the deepest quiet and most solemn devotion pervaded the
whole, only now and then involuntary utterances of intense emotion were heard. What is so often erroneously maintained of such
like undertakings truly and fully applies to this one, that a peculiar
spirit and general higher interest pervaded the concert, that everybody did his duty to the best of his powers, and many did more.
Rietz, for instance, who with the help of his brother and brother-
in-law had undertaken to copy the parts of all the different instruments, refused all pay for himself and the other two. Most singers
declined accepting the tickets offered to them, or else paid for them;
so that for the first concert only six free tickets were issued (of
which Spontini had two), and for the second none at all. Even
before the first concert the many who had not been able to gain
admission raised a loud cry for a repetition, and the industrial
schools petitioned to subscribe; but by this time Spontini was on the
alert, and – with the greatest amiability – tried to prevent a second
performance. Felix and Devrient, however, took the straightest
course, and procured an order from the crown-prince, who from
the beginning had taken a lively interest in the enterprise, and so the
concert was repeated on Saturday, March 21, Bach's birthday: the
same crowd, and a still greater audience, for the ante-room and the

* It was really March 11.

small rehearsal-room behind the audience were added, and all tickets sold. The choruses were perhaps still more exquisite than the first time, the instruments splendid; only one sad mistake of Milder's, and a few slight shortcomings in the solos, put a damp on Felix's spirits – but on the whole I may say that better success could not be desired.

Fanny Mendelssohn, quoted in Sebastian Hensel: *The Mendelssohn Family 1729–1847* (London, 1881), I, pp. 169–73 (with cuts)

BARONIN JENNY VON GUSTEDT

It was in the summer of 1830 that Goethe's daughter Ottilie gave me the news, under a veil of secrecy: Mendelssohn is coming. When I met him for the first time – he going to Goethe's room, I coming from Ottilie's – there crept over me a feeling of mild disappointment: he looked frail, walked with rather a stoop, and his face made no great impression on me. The same afternoon I met him at the Countess Henckel's and felt I was looking at quite a different person: the liveliness of his facial expressions, his gracefulness, but which had nothing feminine about it, his radiant smile, as though someone had drawn a curtain from in front of a window and was now looking out into the loveliest of springs – all this made his appearance one to linger long in the memory. And then his playing, just like the man himself: no feeling that tended towards the bizarre, no disharmony that was not gently absorbed, no virtuoso displays to make us dizzy. Hummel seemed to me to play with more fire, with more external passion, but one did not feel, as one did with Mendelssohn, that his playing was so deeply heartfelt.

Right from the beginning of his stay, Mendelssohn spent most of his time in Goethe's house. He was indeed Goethe's David, because he removed every cloud from our poet's Jovian brow. When I saw Mendelssohn many years later in Berlin, it is true that the laughing, springlike gleam had disappeared from his face, but neither autumn nor winter storms had buffeted him nor wrought havoc with his happy fate. His playing had become richer, calmer, and the stormy Fantasies of his Weimar period were heard no longer. As he remembered those distant years, his eyes lit up and he said to me in tones of the deepest conviction: 'Who knows, without Weimar and without Goethe, what would have become of me!'

Baronin Jenny von Gustedt: 'Felix Mendelssohn-Bartholdy in Weimar', ed. Lily von Kretschman, *Deutsche Rundschau*, lxix (1891), pp. 306–8 (with cuts)

JOHANN WOLFGANG GOETHE
(1749–1832)

Germany's foremost poet and playwright. The following letter refers to Felix's last visit to him in Weimar.

Letter to Carl Friedrich Zelter, Weimar, May 1830
Just now, at half-past nine, with the clearest sky and the brightest sunshine, the excellent Felix, having spent a fortnight with us very pleasantly, and enchanted everybody by the perfection and charm of his art, is driving off with Ottilie, Ulrike, and the children, to Jena, there also to delight his friends, and leaves behind him a memory which deserves to be for ever cherished.

His coming did me a great deal of good, for my feelings about music are unchanged; I hear it with pleasure, interest and reflection; I love its history, for who can understand any subject without thoroughly initiating himself into its origin and progress? It is a great thing that Felix fully recognizes the value of going through its successive stages, and happily his memory is so good as to furnish him with any number of examples of all kinds.

Johann Wolfgang Goethe, quoted in Carl Mendelssohn-Bartholdy: *Goethe und Felix Mendelssohn-Bartholdy* (Leipzig, 1871; Eng. tr. M.E. von Glehn, London, 1872), pp. 77–8 (with cuts)

HENRY FOTHERGILL CHORLEY
(1808–1872)

He joined the staff of *The Athenaeum* in 1833. He was a friend of Browning, Dickens and Sydney Smith. Among his writings on music are *Music and Manners in France and Germany* (1841) and *Thirty Years' Musical Recollections* (1862).

The projected visit to England was duly accomplished in September, 1840; and Mendelssohn conducted the performance of his 'Lobgesang' at the Birmingham Festival. On his return to Leipzig in October, he was accompanied by Moscheles and Chorley.

On the road to Weimar, Mendelssohn recalled an amusing episode of his visit there many years before, as Goethe's guest. The Grand Duchess having expressed a wish to hear him play, an intimation was made to him that he had better call upon the Hof-Marschall; but standing on his dignity, and probably knowing something of that functionary's mode of treating musicians, he declined to do this, expressing at the same time his readiness to accept a formal invitation to the court. Such an invitation was at last sent to him, and he accompanied Madame von Goethe one Sunday evening to the Belvidere. On arriving, he was asked his name by the official in waiting, and on giving it, was separated from his companion, and led 'through a labyrinth of by-passages to a small waiting-room, where cloaks and such ignoble wrappings are deposited,' being directed to wait there until the Hof-Marschall came. After waiting alone for half an hour, the youth began to chafe. 'At last, provoked and indignant, he takes his crush-hat, and rushes out. The servants try to hinder him – he must not go; he will be called upon presently; every one will be very much displeased, and so forth; to which no answer, save that go he will, and go he does, across the fields, in full evening dress, straight to Goethe's house, leaving the formal court to stare and wonder for their pianoforte player; a circle having been convoked expressly to meet him.' Mendelssohn went on to say that this protest had the desired effect, and that the court officials were henceforth instructed to treat Hummel, who had been accustomed to similar indignities, with becoming respect.

Henry Fothergill Chorley: *Autobiography, Memoir and Letters* (London, 1873), I, pp. 322–3 (with cuts)

II

FAMILY PERSPECTIVES AND MARRIAGE

ABRAHAM MENDELSSOHN
(1776–1835)

Felix's father began his career in the Fould banking house in Paris. He moved to Hamburg on marrying Lea Salomon in 1804.

Letter to his daughter Fanny, 1820

M. Leo has played me Felix's last fugue, very imperfectly. He pronounces it very good and in the true style, but difficult. I liked it well; it is a great thing. I should not have expected him to set to work in such good earnest so soon, for such a fugue requires reflection and perseverance. What you wrote to me about your musical occupations with reference to and in comparison with Felix was both rightly thought and expressed. Music will perhaps become his profession, whilst for *you* it can and must only be an ornament, never the root of your being and doing. We may therefore pardon him some ambition and desire to be acknowledged in a pursuit which appears very important to him, because he feels a vocation for it, whilst it does you credit that you have always shown yourself good and sensible in these matters; and your very joy at the praise he earns proves that you might, in his place, have merited equal approval. Remain true to these sentiments and to this line of conduct; they are feminine, and only what is truly feminine is an ornament to your sex.

Abraham Mendelssohn, quoted in Sebastian Hensel: *The Mendelssohn Family 1729–1847* (London, 1881), I, p. 82

IGNAZ MOSCHELES
(1794–1870)

Czech pianist and composer who studied under Albrechtsberger and Salieri. He was piano professor at the Leipzig Conservatory from 1846 until his death.

Diary entry, 1824

This is a family the like of which I have never known. Both parents give one the impression of being people of the highest refinement. They are far from overrating their children's talents; in fact, they are anxious about Felix's future, and to know whether his gift will prove sufficient to lead to a noble and truly great career. Will he not, like so many other brilliant children, suddenly collapse? I asserted my conscientious conviction that Felix would ultimately become a great master, that I had not the slightest doubt of his genius; but again and again I had to insist on my opinion before they believed me. These two are not specimens of the genus prodigy-parents (Wunderkinds-Eltern), such as I must frequently endure.

Ignaz Moscheles, quoted in Charlotte Moscheles: *Aus Moscheles Leben* (Leipzig, 1872; Eng. tr. A.D. Coleridge, London, 1873), II, pp. 97–8 (with cuts)

ADOLF BERNHARD MARX
(1795–1866)

Marx was a composer, writer and theorist – apparently
of a 'solid but rather tendentious' variety.

I soon made the acquaintance of a well-ordered and wisely led family, and learned what incalculable advantages attend one's birth into one, especially when old reputation (Moses Mendelssohn!), wealth, and extended connections are thrown in. I, poor soul, was the product of need and perplexity! Fate had set me down, a naive boy, innocent of all knowledge, at the crossroads of a hundred life paths, and had called out, 'Go! Choose the one you like.' Here I encountered someone whose every step was discussed and watched over by a father's judicious eye. From time to time, even relatively late, Felix would complain to me that his father had once again become doubtful about his profession, dissatisfied with the career of an artist, whose successes must always remain uncertain; that again and again he would suggest to him that he should become a merchant, or enter some other secure career. I would smile and pacify him by pointing out how wisely his father was acting when he encouraged him to examine himself again and again.

Another of his father's comments was to echo strangely in my thoughts, until I recognized the deep life experience out of which it grew. Somewhat later, after the father had become convinced of my loyal devotion to Felix, he once spoke his mind to me, saying that he did not believe his son possessed the highest talent (he meant genius) for music; but that his life might be all the happier as a result.

No doubt he had seen and understood correctly, the discerning son of Moses Mendelssohn. And he was well qualified to speak on the subject of music; his entire life had prepared him for it. In his younger years, he lived in Paris for a time and was exposed to continuous productions of Gluck's operas, which at the time still enjoyed the high esteem of the French and were presented based on unbroken traditions handed down from Gluck's era. He also attended the première of Cherubini's *Der Wasserträger* and often talked about it with pleasure.

Next to the father stood the highly intelligent, perhaps less-feeling mother. In her the traditions or resonances of Kirnberger lived on; she had made the acquaintance of Sebastian Bach's music and in her home she perpetuated his tradition by continually play-ing the *Well-Tempered Clavier*. It is odd that the father's great pre-dilection for Gluck had little impact on his family. Gluck was respected by all, but not really beloved or kept constantly in mind. This honor was reserved for Mozart, Bach, and, to a much lesser extent, Handel. The daughters and Paul, the youngest son, with their similar convictions, drew the family close together in a finely drawn circle. The oldest daughter, Fanny, was closest to Felix and took the liveliest interest in his artistic studies. At the pianoforte, she lacked his skill and strength but not infrequently she surpassed him in tenderness and sensitivity of interpretation, especially of Beethoven. Several of her songs, specifically the duet and some other songs from *Suleika*, found their way into her brother's early published lieder under his name. Other works were published later, as is well known. The younger sister, Rebekka [*sic*], intellectually less remarkable than Fanny, was actually everyone's secret favorite – especially her brother's. The impression she made was like that of a half-veiled maiden; the less clearly she is seen, the richer and ten-derer one imagines her charms to be.

Paul was still very young, and held himself modestly aloof. When

Felix played, which was almost always without sheet music, the youth with the passionate expression and short dark curls would occasionally steal up to his brother after it was over, tap him on the shoulder, and say softly: 'Felix! in the —th bar you played F; it should be F♯. . . .'

Quickness and cheerfulness became the keynotes of his character. This in itself was auspicious and at the same time augured future good fortune. It expressed itself in a peculiar musical trait of his. When he performed one of his compositions for the second or third time, one could observe that with each successive performance he speeded up the tempo – often significantly. Given his extraordinary skill one could not claim that he played slower the first times because of a lack of technique. Fanny was often in despair at this increase in the tempo, which was not always appropriate; but it was the expression of a growing excitement and impatience.

Much more dubious, if equally understandable, was the influence exercised by his pleasure-laden environment and the constant company of his sisters' young female friends. Felix, the clever Klingemann, and I founded a garden newspaper in the expansive park surrounding the house. The capital for this undertaking consisted of a wooden table with a drawer, which stood day and night in one of the long shadowy arbors; whoever had something to contribute would steal over to it. Drawings, tender poems, witty letters, everything imaginable found its way there, to the pleasure of all and sundry, to reveal its clandestine meaning to the lovely maiden who was the object of special veneration. More than once I climbed with Felix – not without danger – onto the roof of an outbuilding, in order to slip delicious peaches or swelling grapes onto the night table of a young lady with a Polish name.

Another characteristic, also a necessary product of those happy circumstances, aroused an eerie feeling in my soul even before I understood its broader implications. It was expressed in a single word, but words express – or betray – events occurring in the soul that are meant to be revealed or sometimes hidden from others, even from the speaker himself. 'That gives me no pleasure!' That was often what I heard when the conversation turned to this or that in music, painting, and so on; and in fact it resounded most often at those very moments in which the most profound and solemn things, the greatest powers of the spirit were being expressed. I remember hearing the devastating expression applied to Dante, Michelangelo, even to Beethoven's compositions – and indeed his profoundest, namely, the Ninth Symphony. And strange! As much as I admired and loved his playing, his interpretation of Beethoven was seldom able to satisfy me. We had words over it on several occasions, specifically over the great B♭ major sonata. But we got nowhere. I was not a strong enough performer, and furthermore I had not achieved sufficiently complete clarity on the matter for the discussion to bear fruit . . .

Undisturbed by such considerations, our union grew so close and fast that scarcely a day passed when we did not exchange visits and notes. The content of the latter was unusual in that it consisted of certain expressions and references that only we understood, musical passages, and a crazy quilt of fantastic pictures; for Felix drew assiduously, especially landscapes, as I, too, practised drawing human figures. We soon discovered that the truly social art is not music, but drawing. For the former imperiously puts an end to all conversation in its vicinity, whereas drawing has the effect of making it even livelier, especially when two dear friends are sitting close together, and if their subject matter should wane, a glance at the work of the other or a request for assistance always offers new material.

But even verbal exchanges between the two of us, whose lives had grown together so closely, could easily take on strange forms, particularly when they turned to subjects like instrumentation that do not permit an exact designation. I can still remember the astonishment in Droysen's look, during a visit to my room, when he overheard me saying to Felix, 'Here pure purple would have to be used; the horns were dampening the splendor of the trumpets'; and Felix replied, 'No! No! That shouts too loud; I want violet.'

Adolf Bernhard Marx: *Erinnerungen aus meinem Leben* (Berlin, 1865), I, pp. 110–17, 131–44; Eng. tr. Susan Gillespie, as 'From the Memoirs of Adolf Bernhard Marx', *Mendelssohn and his World*, ed. R. Larry Todd (Princeton, 1991), pp. 206–13 (with cuts) (© 1991 by R. Larry Todd, reprinted by permission of Princeton University Press)

F. MAX MÜLLER
(1823–1900)

His father was the poet of Schubert's *Die schöne Müllerin* and *Winterreise*. Müller studied Sanskrit and comparative philology at the Universities of Leipzig and Berlin and prepared an edition of the *Rig Veda*, published by Oxford University Press in 1846.

Although Müller studied music in his youth, Mendelssohn advised him to 'stick to Greek and Latin'. Müller later confessed to not enjoying Wagner's music 'except now and then in one of his lucid intervals'.

When I was a student at Berlin, I was much in their house in the *Leipziger Strasse*, and heard many a private concert given in the large room looking out on the garden. Mendelssohn played almost every instrument in the orchestra, and had generally to play the instrument which he was supposed to play worst. When he played the pianoforte, he was handicapped by being made to play with his arms crossed.

F. Max Müller: *Auld Lang Syne* (New York, 1898), pp. 1–33; reprinted in *Mendelssohn and his World*, ed. R. Larry Todd (Princeton, 1991), p. 254

JACOB BARTHOLDY
(1774–1825)

He fought in the Austrian army against Napoleon and was appointed Consul General in Rome in 1815. He was a great patron of painters and scholars. Temperamentally the Mendelssohns considered that Felix took after him in a number of respects.

To his brother-in-law Abraham, Felix's father, c. 1825
I cannot agree that it is right that you should be giving Felix no positive guidance for the future. This would and could not be to the detriment of his aptitude for music, about which everyone is agreed. A professional musician is something I can't bring myself to accept. That is no career, no life, no goal. A musician is as well off

at the beginning as at the end and knows it; indeed, as a rule better off.

Let the boy study in an orderly manner, then finish a law degree at the University, and then make a career as a civil servant.

Jacob Bartholdy, quoted in Hans Gerhard Weiss: *Felix Mendelssohn-Bartholdy: ein Lebensbild* . . . (Berlin, 1947), p. 41

FANNY MENDELSSOHN

In 1822, the whole family made a tour of Switzerland and, on their way home, visited Goethe in Weimar.

The effects of the journey on Felix showed themselves immediately after our return. He had grown much taller and stronger, both features and expression had developed themselves incredibly, and the difference in his way of wearing his hair (the beautiful long curls had been cut off) contributed not a little to change his appearance. His lovely *child's face* had disappeared, and his figure already showed a manliness very becoming to him. He was changed, but no less handsome than before.

In April 1828, a festival was organized in Berlin to mark the 300th anniversary of the death of Albrecht Dürer. Fanny writes to Karl Klingemann, a family friend:

20 April
I could never have believed that we should have to thank the Dürer festival for so happy a day and such charming recollections. Felix in six weeks has written a grand cantata for chorus and full orchestra, with airs, recitatives, and all sorts of things.

The festival began with Felix's Trumpet-overture in C major. Then followed a speech by T., which lasted three quarters of an hour – an age! Hardly ever have I seen an audience more joyfully moved than when he spoke of Dürer's approaching death – a general murmur of applause was heard; and when at last it was really over, all started from their seats in frantic joy. Then followed the cantata, which lasted upwards of an hour and a quarter. The soli were sung by Mmes. Milder and Türrschmiedt, Stümer and

Devrient. Everything went off so successfully, and the reception was so genial, that I do not remember ever passing more agreeable hours. The solemnity was finished by three o'clock, and at four a dinner of about two hundred persons began, mostly artists, learned men, and high-place government officials: we went as guests of Schadow, who presided at the table. I cannot tell you how Felix was honoured and courted by people of distinction, known and unknown; but one thing I must add, that towards the end of the meal Zelter and Schadow took him by the hand, and the latter made a speech to him and solemnly proclaimed him an honorary member of the Artists' Association, of which he received the diploma. But what rejoices me most is that he himself is so pleased with this day, and shows himself more susceptible than hitherto of the honours he received. I assure you he is more excellent and more amiable from day to day; and this is not sisterly affection, but an impartial judgment. I beg you, however, to tell nobody, known or unknown to me, anything of this; for nobody, not even you, will think me impartial, and Felix would be angry if he knew that I have written so much about him.

Letter to Karl Klingemann, Berlin, 8 December 1828
Felix has given me three presents, a 'song without words' for my album (he has lately written several beautiful ones), another piece for the piano composed not long ago and already known to me, and a great work, a piece for four choruses, Antiphona et Respons-orium, about the words 'Hora est, jam nos de somno surgere,' etc. The academy is going to sing it. I will gladly fulfil your request and give you particulars of what Felix is doing, although that is less easy than it may appear. On the whole, I feel no doubt that with every new work he makes an advance in clearness and depth. His ideas take more and more a fixed direction, and he steadily advances towards the aim he has set himself, and of which he is clearly conscious. I know not how to define this aim, perhaps because an idea in art cannot altogether be well expressed in words – other-wise poetry would be the only art – perhaps also because I can only watch his progress with loving eyes, and not on the wings of thought lead the way and foresee his aim. He has full command over all his talents, and day by day enlarges his domain, ruling

like a general over all the means of development art can offer him.

Fanny Mendelssohn, quoted in Sebastian Hensel: *The Mendelssohn Family 1729–1847* (London, 1881), I, pp. 113, 156–8, 163 (with cuts)

EDUARD DEVRIENT

The political ferment which was to explode in Paris during the July following [1830] was much discussed. Hensel's super-loyal opinions often made Felix impatient. Once I heard him exclaim with unusual asperity to Hensel, 'You might show a little more regard for your radical brother-in-law!' Even his father's far-seeing views of Europe's political prospects at that time displeased him. 'It is terrible to see one's father such a conservative!' was the only fault-finding expression I ever heard him utter of his father.

Eduard Devrient: *Meine Erinnerungen an Felix Mendelssohn-Bartholdy* (Leipzig, 1869; Eng. tr. Natalia Macfarren, London, 1869), pp. 97–8

ADOLF BERNHARD MARX

When Mendelssohn declined the new professorship of music at the University of Berlin in 1830, it was given to Marx at his suggestion. Abraham Mendelssohn never liked Marx, and he and Felix quarrelled in the 1830s over early plans for *St Paul*. In July 1830, Felix passed through Munich on his way to Italy:

Letter to Fanny and Rebecka Mendelssohn, Munich, 21 July 1830
What we have done up to this date and are still doing is easily said: we are mylording it. I have deigned to accept the dignity of a viceroy. You may fancy, dear Rebecka, how this becomes me; I accept all homage with the grandest air possible. 'Dear Herr von Marx,' or 'Most honoured sir,' or 'Your honour,' etc – thus they address me on all sides. 'How inestimable,' etc. 'We will carry you on our hands,' 'What can we do for you?' 'If you would but consent to stay a little while.' For (and now you must leave off marvelling) the people here have caught at the idea that my own departure must be

the signal of Felix's. And as the Egyptian mothers and brides sacri-
ficed wine and lambs to the crocodiles, they want to burn incense to
me, that I may not rob them of their pet lamb. If mine were not a
noble nature, but a mercenary one, I might levy a contribution; in
short, I am irresistible, a parvenu! On my way home, however, I
shall not pass Munich, but travel incognito.

But seriously, you cannot have an idea of Felix's position here.
Not a hundredth part of it can come out through his letters, and my
description must, with the very best intentions, fall short of reality.
That they would appreciate his music – that we knew beforehand.
But now, he might make the most wretched music, and they would
all be enchanted. It is worth standing by and watching how he is the
darling in every house, the centre of every circle. From early in the
morning everything concentrates on him. Yesterday, for instance, I
had written as far as 'incognito,' and Felix was still asleep, when the
ambassador's *chasseur* brought a note from the most sweetly writing Betty in all my acquaintance: as Felix could not come to dinner,
would he kindly come at twelve, or some time in the afternoon, or
some time in the morning; at any time she would be very happy, etc.
Again the door opens, and in steps the *chasseur* of some Count
(Protzschy or Prutzschi, or something like that, or unlike that, but
certainly a very queer name), bringing a bouquet of carnations from
Fräulein So-and-so. Then enters Munich's most distinguished
pianoforte-teacher, begging to have a lesson – he has put off his own
lessons as long as Felix is here. Then best compliments from the
grateful Peppi Lang (oh, how much I shall have to tell you of her,
even though she is not yet sixteen!), and she ventures to beg his
pardon for offering him a keepsake (eight charming songs). Fräulein
Delphine Schauroth – of at least sixteen ancestors – having spent the
whole night over a song without words for Felix – nevertheless begs
and entreats him to come at ten, instead of half past, or, if possible,
even earlier still. To deliver this message Count Wittgenstein has to
walk a distance of half an hour. Not to mention Staatsrath Maures,
Kapellmeister Stanz, Moralt, and other dry visits and messages,
there comes an inquiry from Herr von Staudacher to the purpose
that although they had Herr von Mendelssohn's promise to come to
dinner, they begged to make quite sure of it, etc. A confidential note
of Bärmann's follows, notifying that the Staudachers have ordered

two puddings to please Felix. You will think this fragmentary list a sober joke, whereas it is merry earnest, and nothing but a fact.

Adolf Bernhard Marx, quoted in Sebastian Hensel: *The Mendelssohn Family 1729–1847* (London, 1881), I, pp. 260–62

LEA MENDELSSOHN

To Ferdinand David (postscript to letter from Rebecka),
26 January 1832
Felix must have acquired great improvising skill; in Munich he even allowed himself to be persuaded to do it in public, and the King provided themes for him. Felix himself must have shown the singers of the Papal chapel that it was possible to perform the Bach Passion, which until then they had doubted, after looking over the score. When he had solved a number of the problems they had set him to improvise on, they ganged up and devised the most absurd theme in order to trip him up, but he made light work of it.

Like all Germans, he found the state of music in Italy to be beneath contempt; but he was extraordinarily fascinated by the Easter festivals of the Church, together with the wonderful settings and the solemn services. We've also received some very pretty sketchbooks of drawings he's made on his travels.

Letter to Ferdinand David, 29 January 1836
If you have not yet heard Felix playing the Mozart concerto, my dear David, then you have a great pleasure in store. His reading of it is so clear and characteristic of him, I could say so childlike and naive, that one is taken completely by surprise. The cadenzas themselves, in which pianists usually try and exact vengeance on Mozart's patriarchal simplicity by loading it with bursts of cannonshot and fireworks, are inspirations of the moment, and yet at the same time small masterpieces of appropriate taste and analogous sentiment. One thing at least our Abderites* have learned from him, and that is to give public performances of Mozart's and

---

* A reference to Christoph Martin Wieland's widely read comic novel *Geschichte der Abderiten* (1780), a thinly veiled satire on the narrow-mindedness and provincialism of contemporary Germany [RN]

Beethoven's concertos. But so far no one has plucked up the courage to play an unaccompanied sonata, and in this at least they do show some self-knowledge.

Letter to Ferdinand David, 26 April 1836
Dear David, don't be cross with me if I bother you with another task. Namely, that I should like to have a really nice, ready-made waistcoat for Felix; it must be modest, after his fashion, and be suitable for hard labour at the music festival. If Dr Schlemmer is in Leipzig, as I hear, then he will be good enough, as a gentleman, a fashionable dandy and a 'young Frenchman' to choose something really good and fit for said occasion (the lining must not be too thick, otherwise our virtuoso will sweat his soul out. This warning is for Bloggs the tailor.) You and Dr Schlemmer will know how to reconcile the beautiful with the sturdy – what you Latinists refer to as *utile dulci*. Tell Felix also that he is to make sure to take some of his best new shirts and cambric handkerchiefs for the journey, so that his Mama should not have any trouble over his laundry.

Lea Mendelssohn, quoted in Julius Eckardt: *Ferdinand David und die Familie Mendelssohn-Bartholdy* (Leipzig, 1888), pp. 43, 75–7

ABRAHAM MENDELSSOHN

Abraham attended the Lower Rhine Festival at Düsseldorf in 1833, for which Felix had been engaged as conductor. The festival began on 26 May.

Letter to his wife, 22 May 1833
It would be impossible to give you an idea of the incredible kindness and truly antique hospitality these people show me *pour les beaux yeux de – mon fils*, and I cannot deny that I bless the happy coincidence of my meeting Woringen in the street and his recognising me, for I am extremely comfortable here. You shall hear about my travelling adventures and other experiences by-and-by; I must first write of Felix and the festival. When I arrived, he was engaged at rehearsal. Woringen ran at once to tell him that I had come, and quite triumphed at the news of my having taken my abode with

them, to which fact Felix would not at first give credit. After a while he came here, and why should I deny or conceal that he kissed my hand for joy? He looks very well; but, unless my eyes deceive me, this short time has again changed him a good deal: his face is more marked, all the features are more sharply delineated and prominent, the eyes, however, still the same, so that the whole has a very peculiar effect – I have never seen a face like his. Nor have I ever seen anybody so petted and courted as he is here; he himself cannot enough praise the zeal of all the performers, and their perfect confidence in him; and, as it always has been, his playing and his memory astound everybody. His wonderful memory has stood him in good stead, inasmuch as it made them give up a symphony of Beethoven, which had been played here several times already, and put the Pastoral Symphony in its place in the programme. (It makes me melt to think that I shall have to hear it in this dreadful heat the day after to-morrow.) When it was mentioned, he not only instantly played it from memory, but at a small trial on the eve of the rehearsal, when there was no score at hand, conducted it by heart and sang the part of a missing instrument.

Letter to his wife, Whit Sunday 1833
As a musical festival comprehends a conductor, I suppose I must say something about the conductor for this year – Mr Felix – he is hardly called anything else here. Dear wife, this young man gives us much joy. He has indeed got an immense piece of work to do, but he does it with a spirit, energy, seriousness, and cleverness actually miraculous in its effect. To me at least it does appear like a miracle that 400 persons of all sexes, classes, and ages, blown together like snow before the wind, should let themselves be conducted and governed like children by one of the youngest of them all, too young almost to be a friend for any of them, and with no title or dignity whatever. For instance, by one strict injunction (and but for his pronunciation, which he may yet improve, he speaks well) he has brought about what no other conductor to my knowledge has been able to do, the abolition of that disgusting practice of tuning. Another abuse arose from the successive arrival of strangers from all directions, who met for the first time on the orchestra, and found their friends there. It had become the fashion to use the orchestra as

a kind a parlour, where a great deal of talking and gossiping went on, of course highly detrimental to the rehearsal, the conductor having to shout with all his might, and even then without being heard; and since new-comers dropped in up to the very beginning, the disturbance was intolerable. The same kind of thing began this time on the first rehearsal day, and then Felix represented to them that he could not submit to it, that he neither could nor would shout to enable them to hear him, and that he must insist and rely on the most absolute silence and quiet in the orchestra every time he had to speak. He said this for a second time very decidedly and earnestly, and then I assure you that I never saw an order so strictly obeyed. They see that it is right and necessary, and as soon as he knocks and is about to speak, a general pst is heard, and all is dead silence.

By this means he has produced really fine *nuances* both in chorus and orchestra, which all assure me were always wanting before, and which of course gratify the performers and must raise the credit of their execution in their own eyes and ears.

Letter to his wife, 28 May 1833
The young ladies and, I believe, also the matrons of the chorus, had supplied themselves each with a quantity of flowers, and Fräulein Woringen kept hidden under her scarf during the whole second part a velvet cushion with a laurel wreath. The moment Felix descended he received a volley of flowers, and (as I have been *told*, for I sat too far back to see anything, and had not heard a syllable of it before) he made a face half astonished, half angry, when the first bouquet flew about his head. They pushed him, however, up to his place again, where the eldest Miss Woringen wanted to crown him with the wreath. They say he nearly bent down to the floor to escape this homage. But a great strong man from the chorus held him up and stopped him, so that he had to suffer the wreath to be put on his head, after having four times defended himself against it, and to wear it during a continued flourish of the orchestra and cheers of the choir and audience. They say it became him very well.

We were all invited to meet at the Schadows' after the concert. Somebody sat down at the piano and played 'See the conquering hero comes,' and Felix had to put on his wreath again, and they led him in a triumphal procession through the rooms. Hardly had a cup of tea been swallowed when tables and chairs were pushed aside and a wild waltzing and galoping began. Felix had first to play, but by-and-by somebody took his place at the piano and he rushed into the dance. Mme. Decker presumed that he could not dance, being much too grave and engaged with other things, but he soon convinced her to the contrary, and when she rested for the first time she said to me, 'Felix' – he always goes by that name here – 'dances most splendidly.' The important thing Schadow had to say to me was to beg my advice about the choice of a keepsake which the committee want to give Felix. They had had Loos's medal struck in gold for him, but did not like it, and were going to keep it; some proposed a diamond ring, others a set of Handel's scores. I strongly objected to the ring, and was more in favour of the music, but thought it best to ask Felix himself, and Schadow agreed. I instantly did so, and he chose a seal, for daily use. Schadow thought his choice very judicious, and they have ordered a seal, after a design by Schadow, in Berlin, where they say there is now an excellent stone-engraver.

Letter to his wife, 31 May 1833
The consequence of all these doings is highly important for Felix, and I will give you a short account of what is now settled, reserving all particulars for a later time. Felix has been nominated director of all the public and private musical establishments of the town for a period of three years, with a salary of 600 thalers (corresponding to about 800 to 900 thalers at Berlin). His engagement begins on October 1, and he has a three months' leave of absence every year, which he is allowed to take at any time between May and November. His public duty consists in conducting the church-music, his private obligations are the direction of the singing and instrumental associations – hitherto separated but now to be united – and the arrangement of from four to eight annual concerts of these associations, besides the musical festivals. I am sure, dear Lea, that you will agree with me in rejoicing to see Felix in a fixed appointment, occupying him sufficiently but not too much in Germany, not far from us, and on the sure and straight road towards his higher ends, in artistic surroundings, beloved and honoured in a really extraordinary degree, enjoying unlimited confidence, at the head

of established institutions looking entirely to him for their proper
direction and development. I know not what position I could desire
more suitable for him and his future.

> On Felix's fourth visit to Britain, he and Abraham
> remained until 25 August 1833.

Abraham had probably been prevailed on by Felix to come to his
beloved England. The father's letter [to his wife, undated] contains
many pleasant jokes about the son's partiality for that country. For
instance: 'Felix in his enthusiasm calls the shorn sunburnt yellow
meadows "green," the black and gray horizon "blue," which I do
not.' Or in another place: 'this morning at fourteen minutes past
nine the sun was just powerful enough to give a yellow tinge to the
mist, and the air was just like the smoke of a great fire. "A very fine
morning!" said my barber (here called hairdresser). "Is it?" asked I.
"Yes, a *very* fine morning!" and so I learnt what a fine summer
morning here is like. Now, about noon, the mist has carried the
victory, and along with a sultry heat the light is that of a Berlin
November afternoon about four o'clock. I have to move my table
close to the window in order to see, not what I am writing, but *that*
I am writing at all. Felix is gone to St. Paul's to play the organ, whilst
I cannot make up my mind to leave the room. When he comes
home I am sure he will say that nowhere there are such glorious
summer days as in London.'

Abraham Mendelssohn, quoted in Sebastian Hensel: *The Mendelssohn Family 1729–1847*
(London, 1881), I, 280–81, 284–5, 287–8, 291–3 (with cuts)

LEA MENDELSSOHN

> In 1835 she and Abraham, together with Fanny and
> Rebecka and their husbands, attended the Cologne
> Festival which Felix was conducting.

Letter to Rebecka, Berlin, [August 1835]
'Une douce sympathie règne entre nous, chère enfant!' We left
Cologne on the 1st, and arrived here on the 8th. That Lea was well

taken care of in Abraham's bosom you will, I dare say, have learnt through Felix, who has written to you from all the places we passed, with true brotherly affection. But his modesty prevents his telling you that he is a model sick-nurse, real to all intents and purposes, and ideal through his charming, watchful affection. He did not in the most literal sense of the word allow my foot to tread on hard ground, which considering the number of stairs and doorsteps was a difficult task. 'He has a talent for *everything*,' said R. once on a different occasion. Indeed he took rather too much care of me, and kept me somewhat like one of Passalaqua's mummies. Laughing and joking was all he gave me leave for, and that we had plenty of.

Lea Mendelssohn, quoted in Sebastian Hensel: *The Mendelssohn Family 1729–1847* (London, 1881), I, p. 317 (with cuts)

IGNAZ MOSCHELES

Letter to unknown addressee (? London), January 1836
As yet not a word from our friend Felix Mendelssohn; he has not recovered from the shock of his father's death, or he would certainly have written. What I do hear of him is anything but consolatory, they say he cannot work from feeling an indescribable void in the loss of one whom he regarded as the chief mainstay of his life; but such a state of things cannot last. I can well understand his grief when my mind goes back to the autumn days I spent with him in his old home. His father, old, weak, and almost blind, was a man gifted with such activity of mind and clearness of judgment that I could not only understand the deep reverence my friend felt for him, but also share it with him.

Ignaz Moscheles, quoted in Charlotte Moscheles: *Aus Moscheles Leben* (Leipzig, 1872; Eng. tr. A.D. Coleridge, London, 1873), II, pp. 1–2

LEA MENDELSSOHN

Letter to Charlotte Moscheles, Berlin, 12 January 1836
My children, one and all, behave like angels, and I were ungrateful indeed, if, in my hour of agony, I were blind to the many blessings still left to me. Felix's struggle with the sorrow brought on him

made me at first very troubled and anxious; when we are with him, tears seem to give him relief and courage for the battle of life before him. It is a good thing we should have him just now living near us; he has twice visited us since the event. Pray accept, my dear friend, my warmest thanks for all the kindness you showed to my dear one when he was in London; he always spoke of it with emotion and gratitude, at last, when the state of his eyes prevented him from working, he would repeatedly say: 'I don't feel in the least dull, I have seen in the course of my life much that is beautiful and interesting!' And his visits to London, and your friendship, he reckoned his highest enjoyments. He never forgot any of his numerous friends, pray assure them all how deeply sensible I am of their kindness.

Lea Mendelssohn, quoted in Charlotte Moscheles: *Aus Moscheles Leben* (Leipzig, 1872; Eng. tr. A.D. Coleridge, London, 1873), II, p. 3

FANNY MENDELSSOHN

Letter to Charlotte Moscheles, Berlin, (? January) 1836
My anxiety about Felix is at an end, he has collected all his energies, and deep though his sorrow be, it is natural, and not of that distressing kind that deepened our sorrow and made us doubly solicitous on his account. The coming season and travelling will, I trust, completely restore him to that state of mind that he must recover, if he wishes to live up to his father's standard, as he never failed to do whilst they were together. Such intense sympathy as theirs is very rarely found in the world.

Fanny Mendelssohn, quoted in Charlotte Moscheles: *Aus Moscheles Leben* (Leipzig, 1872; Eng. tr. A.D. Coleridge, London, 1873), II, p. 4

EDUARD DEVRIENT

His father [had] often expressed his anxiety lest Felix should let the time pass by when he ought to marry, and thus fail to find the balancing point of his character, the repose of family life for his over-excitable temperament. I recollect the father saying to me, in a conversation about Felix's fidgetiness about an opera libretto: 'I am afraid that Felix's censoriousness will prevent his getting a wife as well as a libretto.' I laughed at the combination, but he continued quite gravely, that he was indeed concerned lest Felix should remain unmarried, like his uncle Bartholdy, with whom, in reference to this question, he had great similarity.

The earnestness of purpose that every well-disposed person carries away from the grave of the honoured dead, the desire to live according to his wish, could not but arise most strongly in Felix. The certainty that he would fulfil this wish by drawing round him family ties, became clear to him during these ten days; he resolved to marry, and told his sister Fanny so before parting.

Eduard Devrient: *Meine Erinnerungen an Felix Mendelssohn-Bartholdy* (Leipzig, 1869; Eng. tr. Natalia Macfarren, London, 1869), p. 193

EDOUARD SOUCHAY

When I went to see my relations one afternoon I met, quite unexpectedly, in the room they call 'la salle', the director of the Städel Institute, the painter Philippe Veit, and a gentleman whom I did not know, but whom Veit introduced as his cousin, the conductor Felix Mendelssohn. Also present were my two charming young nieces, Julie and Cécile Jeanrenaud.

I do not know why I was immediately conscious that this moment was a very fateful one. Herr Mendelssohn was pleasant and very distinguished. The look in Veit's dark, bright eyes seemed significant. Julie was gay, Cécile delightful but a little distant, as she always is. Her eyes were shining with deep enthusiasm.

I heard my father's voice in the next room asking Herr Mendelssohn if he would be kind enough to play. It was only a short time since the death of his father and this seemed to be still affecting him – he seemed almost ill as a result. But, after first declining the invitation to play, he suddenly sat down at the piano as if he wished to express a mood – like Goethe with a poem.

> *Was ich irrte, was ich strebte,*
> *Was ich litt und was ich lebte,*
> *Sind hier Blumen nur im Strauss.*

[All my wandering, all my striving
All my suffering, all my living,
Are here but flowers in the stream.]

The following month my parents were away. Mendelssohn Bartholdy took advantage of the invitation to return and was a frequent visitor at the house of Mme Jeanrenaud, my sister, who lived on the second floor facing the Main. The composer made various sketches from the windows of the house.

Edouard Souchay, quoted in Jacques Petitpierre: *The Romance of the Mendelssohns* (London, 1947), pp. 125–7

CÉCILE JEANRENAUD
(1817–1853)

The daughter of a French Calvinist pastor in Frankfurt, she first met Mendelssohn in 1836, and they were married the following year.

Letter to her cousin Cornélie Schunck (undated)
He [Felix] will talk to you about us when he returns to Leipzig from this seaside stay which he says he is not looking forward to as he fears he will be bored. Mama and I assured him that wouldn't be the case at all. And then we made a little bet . . . I shall be glad if I win . . .

Cécile Jeanrenaud, quoted in Jacques Petitpierre: *The Romance of the Mendelssohns* (London, 1947), pp. 130–31

LEA MENDELSSOHN

Letter to Ferdinand David, 20 July 1836
Try and find out from Schunks or Schlemmer something about the Souchays (the parents of Frau Jeanrenaud) and pass it on to me. I think our butterfly Felix has got his wings burnt again; if only he would take it seriously for once and get married! I don't know any of these flower-children he's fluttering over and feel like warning him of the fate of the lovely Arsène, 'who ended up marrying a charcoal-burner'. On the 25th he's off to Scheveningen; three of

the people he dislikes most in Berlin will also be splashing around there, as luck will have it. I won't tell him, otherwise he would be capable of calling the whole trip off. Man does not escape his fate.

Lea Mendelssohn, quoted in Julius Eckardt: *Ferdinand David und die Familie Mendelssohn-Bartholdy* (Leipzig, 1888), pp. 43, 75–7, 85

FANNY MENDELSSOHN

Letter to her mother (undated, but c. August 1836)
Dear mother, I beseech you not to worry, at the age of sixty, because you think Felix is in love! Couldn't Dr W. give you a sedative to calm such youthful feverishness? I share your emotions and the suspense is making me quite nervy. But we mustn't worry. Felix is a man of taste. I've got a vague suspicion. Is it perhaps a Miss Jeanrenaud or a Miss Souchay?

Fanny Mendelssohn, quoted in Jacques Petitpierre: *The Romance of the Mendelssohns* (London, 1947), pp. 127–8

REBECKA MENDELSSOHN
(1811–1858)

The third of the Mendelssohn children, Rebecka in 1832 married the mathematician Gustav Peter Dirichlet, who became an expert in number theory.

Whilst Dirichlet was making his preparations for leaving his wife and child and going to his parents, arrived the news of Felix's engagement to Cécile Jeanrenaud. Rebecka had been eagerly expecting this event during the whole journey. The family were aware that Felix had set his whole affections on a beautiful girl in the Rhine provinces; but the knowledge was founded only on rumour. Rebecka writes from Gastein that she had taken up the *Allgemeine Zeitung* in the hope of seeing among the paragraphs on the Frankfurt Fair, 'The well-known musician Felix Mendelssohn on such and such a day was betrothed to,' etc.; but all she could find was 'cotton market flat' and a report of the Bundestag. In

Nuremberg Rebecka received a letter from Felix himself with the welcome news. He had returned to Leipzig immediately after his engagement, and thither she followed him, in great delight at the long-looked-for intelligence, and was thus the first of his family to see him in his happiness. She found him very bright but composed, and with an air of profound satisfaction: he was also more communicative than he had been for a long time, and, she says, she could scarcely have believed love would become him so well, for he was more than amiable. So her stay at Leipzig was prolonged from day to day, and what happened in the end may be given in her own words.

Leipzig, 4 October 1836
Yesterday I got up very early, in order to write you a respectable letter, thanking you for your kindness in wishing me to enjoy myself here, whilst you are endeavouring to comfort your afflicted parents. Three pages had I filled when Felix came in. 'Good morning, Rebecka!' 'Good morning, Felix!' 'Well, you are going, of course, to stay on here till Dirichlet comes to fetch you?' I: 'No, I have just written to tell him that it will not do.' Felix: 'Where is the letter?' I: 'Here, do you want to read it?' Felix: 'No.' And with that he walked to the table, took up the letter, and tore it to atoms. I was so startled that I could not make up my mind to write another all yesterday, nor do I yet know what to decide. A week in the hotel would, I am afraid, quite ruin me; on the other hand, it is my maxim never to grudge myself a pleasure, and it is very charming here. Felix is most dear; he plays a great deal to me, and we have no end of chat together. He is kind enough to consider my society as some compensation for his separation from his betrothed.

My letter of yesterday contained a great deal of information now lost, but one piece of news I must repeat. Felix has found a warm friend and patron in Rossini, who takes a great interest in his music, had a very serious conversation with him, and advised him to compose in a more popular style, etc. Moreover, Kalkbrenner's best pupil, Mr. Stamaty, *élève du Conservatoire de Paris*, and popular music-master there, is here in Germany learning music from Felix, and refuses to play until he has learned something better. In fact, except in Berlin and in Aix-la-Chapelle, people are beginning to understand his music. Here he is perfectly adored.

Rebecka Mendelssohn, quoted in Sebastian Hensel: *The Mendelssohn Family 1729–1837* (London, 1881), II, pp. 18–20 (with cuts)

LEA MENDELSSOHN

Letter to Charlotte Moscheles, Berlin, 6 October 1836
You have probably already heard by report, which travels now-a-days so much more rapidly than people or railways and steamers, that Felix is engaged to be married. I cannot, however, deny myself the pleasure of personally communicating to you and your husband, Felix's excellent friend, the news which is a matter of such happiness to us all. You, an affectionate mother, can imagine how strange it seems to me, not to know either his bride elect, or any one of her numerous relations; nor can I recollect ever to have heard the name of the family. As a penalty for excessive liveliness, quite out of place, considering what an old lady I am, I shall be forced to wait a long time before I can see the fair unknown, who is already so precious to me. You know, however, how disinterested are a mother's feelings, and will form a correct estimate of the joy we all feel, for Felix himself seems so completely happy. There is, however, a bitter drop to this cup of joy, and the thought is constantly arising in my mind, had his dear father but lived to share our happiness! He desired such a blessing for Felix so earnestly, and yet scarcely ventured to hope for it. That sad event (his father's death) supplied Felix perhaps with the strongest incentive for taking such a resolve. When he paid us his last Christmas visit, he was so inexpressibly wretched, so thoroughly heartbroken, so absorbed in silent suffering, so vacillating and purposeless even in his art schemes, that his sisters persuaded him he must turn over a new leaf, and give his mind a fresh start.

His acquaintance with a young lady in Frankfurt soon enabled him to shake off the thraldom of low spirits, and he is now happily betrothed to his Cécile.

Lea Mendelssohn, quoted in Charlotte Moscheles: *Aus Moscheles Leben* (Leipzig, 1872; Eng. tr. A.D. Coleridge, London, 1873), II, pp. 3, 17–8

FERDINAND HILLER
(1811–1885)

German composer pianist and conductor. He worked in
a number of German cities including Leipzig, where he
briefly succeeded Mendelssohn in 1841.

The year 1836 was one of the most important of Mendelssohn's life,
for it was that in which he first met his future wife. Madame Jeanrenaud was the widow of a clergyman of the French Reformed
Church in Frankfurt. Her husband had died in the prime of life, and
she was living with her children at the house of her parents, the
Souchays, people of much distinction in the town. Felix had been
introduced to them, and soon felt himself irresistibly attracted by
the beauty and grace of the eldest daughter, Cécile. His visits
became more and more frequent, but he always behaved with such
reserve towards his chosen one, that, as she once laughingly told me
in her husband's presence, for several weeks she did not imagine
herself to be the cause of Mendelssohn's visits, but thought he came
for the sake of her mother, who, indeed, with her youthful vivacity,
cleverness, and refinement, chattering away in the purest Frankfurt
dialect, was extremely attractive. But though during this early time
Felix spoke but little to Cécile, when away from her he talked of her
all the more. Lying on the sofa in my room after dinner, or taking
long walks in the mild summer nights with Dr. S. and myself, he
would rave about her charm, her grace, and her beauty. There was
nothing overstrained in him, either in his life or in his art: he would
pour out his heart about her in the most charmingly frank and
artless way, often full of fun and gaiety; then again, with deep feeling, but never with any exaggerated sentimentality or uncontrolled
passion. It was easy to see what a serious thing it was, for one could
hardly get him to talk of anything which did not touch in some way
upon her. Mendelssohn's courtship was no secret, and was watched
with much curiosity and interest by the whole of Frankfurt society;
and many remarks which I heard showed me that to possess genius,
culture, fame, amiability and fortune, and belong to a family
of much consideration as well as celebrity, is in certain circles
hardly enough to entitle a man to raise his eyes to a girl of patrician

birth. But I do not think that anything of this sort ever came to Mendelssohn's ears.

Ferdinand Hiller: *Felix Mendelssohn-Bartholdy* (Cologne, 1874; Eng. tr. M.E. von Glehn, London, 1874), pp. 59–61 (with cuts)

EDUARD DEVRIENT

In Cecilia Jeanrenaud, the daughter of a Protestant clergyman, he was to find the maiden who was to complete and calm his existence. Schleinitz had introduced him to the house of the young lady's mother, who was a widow, and his relative, not without a secret wish that one of his cousins might win Felix's affections. And so it befell. Felix showed in his dawning affection his characteristic conscientiousness. He tore himself away, and travelled down the Rhine, under pretext of visiting the baths at Scheveningen, in order to test his passion far away from the magic circle of the beloved maiden; but he found his heart so deeply implicated, that he could return with a good conscience in the middle of September and betroth himself.

Cecilia was one of those sweet, womanly natures, whose gentle simplicity, whose mere presence, soothed and pleased. She was slight, with features of striking beauty and delicacy; her hair was between brown and gold; but the transcendent lustre of her great blue eyes, and the brilliant roses of her cheeks, were sad harbingers of early death. She spoke little, and never with animation, in a low soft voice. Shakspeare's words, 'My gracious silence,' applied to her no less than to the wife of Coriolanus. The friends of Felix had every reason to hope that his choice would secure repose to his restless spirit, and happy leisure for thought and work in his home.

Eduard Devrient: *Meine Erinnerungen an Felix Mendelssohn-Bartholdy* (Leipzig, 1869; Eng. tr. Natalia Macfarren, London, 1869), pp. 196–7

FELIX MOSCHELES
(1833–1917)

The son of Ignaz and Charlotte Moscheles, he was also Mendelssohn's godson.

I remember thinking her exceedingly beautiful. Her appearance reminded me of a certain picture of Germania by Kaulbach; but she was not the typical fair-haired German; she was dark, and wore her hair not in classical waves, but according to the fashion of the day, in many ringlets.

Cécile was in many respects a contrast to her husband; she was calm and reserved, where he was lively and excitable. Hers was a deeply emotional nature, but she rarely showed outwardly what moved or impressed her, whereas his emotions would ever rise to the surface, generally to overflow and find expression in words.

Felix Moscheles: *Fragments of an Autobiography* (New York, 1899), pp. 100–01 (with cuts)

REBECKA MENDELSSOHN

Letter to Cécile Jeanrenaud, Berlin, 11 March 1837
(shortly before her marriage to Felix)
What pleasure Felix's different varieties of music will give you! Does he play you any of his funny pieces, or is he too much in love? If he does, ask him for the preludes *à l'enfant* with wrong conclusions: they would make me laugh on my death-bed. Unfortunately we are quite shut out from this musical life, as we have no musical friends now, and have to depend entirely on Fanny's grand performances, which only take place now and then. They are really very beautiful, but after them people are afraid of playing or singing before Fanny, so we have music only when we are by ourselves. My best love to Felix. Does he not look handsome at his conductor's desk? I like to watch him, especially when he is pleased: he nods his head and pushes out his under-lip just as if there were nobody in the room at all.

Rebecka Mendelssohn, quoted in Sebastian Hensel: *The Mendelssohn Family 1729–1847* (London, 1881), II, pp. 29–30

IGNAZ MOSCHELES

Diary entry, 1837 (on first meeting Cécile in Berlin)
Felix's wife is very charming, very unassuming and childlike. Her

mouth and nose are like Sontag's. Her way of speaking is pleasing and simple; her German is quite that of the Frankfurter. She said naïvely at dinner, 'I speak too slowly for my Felix, and he so quickly that I don't always understand him.'

Ignaz Moscheles, quoted in Felix Moscheles: *Fragments of an Autobiography* (New York, 1899), p. 101

WILLIAM STERNDALE BENNETT
(1816–1875)

Bennett was a choirboy at King's College, Cambridge and at the age of ten was studying at the Royal Academy of Music. He became Professor of Music at Cambridge in 1856 and Principal of the Royal Academy ten years later. He was knighted in 1871.

1842

He went for a second time to Berlin. [Journal.] '*Feb. 16th*. Have been spending the evening with Mrs Mendelssohn where I met the whole Mendelssohn family. Mrs Hensel played some of her new compositions and played them charmingly.' Of another evening (Feb. 21) he wrote to Miss Wood: – 'I went to a small music-party at Mendelssohn's where I met all his family and some other musical people. He played three pieces and then insisted on my playing. I *never was so alarmed before*; not at him, for we have played too often together, but at his sister, Mrs Hensel. However, he was getting rather angry, and I played very well as it happened, and they were very generous in their applause. I never was frightened to play to any one before, and to think that this terrible person should be a lady. However, she would frighten many people with her cleverness.'

William Sterndale Bennett, quoted in James Robert Sterndale Bennett: *The Life of William Sterndale Bennett* (Cambridge, 1907), pp. 126–7

MRS. BENECKE

She was Cécile Mendelssohn's aunt.

I may perhaps be allowed to supplement this incident by some further details which Mendelssohn's hostess, Mrs. Benecke, kindly gave
me when I visited her in 1885. We were seated in the room which
Mendelssohn used as his study, overlooking the beautiful garden,
and in which he wrote the *Lied* above referred to ['Chanson de
printemps', op. 62, no. 6, also mentioned below]. Over the old
grand pianoforte, upon which he had often played, was a beautiful
oil-painting of him. In the course of a most interesting conversation,
Mrs. Benecke said that Mendelssohn and his wife intended staying
only a few days till they should find apartments near the concert
rooms, as Mendelssohn had engagements with the Philharmonic
Society, &c. One day on his return from town he said, 'Those lodgings in London are so stuffy after this pleasant house: may we stay
here all the time?' The request was readily granted, and the sojourn
of a few days extended to one of six or seven weeks. As to the pic-nic,
Mr. Benecke thought at the time that the reason of Mendelssohn's
absence from the party was owing to some previous musical
engagement in London. On the long drive to Windsor Mrs. Benecke
said to Frau Mendelssohn: 'Why did not Felix come with us to-
day?' She replied, 'I think he has something in his mind that he
wants to write down.' 'But,' said her hostess, 'there is nothing for
his dinner, only cold meat and rice milk – just the children's dinner.' 'Oh, never mind,' replied Frau Mendelssohn; 'he likes nothing better than rice milk. He will be all right.' On their return home,
Mendelssohn, full of spirits, was waiting in the garden-drive to
receive them, and greeted them with a hearty welcome. When they
were all assembled in his temporary study he played the lovely 'Lied
in A' (No. 30), saying, 'This is what I have been doing while you
have been away.' He was very fond of romping with the children,
and they with him; and the quaver rests in the bass of this *Lied* and
the frequent staccato notes in the treble, represent the constant
withdrawal of his hands from the pianoforte in order to defend
himself against the repeated attacks of the little ones, who, being

alone with him, wanted to drag him away from the pianoforte and into the garden for a romp. The autograph MS. is dated 'London, June 1, 1842,' the day of the pic-nic.

Mrs. Benecke told me of other incidents of this visit. She gave a small musical dinner party, at which William Horsley (the glee writer), Moscheles, Benedict, and others were present. After dinner one of the guests suggested that there should be 'some playing' (pianoforte). 'Oh, yes,' said Mendelssohn, 'we'll have some playing!' And he at once marched the musicians off to play – not the pianoforte – but the game of 'Hen and chickens' in the garden. Horsley, who was not so young as the others, was in fits of laughter as he stood at the window watching the overgrown boys at their 'play,' Mendelssohn being the life and soul of the game.

Although Mendelssohn was thirty-three at the time of his visit to Denmark Hill, he revelled in a game of leap-frog, played with the tutor to Mr. Benecke's sons; and he once practised the horizontal-bar so vigorously as to take the skin off his hands. He composed for the children a very humorous 'Bear's dance' with the following title: 'The real, genuine, warranted Bärentanz, as performed with unbounded applause at the Denmark Hill Chamber Concerts, composed and dedicated (by permission) to the Gooseberry-eaters at Benecke Castle, by their humble colleague and servant, Felix Mendelssohn Bartholdy, usually called Peter Meffert.' This comical little piece, dated 'London, 11th July, 1842,' is on a rapidly re-iterated pedal bass (the lowest F on the pianoforte), and each hand plays at the extreme ends of the keyboard throughout. At the end is the direction: 'Da capo, very often.'

Mrs Benecke, noted in F.G. Edwards: 'Reminiscences of Mendelssohn', *The Musical Times*, 1 August 1892, pp. 466–7

FANNY MENDELSSOHN

Letter to Rebecka, Berlin, 26 December 1843
So far he has played in public twice; once at Molique's concert (he has often played with us lately), when he played Beethoven's sonata in A minor, and again at the subscription-concert, where he took his own concerto in G minor, being applauded both times in a manner

quite exceptional for Berlin. But people are beginning to understand
that the symphonies go in quite a different way to what they did,
and in course of time the audience will make as much progress as
the orchestra. Felix's second psalm for the cathedral choir, *a capella*,
in eight parts, is so beautiful, very Gregorian, and reminding one of
the Sistine. I am curious to hear what will be said about it, that is,
if people listen at all. Felix would prefer composing with the
orchestra, and has got in the thin end of the wedge by introducing
Handel's choruses after those *a capella*, just as he introduced, from
the first, solo-pieces at the subscription-concerts, in the hope of
being able to smuggle part-singing in by-and-by. He sets about it all
so cautiously and prudently that I have no doubt he will get his own
way in everything. And really the moral influence of a distinguished
man tells for so much that something will be done even with the
Philistines and blockheads.

> By 1844, Felix's dislike of Berlin had become obses-
> sional. At the end of September, he came to the city and
> proposed to King Frederick William IV that he should
> undertake only specific commissions, that he should be
> free of the obligation of living in Berlin, and that con-
> sequently his salary should be reduced to 1,000 thalers a
> year. He and his family remained now in Frankfurt.

Diary entry, date unknown [? October 1844]
When I hear him talk about it I cannot help agreeing with him, for
his motives are absolutely noble and worthy of him; but still it is a
pity, and very hard for me, who enjoyed the happiness of living near
him and his family so intensely. And all the music I was looking
forward to! Perhaps we may not see less of Felix himself, though,
for if he comes here several times a year, as he says he will, and we
have him in the house as we have now, we shall certainly see more of
him than if he were living here, but obliged to spend most of his
time away from home, and be worried during the rest. But Cécile
and the children are completely lost to us, and I had grown so fond
of them! Felix is again most dear, and his playing, to my mind, finer
than ever. How contemptible and trumpery amateurishness looks
when one sees what real art is. If I do not give up entirely it is
because, for one thing, I do not seem to myself so stupid when Felix

is away; and for another, my husband would be so distressed. The recital of the way they all – from the cathedral dignitaries down to the last member of the orchestra – have done all in their power to put a spoke in Felix's wheel (with a few exceptions, though), and the total absence of all the little tokens of respect and sympathy to which he is accustomed elsewhere, would fill a volume.

Fanny Mendelssohn, quoted in Sebastian Hensel: *The Mendelssohn Family 1729–1847* (London, 1881), II, pp. 237, 243–4, 300–01 (with cuts)

IGNAZ MOSCHELES

Diary entry, 3 February 1847
We and the Schuncks had combined to celebrate Mendelssohn's birthday. The proceedings were opened with a capital comic scene between two lady's maids, acted, in the Frankfurt dialect, by Cécile and her sister. Then came a charade on the word 'Gewandhaus.' Joachim, adorned with a fantastic wig, à la Paganini, played a hare-brained impromptu on the G string; the syllable 'Wand' was represented by the Pyramus and Thisbe wall-scene from the 'Midsummer Night's Dream;' for 'Haus,' Charlotte acted a scene she had written herself, in which she is discovered knitting a blue stocking, and soliloquizing on the foibles of female authoresses, advising them to attend to their domestic duties. By way of enforcing the moral, she calls her cook – the cook was I myself, and my appearance in cap and dress was the signal for a general uproar. Mendelssohn was sitting on a large straw arm-chair which creaked under his weight, as he rocked to and fro, and the room echoed with his peals of laughter. The whole word 'Gewandhaus' was illustrated by a full orchestra, Mendelssohn and my children playing on little drums and trumpets; Joachim leading with a toy violin, my Felix conducting à la Jullien. It was splendid.

Ignaz Moscheles, quoted in Charlotte Moscheles: *Aus Moscheles Leben* (Leipzig, 1872; Eng. tr. A.D. Coleridge, London, 1873), II, pp. 169–70

FELIX MOSCHELES

The evening of the 8th of October was the last I was to spend at Mendelssohn's house. He, my father, Rietz, and David had been playing much classical music. In the course of an animated conversation which followed, some knotty art question arose and led to a lively discussion. Each of the authorities present was warmly defending his own opinion, and there seemed little prospect of an immediate agreement, when Mendelssohn, suddenly interrupting himself in the middle of a sentence, turned on his heel and startled me with the unexpected question –

'What is the Aoristus primus of τύπτω, Felix?' I was at that time a schoolboy in my fifteenth year, and so, quickly recovering from my surprise, I gave the correct answer.

'Good,' said he, and off we went to supper, the knotty point being thus promptly settled.*

Felix Moscheles: *Fragments of an Autobiography* (New York, 1899), pp. 105–6

SIR JULIUS BENEDICT

The birthday of a child of one of his friends was to be celebrated at Soden, and so he wandered from toy-shop to toy-shop – bought walnuts, goldbeater's-skin, penny trumpets, and, more important than all, a small firtree, to be ornamented after the custom of Germany with sugar-plums, toys, tapers, and what not, hanging from every branch. On returning to Soden, Johann, his faithful, attached servant, was first consulted, and next the whole family went to work decking out the tree, till it looked right cheerful and brilliant. At nightfall the carefully locked doors of the drawing-room were opened, and in poured the happy little folks, screaming with joy. 'Let's have a march,' said Charles – Mendelssohn's eldest son – and all paced round the tree to the same strains I had heard a few months before at the Hanover-Square Rooms, in the presence

---

* The correct answer, ἔτυψα (I struck), is a regular formation. So this was not a trick question: Mendelssohn simply wanted to reassure himself that his godson was being soundly educated. [RN]

of the Queen and Prince Albert, and the élite of London society, for it was the march from 'A Midsummer Night's Dream' which Mendelssohn played.

Sir Julius Benedict: *A Sketch of the Life and Works of the Late Felix Mendelssohn-Bartholdy* (London, 1850), p. 47

III

AS CONDUCTOR

JULIUS SCHUBRING

It was from this period [1829] that Mendelssohn, even at the little rehearsals at home, used the conductor's stick; he had hitherto modestly stated his opinion, from the piano or the desk of the tenor. He assumed a more independent bearing, too, as I remember was the case when, in Haydn's D-major symphony, he required the *tempi* to be taken at a slower rate than that to which we were accustomed. The orchestra kept continually hurrying on, but, with an iron will, and marking the time most forcibly with his stick, he held back, till even the faithful Edward Rietz, the leader, began to grumble. For my own part, I must confess that quite a new light was then thrown upon the Symphony. I had always heard the last movement called the 'Bear's Dance'; but, on the occasion in question, it was a most pleasing piece of composition. Good old father Haydn must not be hurried.

Julius Schubring: 'Reminiscences of Felix Mendelssohn-Bartholdy', *Musical World*, 31 (12 and 19 May 1866); reprinted in *Mendelssohn and his World*, ed. R. Larry Todd (Princeton, 1991), pp. 228–9

REVIEWS

The author conducted it [his First Symphony] in person, and it was received with acclamations. The audience wished the adagio to be repeated, but M. Mendelssohn did not construe the continued applause as an encore. The scherzo and trio, however, were instantly called for a second time, and the band seemed most happy to comply with the demand. It would be an act of injustice to the orchestra not to state, that the execution of this entirely unknown work was as perfect as the most sanguine hopes of the composer could have taught him to expect. He was surprised at such accuracy of performance – which indeed was still more remarkable on the morning of rehearsal than at the concert itself – and expressed his satisfaction in terms that were highly gratifying to this most excellent band.

Review in *The Harmonicon*, July 1829, pp. 173–4, of the seventh Philharmonic Concert, 25 May 1829

Mr M. is not more than 22, his features indicate great vivacity, and his conversation will not disappoint the expectations raised by his face. He speaks English fluently and well, and is in every sense an accomplished gentleman.

Quarterly Music Magazine and Review, 1828–9, p. 297, referring to the same concert

SIR JULIUS BENEDICT

In the spring of 1835 Mendelssohn was invited to come to Cologne, in order to direct the festival. Here we met again, and, thanks to his kindness, I had the pleasure of being present at one of the general rehearsals, where he conducted Beethoven's 8th symphony. It would be a matter of difficulty to decide in which quality Mendelssohn excelled the most – whether as composer, pianist, organist, or conductor of an orchestra; nobody certainly ever knew better how to communicate, as if by an electric fluid, his own conception of a work to a large body of performers. It was highly interesting, on this occasion, to contemplate the anxious attention manifested by a body of more than five hundred singers and performers, watching every glance of Mendelssohn's eye, and following, like obedient spirits, the magic wand of this musical *Prospero*. The admirable allegretto, in B flat, of this symphony, not going, at first, to his liking, he remarked, smilingly, that 'he knew every one of the gentlemen engaged was capable of performing and even of composing a scherzo of his own; but that *just now* he wanted to hear Beethoven's, which he thought had some merits.' It was cheerfully repeated. – 'Beautiful, charming!' cried Mendelssohn, 'but still too loud in two or three instances. Let us take it again from the middle.' 'No, no,' was the general reply of the band; 'the whole piece over again for our own satisfaction'; and then they played it with the utmost delicacy and finish; Mendelssohn, laying aside his baton, and listening with evident delight to the more perfect execution. 'What would I have given,' he exclaimed, 'if Beethoven could have heard his own composition so well understood, and so magnificently performed!' By thus giving alternately praise and blame as required, spurring the slow, checking the too ardent, he obtained orchestral effects seldom equalled in our days. Need I add, that he was able to detect at once, even among a phalanx of performers, the slightest error either of note or accent?

Sir Julius Benedict: *A Sketch of the Life and Works of the Late Felix Mendelssohn-Bartholdy* (London, 1850), pp. 24–6

HEDWIG VON HOLSTEIN

Mendelssohn conducted the first performance of the young Niels Gade's First Symphony at Leipzig in 1843. In October of that year it was repeated under the direction of the composer:

Never had any of Mendelssohn's own works had such a success and yet he was really delighted, like a child, and stroked his young friend's cheeks, after the audience had scattered and the hero of the day was being congratulated in the orchestra.

When he was involved in a rehearsal or a performance, then new life flowed into everything, his eyes flashed sparks, every movement was elastic, stimulating, and through everything there was this noble line of thought, this nobility both of demeanour and of soul. Anyone who had never seen him before would, at a single glance, have picked him out of a thousand others as a spiritually superior being. And how every emotion imprinted itself in an open, lively fashion on his face! There was no greater pleasure than to watch him listening to music, a string quartet, for instance, in which he was not taking part. Every thought in someone else's music could be read on his face, and how heartily he could laugh! Even if he only spoke three words to you, they would offer unlooked-for meaning and stimulation.

Hedwig von Holstein's autobiography, *Die Glückliche*, quoted in Hans Gerhard Weiss: *Felix Mendelssohn-Bartholdy: ein Lebensbild* ... (Berlin, 1947), pp. 172–3

RICHARD WAGNER
(1813–1883)

Wagner settled in Dresden in 1842, when *Rienzi* was accepted for performance by the court theatre. His experiences with the (Old) Philharmonic Society

in London date from 1855, some eight years after
Mendelssohn's death.

Robert Schumann once complained to me, at Dresden, that
Mendelssohn had quite ruined his enjoyment of the Ninth
Symphony by the rapid pace at which he took it, particularly in the
first movement. Myself I once heard Mendelssohn conduct a
symphony of Beethoven's, at a concert-rehearsal in Berlin: it was
the Eighth (in F). I noticed that he would pick out a detail here and
there – almost at random – and polish it up with a certain pertin-
acity; which was of such excellent service to the detail, that I only
wondered why he didn't pay the same attention to other nuances:
for the rest, this so incomparably buoyant (*heitere*) symphony
flowed down a vastly tame and chatty course. As to conducting, he
personally informed me once or twice that a too slow tempo was the
devil, and for choice he would rather things were taken too fast; a
really good rendering was a rarity at any time; with a little care,
however, one might gloss things over; and this could best be done by
never dawdling, but covering the ground at a good stiff pace. Mendelssohn's actual pupils must have heard from the master a little
more, and more in detail, to the same effect; for it can hardly have
been a maxim confided to my ear alone, as I later have had occasion
to learn its consequences, and finally its grounds.

Of the former I had a lively experience with the orchestra of the
Philharmonic Society *in London*. Mendelssohn had conducted that
band for a considerable period, and the Mendelssohnian mode of
rendering had confessedly been raised into a fixed tradition; in fact
it so well suited the customs and peculiarities of this society's concerts, that it almost seemed as if Mendelssohn had derived his mode
of rendering from them. As a huge amount of music was consumed
at those concerts, but only one rehearsal allowed for each performance, I myself was often obliged to leave the orchestra to its tradition, and thereby made acquaintance with a style of execution
which forcibly reminded me at any rate of Mendelssohn's dictum to
myself. The thing flowed on like water from a public fountain; to
attempt to check it was out of the question, and every Allegro
ended as an indisputable Presto. The labour of intervention was
painful enough; for not until one had got the right and rightly-

shaded tempo, did one discover the other sins of rendering that had lain swamped beneath the deluge. For one thing, the orchestra never played else but *mezzoforte*; neither a genuine *forte*, nor a true *piano*, came about. In important cases, as far as possible, I at last insisted upon the rendering that I myself deemed right, as also on the suitable tempo. The good fellows had nothing against it, and expressed sincere delight; to the public, too, it plainly seemed the thing: but the reporters flew into a rage, and so alarmed the Committee that I once was actually asked to be so good as scurry the second movement of Mozart's Symphony in E-flat again, as one had always been accustomed to and as Mendelssohn himself had done.

How scanty is the sense of our modern musicians for this proper grasp of tempo and expression, has set me in sincere amazement; and unfortunately it is precisely with the Coryphæi of our present music-mongering that I have reaped my worst experiences. Thus I found it impossible to convey to Mendelssohn my feeling of the abomination universally put upon the tempo of the *third movement* of Beethoven's Symphony in F (No. 8).

Well, I once was in Mendelssohn's company at a performance of this symphony in Dresden, conducted by the now deceased Kapellmeister Reissiger, and spoke with him about the said dilemma, telling him how – as I believed – I had arranged for its right solution by my colleague of those days, since he had promised open-eyed to take the tempo slower than of wont. Mendelssohn quite agreed with me. We listened. The third movement began, and I was horrified to hear the old familiar Ländler tempo once again. Before I could express my wrath, however, Mendelssohn was rocking his head in pleased approval, and smiled to me: 'That's capital! Bravo!' So I fell from horror into stupefaction. Reissiger was not so much to blame for his relapse into the ancient tempo, for reasons which soon dawned upon me, as I will presently explain; but Mendelssohn's callousness towards this curious artistic contretemps inspired me with very natural doubts as to whether the thing presented any difference at all to him. I fancied I was peering into a veritable abyss of superficiality, an utter void.

Richard Wagner: 'On conducting', *Collected Writings*, ed. William Ashton Ellis, IV (London, 1869), pp. 306–10 (with cuts)

WILHELM ADOLPH LAMPADIUS
(1812–1892)

After gaining his Doctorate in Philosophy at Leipzig, he became a priest and catechist at the Peterskirche and then a teacher at the municipal school.

At the outset, when he took his place at the music-stand, his countenance was wrapped in deep and almost solemn earnestness. You could see at a glance that the temple of music was a holy place to him. As soon as he had given the first beat, his face lighted up, every feature was aflame, and the play of countenance was the best commentary on the piece. Often the spectator could anticipate from his face what was to come. The fortes and crescendos he accompanied with an energetic play of features and the most forcible action; while the decrescendos and pianos he used to modulate with a motion of both hands, till they slowly sank to almost perfect silence. He glanced at the most distant performers when they should strike in, and often designated the instant when they should pause, by a characteristic movement of the hand, which will not be forgotten by those who ever saw it. He had no patience with performers who did not keep good time. His wondrously accurate ear made him detect the least deviation from the correct tone, in the very largest number of singers and players. He not only heard it, but knew whence it came. Repeated and perverse carelessness would provoke him, but never to a coarse or harsh word: he had too much knowledge of the world, and too much grace of character, for that; the farthest he went was to a dash of sarcasm. 'Gentlemen,' he once said to a number of men who insisted on talking together after the signal to begin had been given, 'I have no doubt that you have something very valuable to talk about; but I beg you to postpone it now: this is the place to sing.' This was the strongest reproof that I ever heard him give. Especially kindly was he when he praised the singing of ladies. 'Really,' said he once, when a chorus went passably well at the first singing, 'very good, for the first time exceedingly good; but, because it is the first time, let us try it once again:' on which the whole body broke into a merry peal of laughter, and the second time

they sang with great spirit. All prolonging of the tones beyond the
time designated by the written notes, he would not suffer, not even
at the close of the chorus. 'Why do you linger so long on this note,
gentlemen? it is only a quaver.' He was just as averse to all monotonous singing, 'Gentlemen,' he once said at a rehearsal, 'remember this even when you sing at home; do not sing so as to put any
one to sleep, even if it be a cradle-song.' The pianos could not be
sung too softly for him. Did the chorus only sink in a piano passage
to a mezzo-forte, he would cry out, as if in pain, 'Piano, piano, I
hear no piano at all!' It was one of the remarkable features of his
leading to hear the largest choir sink at the right places into the
faintest breath of sound.

Wilhelm Adolph Lampadius: *Felix Mendelssohn-Bartholdy: ein Denkmal für seine
Freunde* (Leipzig, 1849; Eng. tr. W.L. Gage, New York, 1866), pp. 155–8

IV

AS TEACHER

WILLIAM SMITH ROCKSTRO
(1823–1895)

English pianist, composer and writer about music. He studied at the Leipzig Conservatory for one year (1845–6), taking composition lessons from Mendelssohn. He was highly regarded as a teacher and wrote successful textbooks on harmony and counterpoint.

On the 3rd of January, 1846, he entered upon a course of active service at the Conservatorium; assuming the sole command of two pianoforte classes, and one for composition, and in the management of both fulfilling the duties of a hard-working professor with no less enthusiasm than that which he had so long displayed in his character of conductor at the older institution.

Among the members of the upper classes for the study of the pianoforte and composition were, Mr. Otto Goldschmidt, Mons. Michel de Sentis, Herren Tausch, Kalliwoda, Kahlan, and Wettich, and one or two other pupils, who all met regularly, for instruction, on Wednesday and Saturday afternoons, each lesson lasting two hours. The first pianoforte piece selected for study was Hummel's Septett in D minor: and we well remember the look of blank dismay depicted upon more than one excitable countenance, as each pupil in his turn after playing the first chord, and receiving an instantaneous reproof for its want of sonority, was invited to resign his seat in favour of an equally unfortunate successor. Mendelssohn's own manner of playing grand chords, both in *forte* and *piano* passages, was peculiarly impressive; and now, when all present had tried, and failed, he himself sat down to the instrument, and explained the causes of his dissatisfaction with such microscopic minuteness, and clearness of expression, that the lesson was simply priceless. He never gave a learner the chance of mistaking his meaning; and though the vehemence with which he sometimes expressed it made timid pupils desperately afraid of him, he was so perfectly just, so sternly impartial in awarding praise, on the one hand, and blame on the other, that consternation soon gave place to confidence, and confidence to boundless affection. Carelessness infuriated him. Irreverence for the composer he could never forgive. *'Es steht nicht da!'** he almost shrieked one day to a pupil who had added a note to a certain chord. To another, who had scrambled through a difficult passage, he cried, with withering contempt, *'So spielen die Katzen!'*† But, where he saw an earnest desire to do justice to the work in hand, he would give direction after direction, with a lucidity which we have never heard equalled. He never left a piece until he was satisfied that the majority of the class understood it thoroughly. Hummel's Septett formed the chief part of each lesson, until the 25th of February. After that it was relieved, occasionally, by one of Chopin's studies, or a Fugue from the *Wohltemperirte Klavier*. But it was not until the 21st of March that it was finally set aside, to make room for Weber's *Concert-Stück*, the master's reading of which was superb. He would make each pupil play a portion of this great work in his own way, comment upon its delivery with the most perfect frankness, and, if he thought the player deserved encouragement, would himself supply the orchestral passages on a second pianoforte. But he never played through the piece which formed the subject of the lesson in a connected form. On a few rare occasions – we can only remember two or three – he invited the whole class to his house; and, on one of these happy days, he played an entire Sonata – but not that which the members of the class were studying. And the reason of this reticence was obvious. He wished his pupils to understand the principles by which he himself was guided in his interpretation of the works of the great masters, and at the same time to discourage servile imitation of his own rendering of any individual composition. In fact, with regard to special forms of expression, one of his most frequently reiterated maxims was, 'If you want to play with true feeling, you must listen to good singers. You will learn far more from them than from any players you are likely to meet with.'

Upon questions of simple *technique* he rarely touched, except – as in the case of our first precious lesson upon the chord of D minor – with regard to the rendering of certain special passages. But the members of his pianoforte classes were expected to study these

---

* 'It is not there!'
† 'That's how cats play!'

matters, on other days of the week, under Herren Plaidy, or Wenzel, professors of high repute, who had made the training of the fingers, and wrist, their speciality. It would be impossible to over-estimate the value of this arrangement, which provided for the acquirement of a pure touch, and facile execution, on the one hand, while, on the other, it left Mendelssohn free to direct the undivided attention of his pupils to the higher branches of Art. An analogous plan was adopted with regard to the class for composition. The members of this simultaneously studied the technicalities of harmony under Herr F. Richter; those of counterpoint, and fugue, under Herr Hauptmann, the Kantor of the Thomas-Schule, and the most learned contrapuntist in Europe; and those of form, and instrumentation, under Herr Niels W. Gade.

Mendelssohn himself took all these subjects into consideration, by turns, though only in their higher aspect. For counterpoint, he employed a large black-board, with eight red staves drawn across it. On one of these staves he would write a *Canto fermo*; always using the soprano clef for the soprano part.* Then, offering the chalk to one of his pupils, he would bid him write a counterpoint, above, or below, the given subject. This done, he would invite the whole class to criticise the tyro's work; discussing its merits with the closest possible attention to every detail. Having corrected this, to his satisfaction, or, at least, made the best of it, he would pass on the chalk to some one else – generally, to the student who had been most severe in his criticism – bidding him add a third part to the two already written. And this process he would carry on, until the whole of the eight staves were filled. The difficulty of adding a sixth, seventh, or eighth part, to an exercise already complete in three, four, or five, and not always written with the freedom of an experienced contrapuntist, will be best understood by those who have most frequently attempted the process. It was often quite impossible to supply an additional part, or even an additional note; but Mendelssohn would never sanction the employment of a rest, as a means of escape from the gravest difficulty, until every available resource had been tried, in vain.

* No other clef was ever used at the Conservatorium for the soprano part; nor were the students ever permitted to write alto or tenor parts in any other than their true clefs. This wholesome law was absolute in all the classes.

One day, when it fell to our own lot to write the eighth part, a certain bar presented so hopeless a deadlock, that we confessed ourselves utterly vanquished. 'Cannot you find a note?' asked Mendelssohn. 'Not one that could be made to fit in, without breaking a rule,' said we. 'I am very glad,' said he, in English, and laughing heartily, 'for I could not find one myself.' It was, in fact, a case of inevitable check-mate.

We never knew, beforehand, what form the lessons in this class would assume. Sometimes he would give out the words of a song, to be set to music, by each member of the class, before its next meeting; or a few verses of a psalm, to be set in the form of a Motet. When summoned, towards the end of May, 1846, to direct the Lower Rhine Festival, at Aix-la-Chapelle, the task he left for completion during his absence was a Quartett for stringed instruments. When any trial compositions of this kind pleased him, he had them played by the orchestral class; and would even play the viola himself, or ask Herr Gade to play it, in the chamber music;* striving, by every means of encouragement within his power, to promote a wholesome spirit of emulation among his pupils. It was not often that this kindly spirit met with an unworthy response; but the least appearance of ingratitude wounded him, cruelly. When the Quartetts we have mentioned were sent to him for examination, he found one of them headed 'Charivari.' At the next meeting of the class, he asked for an explanation of the title. 'The time was so short,' stammered the composer, 'that I found it impossible to write anything worthy of a better name. I called it "Charivari," to show that I knew it was rubbish.' We could see that Mendelssohn felt deeply hurt; but he kept his temper nobly. 'I am a very busy man,' he said, 'and am, just now, overwhelmed with work. Do you think you were justified in expecting me to waste my time upon a piece which you yourself knew to be "rubbish"? If you are not in earnest, I can have nothing to say to you.' Nevertheless, he analysed the Quartett with quite as much care as the rest, while the culprit stood by, as white as a sheet; well knowing that not a member of the class would speak to him, for many a long day to come. In pleasant contrast to this, we

* In July, 1846, the writer enjoyed the privilege of having a Double Quartett tried in this way, the two first-violin parts being played by David and Joachim.

cannot refrain from giving publicity to a very different story. One of the best pianoforte players in the class was a handsome young Pole, with a profusion of jet-black hair, which, in true Polish fashion, he allowed to hang half-way down his back. While playing the brilliant passages which form the climax of the *Concert-Stück*, the good fellow shook his head, one day, in such sort as to throw his rich locks over his shoulder, in a tempest of '*Kohlpechrabenschwarze Haare* [jet-black hair].' 'You must have your hair cut,' said Mendelssohn, in German, with a merry laugh. The Pole was very proud of his *chevelure*; but, at the next meeting, his hair was the shortest in the class – and there was not a student then present who would not gladly have had his head shaved, could he thereby have purchased the smile with which the happy student was rewarded for his devotion.

More than once, the lesson was devoted to extemporisation upon given subjects; during the course of which Mendelssohn would sit beside the *improvisatore*, and, without interrupting the perform-ance, suggest, from time to time, certain modes of treatment which occurred to him at the moment.* On other occasions, he would take two well-defined motives, and work them up into a model of the Sonata-form, in order to show how much might be accomplished by very simple means. He insisted strongly upon the importance of a natural and carefully arranged system of modulation; and would frequently call up one pupil after another to pass from a given key to some exceedingly remote one, with the least possible amount of apparent effort. On one occasion, when the writer had failed to satisfy him, in an attempt of this kind, he said, in English, 'I call that modulation very ungentlemanlike.'

When the lesson went well, it was easy to see that he thoroughly enjoyed it. But the work was too hard for him, in addition to his other laborious duties; and the acceptance, by Moscheles, of a pianoforte professorship at the Conservatorium, gave him unmixed satisfaction. But for this, the institution must have suffered terribly, when Mendelssohn's health broke down so suddenly, after the

* He once gave the writer a theme, consisting simply of three Cs – a dotted quaver, a semiquaver, and a crotchet: and afterwards extemporised upon it himself; using the three C's as the initial notes of an enchanting little melody, which he worked up into a species of *Lied ohne Worte*.

completion of *Elijah*. But, when the new professor entered upon his duties, in October, 1846, after sacrificing his splendid position in London for the sole purpose of doing the best he could for the interests of Art, all anxiety on this point was at an end; and the history of the Conservatorium, during the next twenty years, sufficiently proves the wisdom of the offer Moscheles so generously accepted.

William Smith Rockstro: *Felix Mendelssohn Bartholdy* (London, 1884), pp. 104–13

CARL REINECKE
(1824–1910)

Reinecke was a German composer, pianist, conductor and musicologist, and a friend of Schumann. After working in various European cities (including Paris, where he taught Liszt's daughters), from 1860 he lived in Leipzig, where he conducted the Gewandhaus Concerts. In 1885 he became a professor at the Conservatory and its Director in 1897. Grieg, Sinding and Sullivan were among his pupils.

Reinecke visited Mendelssohn once, in Leipzig in October 1843, and immediately wrote home to his father describing the occasion. He found the letter years later after his father's death. Mendelssohn received him with the following words:

'I enjoyed your compositions very much; you have a quite definite talent for composition. That's no empty comment on my part (I never make those in such cases); each of your pieces shows that talent, especially the Quartet. But you must go on being very diligent, because there is still one great failing in all your work. You always start off quite attractively, but after the initial exposition it doesn't remain interesting enough. You must summon up more energy and be severe with yourself, to see that you don't write a single bar that you yourself do not find interesting. On the other hand, you must not be so self-critical that you end up writing nothing at all.

Your playing has a fault too, namely that you play too much with an ear to the general effect. You must pay more attention to the details of the piece, but after that you can go for the general effect. But be diligent, young man! You have the youth, strength, health and talent for it. You will already be easily finding the greatest admiration and praise in all the salons, whether in Hamburg or Leipzig. But that's of no help to us. There's always enough admiration and praise around, but there are not enough competent artists, and it is up to you to become one – you have now got to choose. But a young artist like you must never let it happen that he produces a whole volume of songs, all in triple metre.'

When I replied that I had not noticed this aspect of my songs, Mendelssohn countered: 'But it's your job to do so! You must now write quantities of music, every day. If you will only be diligent and severe, very severe with yourself, in a few years you will already be producing fine works for us to listen to.'

> Reinecke did not study with Mendelssohn, who gave no regular lessons outside the Leipzig Conservatory. But some information about Mendelssohn's methods of composition teaching came to Reinecke from his friend Josef von Wasielewski:

In his composition lessons, Mendelssohn looked through the exercises that had been submitted to him and corrected the mistakes in them, for which he would offer explanations as he went along. To one pupil, in whose composition he detected hidden fifths, he said: 'To be on the safe side, you've decorated your fifths with garlands of flowers. But that's no solution: they still offend a discriminating ear.' Another pupil asked him how he should set about writing a quartet. Mendelssohn replied: 'Take a quartet by Haydn or Mozart, and copy the form. That's what my teacher Zelter used to make me do.'

Carl Reinecke: *Neue Zeitschrift für Musik*, 78/1 (1911), pp. 2, 3 (with cuts)

V

AS PERFORMER AND IMPROVISER

IGNAZ MOSCHELES

Diary entry, 22 November 1824

'This afternoon, from two to three o'clock, I gave Felix Mendelssohn his first lesson, without losing sight for a single moment of the fact that I was sitting next to a master, not a pupil. I feel proud that after so short an acquaintance with me his distinguished parents entrust me with their son, and congratulate myself on being permitted to give him some hints, which he seizes on and works out with that genius peculiar to himself.' Six days later he says: 'Felix Mendelssohn's lessons are repeated every second day; to me they are subjects of ever-increasing interest; he has already played with me my Allegri di Bravura, my concertos, and other things, and how played! The slightest hint from me, and he guesses at my conception.'

Ignaz Moscheles, quoted in Charlotte Moscheles: *Aus Moscheles Leben* (Leipzig, 1872; Eng. tr. A.D. Coleridge, London, 1873), II, pp. 99–100

HEINRICH FRIEDRICH LUDWIG RELLSTAB
(1799–1860)

German music critic and poet. He met Beethoven in 1825 and in 1828 Schubert set ten of his poems (including seven in *Schwanengesang*). From 1826 he was prominent as a music critic, promoting the music of Cherubini, Spohr, Weber and Mendelssohn.

In the evening, we assembled in Goethe's rooms to tea; for he had invited a large party of his Weimar musical acquaintances to make them acquainted with the boy's extraordinary talents. A certain solemnity was visible among the guests, prior to the entrance of the great poet; and even those who stood on terms of intimacy with him underwent a feeling of veneration. His slow, serious walk, his impressive features, which expressed the strength rather than weakness of old age; the lofty forehead; the white, abundant hair;

lastly, the deep voice, and slow way of speaking, – all united to produce the effect. His 'good evening' was addressed to all; but he walked up to Zelter first, and shook his hand cordially. Felix Mendelssohn looked up, with sparkling eyes, at the snow-white head of the poet. The latter, however, placed his hands kindly on the boy's head, and said, 'Now you shall play us something,' Zelter nodded his assent.

The piano was opened, and lights arranged on the desk. Mendelssohn asked Zelter, to whom he displayed a thoroughly childish devotion and confidence, 'What shall I play?'

'Well, what you can,' the latter replied, in his peculiarly sharp voice; 'whatever is not too difficult for you.'

To me, who knew what the boy could do, and that no task was too difficult for him, this seemed an unjust depreciation of his faculties. It was at length arranged that he should play a fantasia; which he did to the wonder of all. But the young artist knew when to leave off; and thus the effect he produced was all the greater. A silence of surprise ensued when he raised his hands from the keys after a loud finale.

Zelter was the first to interrupt the silence in his humorous way, by saying aloud, 'Ha! you must have been dreaming of kobolds and dragons: why, that went over stick and stone!' At the same time there was a perfect indifference in his tone, as if there were nothing remarkable in the matter. Without doubt, the teacher intended to prevent, in this way, the danger of a too brilliant triumph. The playing, however, as it could not well be otherwise, aroused the highest admiration of all present; and Goethe, especially, was full of the warmest delight. He encouraged the lad, in whose childish features joy, pride, and confusion were at once depicted, by taking his head between his hands, patting him kindly, and saying jestingly, 'But you will not get off with that. You must play more pieces before we recognise your merits.'

'But what shall I play?' Felix asked: 'Herr Professor,' – he was wont to address Zelter by this title, – 'what shall I play now?'

I cannot say that I have properly retained the pieces the young virtuoso now performed; for they were numerous. I will, however, mention the most interesting.

Goethe was a great admirer of Bach's fugues, which a musician of Berka, a little town about ten miles from Weimar, came to play to him repeatedly. Felix was therefore requested to play a fugue of the grand old master. Zelter selected it from the music-book; and the boy played it without any preparation, but with perfect certainty.

Goethe's delight grew with the boy's extraordinary powers. Among other things, he requested him to play a minuet.

'Shall I play you the loveliest in the whole world?' he asked, with sparkling eyes.

'Well, and which is that?'

He played the minuet from 'Don Giovanni.'

Goethe stood by the instrument, listening; joy glistening in his features. He wished for the overture of the opera after the minuet; but this the player roundly declined, with the assertion, that it could not be played as it was written, and nobody dared make any alteration in it. He, however, offered to play the overture to 'Figaro.' He commenced it with a lightness of touch, – such certainty and clearness as I never heard again. At the same time he gave the orchestral effects so magnificently that the effect was extraordinary; and I can honestly state, that it afforded me more gratification than ever an orchestral performance did. Goethe grew more and more cheerful and kind, and even played tricks with the talented lad.

'Well, come,' he said, 'you have only played me pieces you know; but now we will see whether you can play something you do not know. I will put you on trial.'

Goethe went out, re-entered the room in a few moments, and had a roll of music in his hand. 'I have fetched something from my manuscript collection. Now we will try you. Do you think you can play this?'

He laid a page, with clear but small notes, on the desk. It was Mozart's handwriting. Whether Goethe told us so, or it was written on the paper, I forget, and only remember that Felix glowed with delight at the name; and an indescribable feeling came over us all, partly enthusiasm and joy, partly admiration and expectation. Goethe, the aged man, laying a manuscript of Mozart, who had been buried thirty years, before a lad so full of promise for the future, to play at sight, – in truth such a constellation may be termed a rarity.

The young artist played with the most perfect certainty, not making the slightest mistake, though the manuscript was far from easy reading. The task was certainly not difficult, especially for Mendelssohn, as it was only an adagio: still there was a difficulty in doing it as the lad did; for he played it as if he had been practising it for years.

Goethe adhered to his good-humoured tone, while all the rest applauded. 'That is nothing,' he said: 'others could read that too. But I will now give you something over which you will stick; so take care.'

With these words, he produced another paper, which he laid on the desk. This certainly looked very strange. It was difficult to say if they were notes or only a paper, ruled, and splashed with ink and blots. Felix Mendelssohn, in his surprise, laughed loudly. 'How is that written? who can read it?' he said.

But suddenly he became serious; for while Goethe was saying, 'Now, guess who wrote it?' Zelter, who had walked up to the piano, and looked over the boy's shoulder, exclaimed, 'Why, Beethoven wrote that! any one could see it a mile off. He always writes with a broomstick, and passes his sleeve over the notes before they are dry. I have plenty of his manuscripts. They are easy to know.'

At the mention of the name, as I remarked, Mendelssohn had suddenly grown serious, – even more than serious. A shade of awe was visible on his features. Goethe regarded him with searching eyes, from which delight beamed. The boy kept his eyes immovably fixed on the manuscript; and a look of glad surprise flew over his features as he traced a brilliant thought amid the chaos of confused blurred notes.

But all this lasted only a few seconds; for Goethe wished to make a severe trial, and give the performer no time for preparation. 'You see,' he exclaimed, 'I told you that you would stick. Now try it: show us what you can do.'

Felix began playing immediately. It was a simple melody; if clearly written, a trifling, I may say no task, for even a moderate performer. But to follow it through the scrambling labyrinth required a quickness and certainty of eye such as few are able to attain. I glanced with surprise at the leaf, and tried to hum the tune; but many of the notes were perfectly illegible, or had to be sought at the most unexpected corners, as the boy often pointed out with a laugh.

He played it through once in this way, generally correctly, but stopping at times, and correcting several mistakes with a quick 'No, so:' then he exclaimed, 'Now I will play it to you.' And, this second time, not a note was missing. 'This is Beethoven, this passage,' he said once turning to me, as if he had come across something which sharply displayed the master's peculiar style. 'That is true Beethoven. I recognise him in it at once.'

With this trial-piece Goethe broke off. I need scarcely add, that the young player again reaped the fullest praise, which Goethe veiled in mocking jests, that he had stuck here and there, and had not been quite sure.

H.F. Ludwig Rellstab, quoted in Wilhelm Adolph Lampadius: *Felix Mendelssohn-Bartholdy: ein Denkmal für seine Freunde* (Leipzig, 1849; Eng. tr. W.L. Gage, New York, 1866), pp. 204–8

FERDINAND HILLER

Felix made his third and last visit to Paris between December 1831 and April 1832:

Mendelssohn had brought with him to Paris the draught-score of the 'Hebrides' Overture. He told me that not only was its general form and colour suggested to him by the sight of Fingal's Cave, but that the first few bars, containing the principal subject, had actually occurred to him on the spot. The same evening he and his friend Klingemann paid a visit to a Scotch family. There was a piano in the drawing-room, but being Sunday, music was utterly out of the question, and Mendelssohn had to employ all his diplomacy to get the instrument opened for a single minute, so that he and Klingemann might hear the theme which forms the germ of that original and masterly Overture, which, however, was not completed till some years later at Düsseldorf.

It was through Habeneck and his 'Société des Concerts' that

Mendelssohn was introduced to the Parisian public. He played the Beethoven G major Concerto – with what success may be seen from his published letters.* The 'Midsummer Night's Dream Overture' was also performed and much applauded. I was present at the first rehearsal. The second oboe was missing – which might have been overcome; but just as they were going to begin, the drummer's place was also discovered to be empty. Upon which, to everybody's amusement, Mendelssohn jumped on to the orchestra, seized the drumsticks, and beat as good a roll as any drummer in the Old Guard. For the performance a place had been given him in a box on the grand tier, with a couple of distinguished musical amateurs. During the last *forte*, after which the fairies return once more, one of these gentlemen said to the other: 'C'est très-bien, très-bien, mais nous savons le reste;' and they slipped out without hearing the 'reste,' and without any idea that they had been sitting next the composer.

The termination of Mendelssohn's connection with that splendid orchestra was unpleasant, and hurt him much. It was proposed to give his Reformation Symphony, and a rehearsal took place. I was not present, but the only account which our young friends gave me was that the work did not please the orchestra: at any rate it was not performed. Cuvillon's description was that it was 'much too learn-ed, too much *fugato*, too little melody,' &c., &c. To a certain extent the composer probably came round to this opinion, for the Symphony was not published during his lifetime. But at the time I am writing of he was very fond of it, and the quiet way in which it was shelved certainly pained him. I never referred to the occurrence, and he never spoke of it to me.

Ferdinand Hiller: *Felix Mendelssohn-Bartholdy* (Cologne, 1874; Eng. tr. M.E. von Glehn, London, 1874), pp. 18–22 (with cuts)

HENRY FOTHERGILL CHORLEY

In the final concert of the 1839 Brunswick Festival, Mendelssohn played his Piano Concerto in D minor and his *Serenade and Allegro giocoso* in B minor:

* To his mother, Paris, 15 and 31 March 1832

The pianoforte playing was of course the chief treat. It is rarely that I have been so delighted, without novelty or surprise having some share in the delight. It would have been absurd to expect much *pianism*, as distinct from music, in the performance of one writing so straightforwardly, and without the coquetries of embroidery, as Mendelssohn. Accordingly, his performance had none of the exquisite *finesses* of Moscheles, on the score of which it has been elsewhere said that 'there is wit in his playing;' none of the delicate and plaintive and spiritual seductions of Chopin, who swept the keys with so insinuating and gossamer a touch, that the crudest and most chromatic harmonies of his music floated away under his hand, indistinct, yet not unpleasing, like the wild and softened discords of the Æolian harp; none of the brilliant extravagances of Liszt, by which he illuminates every composition he undertakes with a living but lightening fire, and imparts to it a soul of passion, or a dazzling vivacity, the interpretation never contradicting the author's intention, but more poignant, more intense, more glowing, than ever the author dreamed of. And yet no one that ever heard Mendelssohn's pianoforte playing could find it dry, could fail to be excited and fascinated by it, despite of its want of all the caprices and colourings of his contemporaries. Solidity, in which the organ-touch is given to the piano without the organ ponderosity; spirit (witness his execution to the finale of the 'D-minor Concerto') animating, but never intoxicating, the ear; expression, which, making every tone sink deep, required not the garnishing of trills and appoggiature, or the aid of changes of time, – were among its outward and salient characteristics.

Henry Fothergill Chorley: *Modern German Music* (London, 1854), I, pp. 50–51

ELISE POLKO
(1823–1899)

A writer on music. Sir George Grove condemned this volume of Mendelssohn reminiscences as 'a poor gushing book'.

It was Mendelssohn who first originated the idea of erecting a monument to the memory of the venerable Father of German church music, to be placed opposite the scene of his labours within the precincts of the Thomas School. He forthwith applied himself with the greatest energy to the execution of this scheme, and arranged a series of organ-concerts, the profits of which were to be devoted to the erection of a Bach monument. A reverent assemblage crowded every place and corner of the ancient time-honoured church of St Thomas on the 6th of August, 1840, for the purpose of hearing Mendelssohn for the first time play the organ. The programme was exclusively made up of his own performances, thus devoting his powers to the fulfilment of his cherished wish. Bach's splendid fugue in E-flat major came first; then his Fantasia on the Chorale 'Schmücke dich, o liebe Seele;' a Prelude and Fugue in A minor, with twenty-one variations; the Pastorella and the Trinata, in A minor; and finally, Mendelssohn wound up the concert by extemporising on the most deeply touching choral-melody in the world –

O Haupt voll Blut und Wunden!

No musician of the modern time was seated above in the organ-loft. No! it was the old and marvellous Sebastian Bach himself playing there! Sacred awe pervaded the souls of the hearers, and tears rushed to eyes that had long since ceased to weep. The worthy old Rochlitz embraced the young master at the close of the concert, saying, 'I can now depart in peace, for never shall I hear anything finer or more sublime.'

Elise Polko: *Erinnerungen an Felix Mendelssohn-Bartholdy* (Leipzig, 1868; Eng. tr. Lady Wallace, London, 1869), pp. 86–7 (with cuts)

JOSEPH JOACHIM
(1831–1907)

After studying violin with Ferdinand David at the Leipzig Conservatory, he became Concertmaster under Liszt at Weimar in 1849 and Director of the Berlin Hochschule in 1868. Schumann, Max Bruch, Brahms and Dvořák dedicated their concertos to him.

Dr. Joachim refers to the friendly relations which existed between Mendelssohn and Schumann. 'Schumann is one of the finest men I know,' Mendelssohn remarked to his young friend; and on the occasion of one of Joachim's visits, he said: 'We won't have any music to-day; I am going to take you to hear Schumann's "Paradise and the Peri."' Thither we went, Mendelssohn paying for his ticket and mine. One of the nicknames he bestowed upon me was "Teufelsbraten" ("Devil's tit-bit"), I suppose because I was a fat boy! Another nickname was "Posaunen-Engel" ("trombone cherub").' Dr. Joachim speaks enthusiastically of Mendelssohn's remarkable pianoforte playing. 'No one could equal his *staccato*, its crispness was extraordinary. I once heard him play the Overture to "Coriolan" on the pianoforte, when he brought out the effects of the orchestral score in a most astonishing manner.'

At a concert given by a Mr. Purdy, at Radley's Hotel, Bridge Street, Blackfriars, on June 5, 1844, Mendelssohn was announced to play his D minor Trio with Master Joachim and Mr. Hancock. 'It so happened,' relates Dr. Joachim, 'that only the violin and violoncello parts had been brought to the concert-room, and Mendelssohn was rather displeased at this; but he said, "Never mind, put any book on the piano, and someone can turn from time to time, so that I need not look as though I played by heart." Now-a-days, when people put such importance on playing or conducting without a book, I think this might be considered a good moral lesson of a great musician's modesty. He evidently did not like to be in too great a prominence before his partners in the Trio. He was always truly generous!'

Joseph Joachim: interview in *The Musical Times*, 1 April 1898, pp. 226–7 (with cuts)

FELIX MOSCHELES

One of Mendelssohn's earliest gifts to him was an album containing the *Wiegenlied* ('Slumber Song').

In due course of time, and after full enjoyment of the Slumber Song, I got out of my cradle and on to my legs, and it is from that stage in my development that I really date my recollections of my godfather.

Some are hazy, others distinct. I am often surprised when I realise that he was short of stature; to me, the small boy, he appeared very tall. I looked upon him as my own special godfather, in whom I had a sort of vested interest, and I showed my annoyance when I was not allowed to monopolise him, or at least to remain near him. Being put to bed was at best a hateful process; how much more so, then, when I was just happily installed on my godfather's knee; occasions of that kind are connected in my mind with vociferous protests, followed by ignominious expulsion.

There were, however, happier times soon to follow, times which recall to me our exploits in the Park. He could throw my ball farther than anybody else; and he could run faster too, but then, to be sure, for all that, *I* could catch him.

One of my achievements, when I was a little boy in a black velvet blouse, was the impersonation of what we called 'the dead man'; the dying man would have been more correct. From my earliest days I evidently pitied the soldier dying a violent death on the battle-field. Since then I have learnt to extend my commiseration to the tax-payer, and to the many innocent victims of a barbarous and iniquitous system. Well, the dying man in the blouse was stretched full length – say some three feet – on the Brussels carpet. Mendelssohn or my father were at the piano improvising a running accompaniment to my performance, and between us we illustrated musically and dramatically the throes and spasms of the expiring hero.

The dead-man improvisations remind me of the marvellous way in which my father and godfather would improvise together, play-ing *à quatre mains*, or alternately, and pouring forth a never-failing stream of musical ideas. I have spoken of it before, but it was in a preface, and who reads a preface? So I may perhaps once more be allowed to describe it. A subject started, it was caught up as if it were a shuttlecock; now one of the players would seem to toss it up on high, or to keep it balanced in mid-octaves with delicate touch. Then the other would take it in hand, start it on classical lines, and develop it with profound erudition, until perhaps the two joining together in new and brilliant forms, would triumphantly carry it off to other spheres of sound. Four hands there might be, but only one soul, so it seemed, as they would catch with lightning speed at each other's ideas, each trying to introduce subjects from the works of the other.

It was exciting to watch how the amicable contest would wax hot, culminating occasionally in an outburst of merriment, when some conflicting harmonies met in terrible collision. I see Mendelssohn's air of triumph when he had succeeded in twisting a subject from a composition of his own into a Moscheles theme, while the latter was obliged to second him in the bass. But not for long. 'Stop a minute,' said the next few chords that my father struck. 'There I have you, you have taken the bait.' Soon they would be again fraternising in perfect harmonies, gradually leading up to the brilliant finale that sounded as if it had been so written, revised and corrected, and were now being interpreted from the score by two masters.

Following the example of the parents, the children of the two families soon fraternised too. I recollect a very lively children's party at our house. Mendelssohn came in and joined in the games; then he went to the piano and set us all a dancing as only the rhythm of his improvisation could. When he ended, we clamoured for more. Give any child a Mendelssohn finger and no wonder it wants the ten. We got another splendid waltz that glided into a galop, but when that too came to an end, we insatiable little tyrants would not let him get up from the piano.

'Well,' he said, 'if all the little girls will go down on their knees and beg and pray of me, I may be induced to give you one more dance.' A circle was soon formed around him, and they had to beg hard, harder, and hardest, before he allowed himself to be softened.

Felix Moscheles: *Fragments of an Autobiography* (New York, 1899), pp. 35–8, 101–2 (with cuts)

WILHELM ADOLPH LAMPADIUS

Mendelssohn's skill as a virtuoso was no mere legerdemain, no enormous finger facility, that only aims to dazzle by trills, chromatic runs, and octave passages; it was that true, manly *virtus* from which the word virtuoso is derived; that steadfast energy which overcomes all mechanical hindrances, not to produce musical noise, but music, and not satisfied with anything short of exhibiting the very spirit of productions written in every age of the musical art. The characteristic features of his playing were a very elastic touch, a wonderful trill, elegance, roundness, firmness, perfect articulation, strength, and tenderness, each in its needed place. His chief excellence lay, as Goethe said, in his giving every piece, from the Bach epoch down, its own distinctive character; and yet, with all his loyalty to the old masters, he knew just how to conceal their obsolete forms by adding new graces in the very manner of his playing. Especially beautiful was his playing of Beethoven's compositions, and the adagios most of all, which he rendered with unspeakable tenderness and depth of feeling. The soft passages were where his strength lay, in his performance upon the pianoforte, as they were in his leading of a great choir; and in this no man has surpassed him, I might say no one has approached him. His skill on the tenor-viol has already been spoken of. He possessed a pleasant, but not strong tenor voice; but he never used it, except at the chorus rehearsals, or, at the practice of a soloist, to give an idea of a phrase or an interval, or, at the most, to sing a brief recitative.

Wilhelm Adolph Lampadius: *Felix Mendelssohn-Bartholdy: ein Denkmal für seine Freunde* (Leipzig, 1849; Eng. tr. W.L. Gage, New York, 1866), pp. 158–9

MR BEATTY-KINGSTON

In his recently published volume of reminiscences, entitled 'Men, Cities, and Events,' Mr. Beatty-Kingston gives a circumstantial account of his introduction to Mendelssohn, before whom he played at the age of nine. To mark his appreciation of the boy's effort, Mendelssohn offered to extemporise on any theme which was given to him. Master Beatty-Kingston – we speak retrospectively, *bien entendu* – accordingly suggested 'The Blue Bells of Scotland,' and Mendelssohn extemporised some twenty Variations, 'each illustrating a special method of subject-treatment or branch of technical proficiency . . . Amongst other amazing feats, I remember the "canonisation" of the melody *alla seconda* and *alla settima*; two versions differently harmonised, in the minor mood; an inimitable left hand *étude* in the Chopinesque manner, and a tremendous four-part fugue, with episodical inversion of the subject, leading into a stately chorale, at the close of which Mendelssohn fairly broke out into one of those fanciful, incomparable *cadenze* in which he notoriously delighted to "let himself go," and which may fairly be said to have exhausted the difficulties of pianoforte playing. This paramount achievement, which lasted fully three minutes, culminated in a triumphal March, with which the improvisation closed, and which sounded throughout as though it were being played by four hands instead of two.'

Mr Beatty-Kingston, quoted in *The Musical Times*, 1 December 1895

SIR GEORGE GROVE
(1820–1900)

Civil engineer, Biblical scholar and writer on music. For fifteen years he was editor of *Macmillan's Magazine* until, in 1883, he became the first Director of the Royal College of Music and was knighted.

'His mechanism,' says another of his Leipzig pupils, [Otto Goldschmidt] 'was extremely subtle, and developed with the lightest of wrists (never from the arm); he therefore never strained the instrument or hammered. His chord-playing was beautiful, and based on a special theory of his own. His use of the pedal was very sparing, clearly defined, and therefore effective; his phrasing beautifully clear. The performances in which I derived the most lasting impressions from him were the 32 Variations and last Sonata (Op. 111) of Beethoven, in which latter the Variations of the final movement came out more clearly in their structure and beauty than I have ever heard before or since.' Of his playing of the 32 Variations, Professor Macfarren remarks that 'to each one, or each pair, where they go in pairs, he gave a character different from all the others. In playing at sight from a MS. score he characterised every incident by the peculiar tone by which he represented the instrument for which it was written.' In describing his playing of the 9th Symphony, Mr. Schleinitz testified to the same singular power of representing the different instruments.

His adherence to his author's meaning, and to the indications given in the music, was absolute. Strict time was one of his hobbies. He alludes to it, with an eye to the sins of Hiller and Chopin, in a letter of May 23, 1834, and somewhere else speaks of 'nice strict tempo' as something peculiarly pleasant. After introducing some *ritardandos* in conducting the Introduction to Beethoven's 2nd Symphony, he excused himself by saying that 'one could not always be good,' and that he had felt the inclination too strongly to resist it. In playing, however, he never himself interpolated a *ritardando*, or suffered it in any one else. It especially enraged him when done at the end of a song or other piece. 'Es steht nicht da!' he would say; 'if it were intended it would be written in – they think it expression, but it is sheer affectation.' But though in playing he never varied the *tempo* when once taken, he did not always take a movement at the same pace, but changed it as his mood was at the time. We have seen in the case of Bach's A minor Fugue that he could on occasion introduce an individual reading; and his treatment of the arpeggios in the Chromatic Fantasia shows that, there at least, he allowed himself great latitude. Still, in imitating this it should be remembered how thoroughly he knew these great masters, and how perfect his sympathy with them was. In conducting, as we have just seen, he was more elastic, though even there his variations would now be condemned as moderate by some conductors. Before he conducted at the Philharmonic it had been the tradition in the Coda of the Overture to Egmont to return to a *piano* after the *crescendo*; but this he would not suffer, and maintained the *fortissimo* to the end – a practice now always followed.

He very rarely played from book, and his prodigious memory was also often shown in his sudden recollection of out-of-the-way pieces.

His extemporising was however marked by other traits than that of memory. 'It was,' says Prof. Macfarren, 'as fluent and as well planned as a written work,' and the themes, whether borrowed or invented, were not merely brought together but contrapuntally worked. Instances of this have been mentioned at Birmingham and elsewhere. His tact in these things was prodigious. At the concert given by Jenny Lind and himself on Dec. 5, 1845, he played two Songs without words – Bk. vi, No. I, in E♭, and Bk. v, No. 6, in A major, and he modulated from the one key to the other by means of a regularly constructed intermezzo, in which the semiquavers of the first song merged into the arpeggios of the second with the most consummate art, and with magical effect. But great as were his public displays, it would seem that, like Mozart, it was in the small circle of intimate friends that his improvisation was most splendid and happy. Those only who had the good fortune to find themselves (as rarely happened) alone with him at one of his Sunday afternoons are perhaps aware of what he could really do in this direction, and he 'never improvised better' or pleased himself more than when *tête à tête* with the Queen and Prince Albert.

Sir George Grove: *Dictionary of Music and Musicians*, first edition (London, 1880), pp. 299–300 (article on Mendelssohn; with cuts)

CLARA SCHUMANN
(1819–1896)

As Clara Wieck, she toured Europe successfully as a pianist from the age of thirteen. In 1840 she married Robert Schumann.

My recollections of Mendelssohn's playing are among the most delightful things in my artistic life. It was to me a shining ideal, full of genius and life, united with technical perfection. He would sometimes take the *tempi* very quick, but never to the prejudice of the music. It never occurred to me to compare him with virtuosi. Of mere effects of performance he knew nothing – he was always the great musician, and in hearing him one forgot the player, and only revelled in the full enjoyment of the music. He could carry one with him in the most incredible manner, and his playing was always stamped with beauty and nobility. In his early days he had acquired perfection of technique; but latterly, as he often told me, he hardly ever practised, and yet he surpassed every one. I have heard him in Bach, and Beethoven, and in his own compositions, and shall never forgot the impression he made upon me.

Clara Schumann, quoted in Sir George Grove: *Dictionary of Music and Musicians*, first edition (London, 1880), p. 298 (article on Mendelssohn)

FERDINAND HILLER

Mendelssohn's playing was to him what flying is to a bird. No one wonders why a lark flies, it is inconceivable without that power. In the same way Mendelssohn played the piano because it was his nature. He possessed great skill, certainty, power, and rapidity of execution, a lovely full tone – all in fact that a virtuoso could desire, but these qualities were forgotten while he was playing, and one almost overlooked even those more spiritual gifts which we call fire, invention, soul, apprehension, etc. When he sat down to the instrument music streamed from him with all the fullness of his inborn genius, – he was a centaur, and his horse was the piano. What he played, how he played it, and that he was the player – all were equally rivetting, and it was impossible to separate the execution, the music, and the executant. This was absolutely the case in his improvisations, so poetical, artistic, and finished; and almost as much so in his execution of the music of Bach, Mozart, Beethoven, or himself. Into those three masters he had grown, and they had become his spiritual property. The music of other composers he knew, but could not produce it as he did theirs. I do not think, for instance, that his execution of Chopin was at all to be compared to his execution of the masters just mentioned; he did not care particularly for it, though when alone he played everything good with interest. In playing at sight his skill and rapidity of comprehension were astonishing, and that not with P.F. music only, but with the most complicated compositions. He never practised, though he once told me that in his Leipzig time he had played a shake (I think with the 2nd and 3rd fingers) several minutes every day for some months, till he was perfect in it.

Ferdinand Hiller, quoted in Sir George Grove: *Dictionary of Music and Musicians*, first edition (London, 1880), pp. 298–9 (article on Mendelssohn)

VI

MUSICAL TASTES AND ATTITUDES
– AND STRUGGLES WITH OPERA

JOHANN CHRISTIAN LOBE
(1797–1881)

German composer and theorist, highly regarded by
Goethe and his circle.

I do not know whether there is anyone who can boast of having had
long conversations with Mendelssohn. So far as I knew him, they
were not his cup of tea. Men of small knowledge and fine-sounding
words tried in vain to draw him into conversation. He eluded them
with a remark, or, if they attempted to hold him against his will,
broke off curtly. Many an unsympathetic judgment about his works
may have flowed from just such conversations rebuffed. People
declared that he was proud and took their revenge in journalistic
attacks.

On a walk our conversation once turned to the 'school' and the
disdain with which people were now (then) beginning to inveigh
against it, as a drag on genius.

'This opinion,' he exclaimed, 'is an insult to both reason and
experience! What concept do such people attach to the word
'school'? If someone has the greatest musical genius – can he compose without knowledge of chords and the rules governing their
relationships? Can he form a piece of music without having studied
the laws of musical form? Can he orchestrate without knowing the
instruments, without having had a hundredfold the experience of
their inexhaustible combinations? And is all of this not schooling?'

'But you must admit,' I objected, 'that many artists who have
their schooling completely under control do not create any significant works, while there are artists lacking schooling who accomplish important things.'

'Well,' he replied, 'school cannot make talent; and if you do not
have any, it will not help you. But that one can make anything
sensible without schooling is something you will have to prove to
me. I do not know of any examples. Someone can show talent without schooling, but so far as creating a genuine work of art, he
should forget about it. Too bad, we say, that this artist has studied
so little, or has so little true artistic insight. How much more

important his works would have become *if he had learned more.*
And such talents, who have never matured on account of their lack
of study, have invented that sentence as consolation for their own
inner accusations, and other lazybones have adopted it.'

On another occasion I tried to obtain clarification on a point that
was very important to me.

'I am told,' I said, 'that in your compositions you make many
changes, often right up until the moment when you hand in the
manuscript. Unfortunately, it is the same with me, and much worse;
for I could not name a single one of my works in which I have not
found deficiencies to complain about after it was printed, passages
that now come to me more clearly, but that can no longer be
banished.'

Mendelssohn had two main ways of smiling. One was the
incomparably lovely smile that played about his face when he had a
satisfied, cheerful thought; the other contained a slight sarcastic
admixture on occasions when he had something to criticise, without its seeming severe enough to make him feel bitter. The latter
occurred very seldom with him in any case – or else, as a finely
cultivated man of the world, he had learned to suppress it.

'The misfortune you complain about happens to me, too,' he
said. 'In everything I have written down there is at least as much
deleted as there is allowed to stand. We should take comfort from
the greatest masters, who suffered no better fate. Ah, if it were only
weak passages that the imagination, that wily dissembler, smuggled
past an intoxicated judgment onto paper! She plays worse tricks
than that on me! Sometimes she seduces me into writing an entire
work that I later have to recognize is a piece of shoddy merchandise!
Among twelve songs that I put together, I considered only six
worthy of print, and threw out the other six. My *St. Paul* originally
had a third more numbers, which never saw the light of day. What
do you say to that?' he asked, smiling sarcastically.

'The world *forgets very easily*,' he remarked, 'and the artist, once
he has appeared in public, must try to forestall that forgetfulness
through continuous publication of new works. He must not be
absent from any fair catalog. In each one, his name must come
before the eyes of the public, for it often takes a long time before the

public responds to something. There are more and more composers. Disappear from the music catalogs for a few years, and you are lost, because forgotten.

'And since not every work the artist creates succeeds, and since he must always demonstrate that he is productive, he can and must let a weak performance get out from time to time along with the others, just to hold his place. If the thing is nothing special, he has nevertheless shown himself to be a vigorous worker, and so one hopes he will produce something better the next time. You can forgive someone you are interested in if he has a bad mood or is dry, but you will become indifferent to him if he comes too seldom, and finally you will not care about him at all, if he stays away entirely.'

'How is it,' he asked me once, 'that you have fallen silent as a composer? I have the impression that you have not published anything for several years now? That is a great mistake, as I have said to you previously. Your productivity can hardly have run out already?'

'The productivity perhaps not,' I responded, 'but the desire to produce. A single comment from a critical journal has frightened me off from composing, I believe forever, since unfortunately it seemed to me to be correct.'

'Good gracious, what kind of a comment can that have been?' he asked wit a smile.

' "He has talent, *but he will not break any new ground.*" '

'Hmmm!' he said, 'that frightened you off?'

'Indeed,' I replied, 'I found that everything I had done not only failed to surpass the best that was already in existence, but did not even come close to it. Now I really tried to improve. I resolved to be exceedingly original, from the first thought to the last, and to write more beautifully than could ever be expected. But my imagination did not bring forth what I desired. It did not show me a single thought that satisfied my demands, that would have made me appear as a traveler down a new path, so the pen finally dropped from my hand and I became resigned.'

'Yes, yes,' he said, 'I know how that is. When you first start a composition you have a lofty idea of what you can and will create this time! The ideas for which you search always appear more beautiful in their vague presentiment than they are later on paper. I have experienced similar things, but I soon got a grip on myself. If we only wanted to accept the ideas that agreed *perfectly* with our desires, then we would accomplish nothing at all, or at most very little. For this reason I, too, have sometimes left works I had started unfinished and not completed them.'

'That means nothing,' I commented. 'All artists have left torsos behind, as a result of the realization that they have blundered.'

'That may be,' he replied. 'Such an unfinished work makes me extremely discomfited and hesitant to start another. I regret the time I have wasted on it. So I called a halt and swore that I would not stop working on any work I had begun, but would finish every one, no matter how it turns out. If it does not become a work of art in the highest sense, at least it is an exercise in forming and portraying ideas. Here you have the reason why I have made so many composi-tions that have not been published and never will be published.'

'But *your* reason for not wanting to write any more, because you do not hope to break any new ground, is – if you will pardon me – not reasonable. What does this phrase mean, actually? To clear a path that no one has walked before you? But first this new path would have to lead to much more beautiful, more charming terri-tory. For just clearing a new path can be done by anyone who knows how to wield a shovel and move his legs. In every nobler sense, however, I deny forthwith that there are new paths to be cleared, for there are no more new artistic territories. All of them have long since been discovered. New ground! Vexatious demon for every artist who submits to it! Never, in fact, did an artist break new ground. In the best case he did things imperceptibly better than his immediate predecessors. Who should break the new ground? Surely no one but the most sublime geniuses? Well, did Beethoven open up new ground completely different from that of Mozart? Do Beethoven's symphonies proceed down completely new paths? No, I say. Between the first symphony of Beethoven and the last of Mozart I find no extraordinary [leap in] artistic value, and no more than ordinary effect. The one pleases me and the other pleases me. Today, if I hear Beethoven's Symphony in D major, I am happy, and tomorrow, if I hear the C-major of Mozart, with the final fugue, I am happy too. I do not think about a new path in Beethoven's case, and there is nothing to remind me. What an opera *Fidelio* is! I do not say that every idea in it appeals to me completely, but I would like to know the name of the opera that could have a more profound effect, or offer more enchanting pleasures to the listener. Do you find in it a single number with which Beethoven broke new ground? I do not. I look at the score and listen to the performance, and everywhere I find Cherubini's dramatic musical style. Beethoven was not imitating it, but he had it in mind as a favorite musical model.'

'And Beethoven's last period?' I asked. 'His last quartets, his Ninth Symphony? His mass? Here one cannot speak of a comparability with Mozart, or with any other artist before or after him.'

'That may be, in a certain sense,' he continued animatedly. 'His forms are wider and broader, the style is more polyphonic, more artificial, the ideas for the most part darker, more melancholy, even when they want to be cheerful; the instrumentation is fuller, and *he went somewhat farther along the path he had already embarked on, but he did not clear a new one.* And let us be honest; where did he lead us? To regions that are really *more beautiful*? As *artists*, is the pleasure that we feel at the Ninth Symphony absolutely *greater* than what we feel at most of his other symphonies? As far as I am concerned, I will say quite openly: no! When I listen to it, I celebrate a joyous hour, but the C-minor symphony gives me occasion for a similar celebration, and what I experience with the former is perhaps not quite so unsullied, so pure, as with the latter.'

On a subsequent occasion, I again brought the conversation around to the question of 'new ground.' The thought tormented me, and Mendelssohn's reasoning had not convinced or pacified me at all.

'Recently,' I began, 'I heard your overture to *A Midsummer Night's Dream* for the first time. It seems to me to surpass all your earlier works in its originality, and I cannot compare it with any other piece; it has no sisters, no family resemblance. So one would probably be justified in saying that you have broken new ground with it?'

'Not at all,' he retorted. 'You have forgotten that what I understand by "new ground" is creations that obey newly discovered and at the same time more sublime artistic laws. In my overture I have not given expression to a single new maxim. For example, you will find the very same maxims I followed in the great overture to Beethoven's *Fidelio*. My *ideas* are different, they are Mendelssohnian, not Beethovenian, but the *maxims* according to which I composed it are also Beethoven's maxims. It would be terrible indeed if, walking along the same path and creating according to the same principles, one could not come up with new ideas and images. What did Beethoven do in his overture? He painted the content of his piece in tone pictures. I tried to do the same thing. He did it in a broader overture form, and used more extended periods; so did I. But basically, the form of our periods follows the same laws under which the concept 'period' generally presents itself to human intelligence. And you can examine all the musical elements; nowhere will you find in my overture anything at all that Beethoven did not have and practice, unless' – he smiled roguishly – 'you want to consider it as new ground that I used the ophicleide.

'If I am considered to have originality, I realize that I owe *most* of it to my strict self-criticism and my drive to change and better myself. I have turned and tested my ideas – how frequently I altered each one! – in order to transform their originally ordinary physiognomy into a more original, more meaningful and effective one. Just as it can happen that one or several notes, if their pitches or rhythms are treated differently, can give a particular idea an entirely different physiognomy and expression, so, in a larger context, a period that is inserted or omitted can make something ordinary and ineffective into something unusual and effective. My God, take a look at Beethoven's sketchbooks; just look at the sketch of "Adelaide." Why did he make the change right at the beginning? Because the first variant was dull and ordinary, while the second is more lively, expressive and melodically pleasing. Give me an idea of the most ordinary kind, you may wager that I will turn it and twist it in shape and accompaniment and harmony and instrumentation long enough to make it into a decent piece. And as with a single idea, I believe I am capable, by means of changes and improvements, of turning an entire ordinary piece into an interesting one.'

'I believe you,' I said with complete conviction.

'And so?' he said, 'What do you want? Roasted fowl do not fly into the mouth of even the most talented artist. It can happen occasionally, but seldom; as a rule, one must first catch and behead them, and then roast them!'

'And still you have set aside entire pieces because they were not particularly successful?' I asked.

'Yes,' he replied, 'Sometimes they come into the world so sickly that to turn them into healthy ones would require too much time, perhaps more than one would need to write a new one. Then it is preferable to make a new one.'

'And is it not possible,' I asked again, 'that through excessive improvements, instead of making a work better, one can make it worse? Is not Goethe right when he says, "You roasted your chestnuts too long in the fire; now they have all turned to charred embers"?'

'That too,' he said laughing. 'Would Goethe have said something that did not have a basis in reality? But I prefer to roast a dish too long and have it turn to charcoal once in a while than to bring all my courses to the table raw.'

'I cannot remember any occasion when I ever thought to myself, "You want to write a trio like this one or that one by Beethoven, or by Mozart, or by any other master." I wrote them according to my taste: in other words, whatever I imagined in general to be pleasing. For example, I do not like blaring brass instruments and have never emphasized them, although I often enough had occasion to notice the effect they have on many members of the audience. I love the finely woven voices, the polyphonic movement, and here my early studies in counterpoint with Zelter and my study of Bach may have had their principal impact; purely homophonic methods of composition appeal to me less. And in this way, as I have tried to develop what satisfies me, what is part of my nature, whatever originality one will concede to me may have developed.

'Do you think I am not aware that for a considerable time I found *no real interest*? True, there was no lack of apparent interest *when I was present*, but basically there was not much to it. I had to produce my own things; seldom did I find them already *there* when I arrived. And this experience was in truth not terribly encouraging. But I thought, "*What you have done you have done; and now it will have to go forth and see how well it makes out in the world.*" Eventually, even if it takes a long time, it will find the people who are sympathetic; after all, the world is so big and full of variety. And that is in fact how it happened. And it happened that way because I continued on my own path, without paying much heed to whether and when my works would find general acceptance.'

'And would you really have held out if that acceptance had never come?' I asked. 'Or were you not convinced, quite naturally, that your way really had value and *had to* prevail?'

'I do not want to make myself out to be stronger than I am,' he said. 'It is true that I never lost this conviction, or at least powerful hope. A single blow of the axe never fells a tree, I told myself, and if it is a strong one, sometimes several will not suffice. What every artist needs is *a single éclat*, one work that really makes an impact on the public. Then the matter is solved. Then he has captured attention, and from that point on the public is not only concerned with all the following works, it even inquires about the earlier ones that it has previously passed over without notice, and thus the whole thing begins to move. This, too, is what all music publishers count on. They continue for long periods to publish works by talented composers without expecting any return. They hope for the work, the éclat, that will make the earlier ones profitable too.'

'And this éclat is what you demonstrated in the most fortunate way with your overture to *A Midsummer Night's Dream*,' I said. 'I remember very well what excitement this overture caused due to your surprising originality and honesty of expression, and how from that moment on you rose high in the opinions of musicians and lay people alike.'

'I, too, believe that,' he said, 'and hence one must put a little trust in luck, too.'

'Luck?' I asked. 'I should think that such an overture is created not by luck, but by the artist's genius?'

'Talent,' Mendelssohn said, modestly altering my expression, 'is naturally part of it, but what I call luck here is the idea for the *subject* of this overture, which had the ability to provide me with musical ideas and forms that could appeal to the general public. What I was able to do as a composer, I was able to do before then.

But I had never had a similar subject before my imagination. That was an inspiration, and a lucky one.'

'In recent times one hears much about the influence that a composer's *Weltanschauung* is supposed to have on his works,' I said to Mendelssohn. 'I admit that I am unable to form a clear concept based on this sentence. You are a contemporary composer; what do you think of it?'

'Ah, there even I am unable to help you,' he replied with a smile. 'I do not have the addiction, or, if you prefer, the spirit of making profound connections between heterogeneous things. Certainly many things that appear to be unrelated have an effect on one another and are mutually interdependent, but it is equally true that others have nothing to do with one another and have absolutely no interconnection.

'The artist, when he is creating, flees from ordinary life with its competing interests and enters the loftier, pure kingdom of art. What interconnection can exist for a political fanatic at the moment when he is to set his *love aria* to music? Is he permitted, in this moment of creation, to think of his democratic or aristocratic opinions, to awaken the hatred in his breast, and with this feeling to begin the musical description of the love of a tender maiden?'

'I guess I agree with you,' I said, 'but then one must ask where an idea can come from, and find so many adherents, if there is basically nothing real in it?'

'It comes from a one-sided view of things. Because Auber wrote a *Muette de Portici*, Beethoven an *Eroica* Symphony, Rossini a *Wilhelm Tell*, people have seen fit to extrapolate political music from them and to demonstrate that the composers must have *had* to write these pieces as a consequence of their political *Weltanschauung* and the times in which they lived. That Auber wrote a *Maurer und Schlosser*, a *Fra Diavolo*, Rossini an *Othello*, a *Tancredi*, and so on; that Beethoven wrote a hundred works that have nothing to do with political *Weltanschauung*, is overlooked.'

'If your reasoning is correct,' I said, 'then there is a further conclusion that can be drawn from it. Because the artist's work is made dependent upon his *Weltanschauung*, many people want to bring the development of art itself into a necessary relationship with political and religious life; political and religious ideas develop in such and such a way; *therefore* music had to develop in such and such a way. Handel *had* to write in a certain way in his time, because life was as it was; Gluck had to write the way he did; so did Haydn, Mozart, and so on, in conformity with the overall development of the general *Weltanschauung*.'

'An opinion just as untenable,' Mendelssohn said, 'as the one about the works of the individual artist! The fact that Beethoven's genius took the shape it did is a consequence of the sequence in which it appeared. In Handel's time he would not have become our Beethoven. Haydn and Mozart would have been different people if they had come after Beethoven. And all this would most certainly have come about no matter how the world might have looked from a political or religious viewpoint. Whether we have this dogma or that political belief, war or peace, absolutism, constitutionalism, or a republic, it has *no effect whatsoever on the evolution of the art of music.* This evolution has only one cause – the fact that *the artist cannot develop and train himself otherwise than in keeping with the artistic moment in which he appears.* Imagine for a moment that today, for some reason, is the beginning of *a hundred-year hiatus in musical creation*, while the political, religious, philosophical world continues to march forward unchecked. Would the art of music, when it awoke from its long sleep, have moved forward along with the rest of the world; would the works of the next master be a hundred years ahead of the best works of our time? Not by a single step. In the best case, they would pick up where our best works left off, and continue the series that had been interrupted, no matter how far the world had progressed in every [other] area.

'In short, the development of the art of music has nothing in common with the development of science, of philosophy, of religion, of politics – it develops according to the natural laws of progression of the art in question, following the laws of creation, growth, and decay.'

Johann Christian Lobe: *Fliegende Blätter für die Musik*, 1, no. 5 (1855), pp. 280–96; Eng. tr. Susan Gillespie, as 'Conversations with Felix Mendelssohn', *Mendelssohn and his World*, ed. R. Larry Todd (Princeton, 1991), pp. 188–203 (with cuts) (© 1991 by R. Larry Todd, reprinted by permission of Princeton University Press)

ADOLF BERNHARD MARX

Mendelssohn had returned from his trips to England and Italy a different man from the one he had been during the time of our intimate friendship. When I made his acquaintance, he was deeply imbued with the power, profundity and truth of Sebastian Bach; repeatedly, with feeling, he had striven to demonstrate to me, for whom the pivotal works of the master had been unavailable up until then, the superiority of Bach over Handel. What I say here reflects his and perhaps also my thinking at that time; I have long since distanced myself sufficiently from such measuring of intellects against each other. At that time, too, Felix struggled for veracity and truthfulness in his own works. I can still see him [in 1826] entering my room with a heated expression, pacing up and down a few times, and saying: 'I have a terrific idea! What do you think of it? I want to write an overture to *A Midsummer Night's Dream.*' I expressed warm support for the idea. A few days later he, the happy, free one, was back again with the score, complete up to the second part. The dance of the elves with its introductory chords was as one would later know it. Then – well, then there followed an overture, cheerful, pleasantly agitated, perfectly delightful, perfectly praiseworthy – only I could perceive no *Midsummer Night's Dream* in it. Sincerely feeling that it was my duty as a friend, I told him this in candor. He was taken aback, irritated, even hurt, and ran out without taking his leave. I let that pass and avoided his house for several days, for since my last visit, following that exchange, his mother and Fanny had also received me coldly, with something approaching hostility.

A few days later, the Mendelssohns' slim manservant appeared at my door and handed me an envelope with the words 'A compliment from Mr. Felix.' When I opened it great pieces of torn-up manuscript paper fell to the ground, along with a note from Felix reading: 'You are always right! But now come and help.' Perhaps the very understanding, thoughtful father had made the difference; or perhaps the hotheaded young man had come to himself.

I did not fail to respond; I hurried over and explained that, as I saw it, such a score, since it serves as a prologue, must give a true and complete reflection of the drama. He went to work with fire and absolute dedication. At least the wanderings of the young pairs of lovers could be salvaged from the first draft, in the first motive (E, D♯, D, C♯); everything else was created anew. It was pointless to resist! 'It's too full! too much!' he cried, when I wanted him to make room for the ruffians and even for Bottom's lovesick ass's braying. It was done; the overture became the one we now know. Mother and sister were reconciled when they saw the composer rushing around in high excitement and pleasure. But during the first performance at his house, the father declared in front of the numerous assembly that it was actually more my work than Felix's. This was naturally quite unjustified, whether it was merely to express his gratification at my behavior, or perhaps to give me satisfaction for the earlier defection of the womenfolk. The original idea and the execution belonged to Felix; the advice I had given was my duty and my only part in it.

Once, when we were taking our leave before his trip to England, Felix spoke to me with great emotion: 'Listen. If anything should reach your ears over here that doesn't seem right to you, don't judge too hastily! I shall return.' I did not understand his comment, but it gradually became clear to me.

In England he had performed his C-minor symphony, but in place of the minuet he had inserted the scherzo from the Octet; it did not fit the character of the whole, but it seemed for him to be more attention-getting. How often he and I had earlier laughed and made fun of the bad habit the French had of mixing in foreign movements, for example of transplanting the scherzo of Beethoven's A-major symphony into that in D major!

Adolf Bernhard Marx: *Erinnerungen aus meinem Leben* (Berlin, 1865), II, pp. 229–38; Eng. tr. Susan Gillespie, as 'From the Memoirs of Adolf Bernhard Marx', *Mendelssohn and his World*, ed. R. Larry Todd (Princeton, 1991), pp. 216–7

EDUARD DEVRIENT

In August 1825, Felix finished his two-act opera, *Camacho's Wedding*, on a libretto by Karl Klingemann, based on Cervantes' *Don Quixote*. Devrient was tactful enough to conceal his disappointment with the work:

One point, however, I warmly contested with Felix, because he set store by it, and this was the musical treatment of the character of Don Quixote. Throughout the opera, every speech of the Don, bearing upon his boastful knighthood, was ushered in by an imposing flourish of trumpets; no real hero could have been announced with greater dignity. But here, where the intention was to characterise a crazy knight-errant (however loyal in his self-imposed mission), I thought he ought to have chosen such instrumentation as would convey an ironical sense of knight-errantry. Felix, on the contrary, maintained that the knight of the rueful countenance believed himself to be a genuine hero, capable of all glorious deeds, and that the composer ought to express the feelings of his dramatic personage, not his own. In answer to this, I drew his attention to the fact that Cervantes himself everywhere places the grotesqueness of antiquated chivalry in the strongest light; I urged that the composer might safely follow the poet, and that no actor would think of personating the old knight as a veritable hero, but always as the vainglorious boaster; and how was this universal interpretation of the character to be reconciled with the grandiose instrumentation of Felix?

This fertile subject was much discussed; I was surprised to find that Felix's father took his son's view of the matter; this was, probably, because it was now beyond recall.

> In 1827, Devrient offered Felix a libretto on the legend of *Hans Heiling*:

Felix avoided all allusion to 'Hans Heiling;' in the autumn, one day when we were chatting confidentially in his room on the *entresol*, I asked for his opinion about it, and he admitted that he found himself unable to warm to the subject, and unless he could do that the work could never become what it ought to be.

He spoke of a similarity in the subject to that of 'Freischütz.' He was probably quoting Marx's opinion, and thought this class of tale had better be avoided for some time to come; this we fully discussed. I defended popular legends as furnishing the best scope for music, the art best fitted to deal with the marvellous and supernatural, and rejected historical subjects, as in their very nature unmusical. Felix did not attempt a defence of Marx's point of view, he even agreed that legends were operatic subjects, but Heiling did not please him, he had no sympathy with the leading character, my verses did not appear to him suggestive, and he returned to his original argument, that faith in the subject was the first condition from which a work of art should spring, and that it was a crime to art, and consequently to mankind, to enter upon a work without it. What he said then he afterwards repeated in a letter that he wrote me in 1831 from Venice, – a beautiful, ideal creed, which however is scarcely fitted to be applied in real life, as he was afterwards to prove.*

(c. 1829)
From all sides he was besought, about this time, to devote himself to dramatic composition; I, not less than others, joining in the general desire. He still believed in commissions from England, in which I had no faith at all; meanwhile he entered into relations with Holtei, who proposed various subjects and discussed how they might be treated. He gave it up however at last, with this declaration: 'Mendelssohn will never find an operatic subject that contents him; he is much too acute.' And his words have been fulfilled.

Eduard Devrient: *Meine Erinnerungen an Felix Mendelssohn-Bartholdy* (Leipzig, 1869; Eng. tr. Natalia Macfarren, London, 1869), pp. 26–7, 42–3, 94

JULIUS SCHUBRING

How he composed, I enjoyed only one opportunity of witnessing. I went one morning into his room, where I found him writing music. I wanted to go away again directly so as not to disturb him. He asked me to stop, however, remarking: 'I am merely copying out.' I remained in consequence, and we talked of all kinds of subjects, he continuing to write the whole time. But he was not copying, for there was no paper but that on which he was writing. The work whereon he was busy was the grand Overture in C major, that was

* Devrient then offered the libretto to Marschner. His opera on the subject was produced with great success in Berlin and Leipzig in 1833, with Devrient singing the name part. [RN]

performed at that period but not published. It was, too, a score for full band. He began with the uppermost octave, slowly drew a bar-line, leaving a pretty good amount of room, and then extended the bar-line right to the bottom of the page. He next filled in the second, then the third stave, etc., with pauses and partly with notes. On coming to the violins, it was evident why he had left so much space for the bar; there was a figure requiring considerable room. The longer melody at this passage was not in any way distinguished from the rest, but, like the other parts, had its bar given in, and waited at the bar-line to be continued when the turn of its stave came round again. During all this, there was no looking forwards or backwards, no comparing, no humming-over, or anything of the sort; the pen kept going steadily on, slowly and carefully, it is true, but without pausing, and we never ceased talking. The copying out, therefore, as he called it, meant that the whole composition, to the last note, had been so thought over and worked out in his mind, that he beheld it there as though it had been actually lying before him.

Julius Schubring: 'Reminiscences of Felix Mendelssohn-Bartholdy', *Musical World*, 31 (12 and 19 May 1866); reprinted in *Mendelssohn and his World*, ed. R. Larry Todd (Princeton, 1991), p. 226

EDUARD DEVRIENT

His most serious occupation during this winter [1829–30] was the Reformation Symphony. He talked over the plan of it with me, and played the leading subjects in their characteristic application. With the greatest expectations I saw the work arise. In this work he tried a strange experiment in writing down the score, which I had scarcely deemed practicable. It is well known that scores are generally written by noting down only the bass, the leading phrases and effects in their appropriate lines, thus giving a complete outline of a movement, and leaving the remainder of the instrumentation to be filled in afterwards. Felix undertook to write bar by bar, down the entire score, the whole of the instrumentation. It is true that he never wrote out a composition until it was quite completed in his head, and he had played it over to those nearest to him; but nevertheless this was a gigantic effort of memory, to fit in each detail, each doubling of parts, each solo effect barwise, like an immense mosaic. It was wonderful to watch the black column slowly advance upon the blank music paper. Felix said it was so great an effort that he would never do it again; he discontinued the process after the first movement of the symphony. It had proved his power, however, mentally to elaborate a work in its minutest details.

Eduard Devrient: *Meine Erinnerungen an Felix Mendelssohn-Bartholdy* (Leipzig, 1869; Eng. tr. Natalia Macfarren, London, 1869), pp. 96–7

FERDINAND HILLER

When he liked a thing he liked it with his whole heart, but if it did not please him, he would sometimes use the most singular language. One day when I had been playing him some composition of mine, long since destroyed, he threw himself down on the floor and rolled about all over the room. Happily there was a carpet! Many an evening we spent quite quietly together talking about art and artists over the cheerful blazing fire. On great things we always agreed, but our views on Italian and French composers differed considerably, I being a stronger partizan for them than he. He sometimes did not spare even the masters whom he thought most highly of. He once said of Handel that one might imagine he had had his different musical drawers for his choruses, one labelled 'warlike,' another 'heathen,' and a third 'religious,' and so on.

Speaking of the Opera in general he said that he thought it had not yet produced so perfect and complete a masterpiece as 'William Tell' and others of Schiller's dramas, but that it must be capable of things equally great, whoever might accomplish them. Though fully alive to the weak points in Weber's music, he had a very strong and almost personal affection for him. He declared that when Weber came to Berlin to conduct the performance of Freischütz, he did not dare to approach him, and that once when Weber was driving to the Mendelssohns' house after a rehearsal, and wanted to take Felix with him, he obstinately refused the honour, and then ran home by a short cut at such a pace as to be ready to open the door for the Herr Hof-Capellmeister on his arrival.

Of all Mozart's works, I think the Zauberflöte was the one he liked best. It seemed to him inexpressibly wonderful that Mozart had been able to express so exactly what he wanted, neither more nor less, with perfect artistic consciousness, and at once with simplest means, and the greatest beauty and completeness.

Ferdinand Hiller: *Felix Mendelssohn-Bartholdy* (Cologne, 1874; Eng. tr. M.E. von Glehn, London, 1874), pp. 31–3

EDUARD DEVRIENT

In the latter half of 1841, Mendelssohn set to music the choruses from Sophocles' *Antigone*. They were first performed in the King of Prussia's private theatre in Potsdam:

The musical treatment of the choruses was much discussed between us; every praise and every censure that the composition afterwards met with was then foretold and weighed; Felix did not enter upon his task without the fullest consideration. The first suggestion was to set the chorus in unison throughout, and to recitative interspersed with solos; as nearly as possible to intone or recite the words, with accompaniment of such instruments only as may be supposed in character with the time of Sophocles, flutes, tubas, and harps, in the absence of lyres. I opposed to this plan that the voice parts would be intolerably monotonous, without the compensatory clearness of the text being attained.

Nevertheless Felix made the attempt to carry out this view, but after a few days he confessed to me that it was impracticable; that I was right in maintaining the impossibility of making the words clear in choral singing, except in a few places that are obviously suited for recitative; that the chanting of a chorus would be vexatiously monotonous, tedious and unmusical; and that accompaniments for so few instruments would give so little scope for variety of expression, that it would make the whole appear as a mere puerile imitation of the ancient music, about which after all we knew nothing. He concluded therefore that the choruses must be sung, as the parts must be recited, not to assimilate themselves with the usages

of Attic tragedy (which might easily lead us into absurdity), but as
we would now express ourselves in speech and song.

Eduard Devrient: *Meine Erinnerungen an Felix Mendelssohn-Bartholdy* (Leipzig, 1869;
Eng. tr. Natalia Macfarren, London, 1869), pp. 224–6 (with cuts)

FERDINAND HILLER

He also accompanied us to the opera a few times, and I may here
recall a gay remark of his as we were listening to a performance of
the 'Favorita' for the first time. In the opening scene, if I am not
mistaken, there is a chorus of monks, which begins with an ascend-
ing scale, accompanied by the orchestra in rather an old-fashioned
style. 'Now they will sing the descending scale,' said Felix; and he
was right.

Ferdinand Hiller: *Felix Mendelssohn-Bartholdy* (Cologne, 1874; Eng. tr. M.E. von Glehn,
London, 1874), p. 186

EDUARD DEVRIENT

If one reviews this constant urging and praying for an opera
libretto, extending as it did over a period of more than ten years, it
may appear unfriendly in me that I did not long before then procure
him one. But on a closer consideration of his requirements in the
matter, it will be seen that, though they were in semblance so small,
yet in fact they were very great.

Nothing but a plot sketched out upon two pages, but a sound
plot, formed upon an appropriate and promising subject, and just
this is the chief and only thing for a dramatic poem. To give such
a sketch into strange hands is a doubtful thing, for the effect of
each scene must greatly depend upon the way in which it is
worked out in detail. How would the second worker find the
exact clue of the original intention and follow it out? The method
of proceeding proposed by Felix was very precarious. And what
demands he made on a libretto! I had no expectation of satisfying
them. Besides Heiling, I had proposed to him the legends of Blue-
beard, of King Thrushbeard, the Musk Apple (Bisamapfel), the
Loreley, a plot of my own, of two friends, whose estrangement

and reconciliation was to unfold itself in Germany, in the Italian Carnival, and in the Swiss Alps; then Kohlhas, Andreas Hofer, and an episode of the Peasants' War; in each of these I had done my best to bring the musical points in relief yet not one could win his entire sympathy.

Eduard Devrient: *Meine Erinnerungen an Felix Mendelssohn-Bartholdy* (Leipzig, 1869; Eng. tr. Natalia Macfarren, London, 1869), pp. 262–3

BENJAMIN LUMLEY
(1812–1875)

He managed the Drury Lane Theatre from 1841 to 1852 and again from 1856 to 1858. Among his productions were operas by Donizetti, Verdi and Halévy.

Dr. Mendelssohn had long had 'The Tempest' in view as a subject for operatic treatment. On the 19th of January, 1847, Dr. Mendelssohn announces the receipt of the *libretto* from Scribe, but feels now the 'responsibility' of finishing the opera in time. He adds, however, 'I shall try to do it, try with all my heart, and as well as I can.'

It is clear, at the same time, from the correspondence with Monsieur Scribe, that the author of the *libretto* was willing to modify his plan and effect several changes in order to meet the views of the composer, much as he might wish to defend the dramatic propriety of his own conceptions. It is evident, however, from this singular and interesting correspondence (into which, unfortunately, it would lead us too far to enter in detail), that, much as composer and author might admire and respect the talent of each other, it was impossible to reconcile their peculiar idiosyncrasies. The German and French natures were in conflict. The more strictly logical and analytical spirit of the former seemed strangely hypercritical to the latter. The facile imagination of the Frenchman, however fertile in scenic resources (as was evidenced by the changes he proposed) found no response in the less flexible tenets of the German. Great in true poetical feeling as was the mind of Mendelssohn, he clung, in this instance, to a rigidity of sequence which it was impossible for the French dramatist to admit or comprehend, in a subject of 'féerie.' And the two went asunder.

Benjamin Lumley: *Reminiscences of the Opera* (London, 1864), pp. 166–8 (with cuts)

SIR GEORGE MACFARREN
(1813–1887)

Macfarren entered the Royal Academy of Music in London in 1829 and studied under Cipriani Potter. He returned as Professor of Composition in 1837, but resigned over the controversy concerning Alfred Day's theoretical system (see below) in 1847. He was reinstated by Potter in 1851.

I have heard Macfarren say that no pianoforte playing ever gave him so much pleasure as that of Mendelssohn. There was no sympathy, I believe, on the part of Mendelssohn, with Macfarren's theoretical views; perhaps it would be more just to say, his theorizing habit of mind. The whole thing was distasteful to him. When I related to Macfarren the anecdote of Mendelssohn's reply to an inquirer as to the root of the first chord in the 'Wedding March,' – 'I don't know, and don't care,' – he said: 'I never heard that story, but I can quite believe it, for Mendelssohn had such a dislike to all theorizing.' Macfarren's theoretical system may have led him to write unusual chords and progressions; certainly it led him to use unusual notation. Mendelssohn did not argue these matters with him, it may well be believed; but, when playing from Macfarren's manuscript, would, on coming to such cases, cry out, in that quick way which is not to be forgotten by those who once heard it: 'Mac, Mac, do you mean this?' On an affirmative answer being given, he would simply say, 'Very well, all right, go on,' to the rest of the performers.

One great Master, indeed, Dr. Day sought to enlist as an adherent – Felix Mendelssohn Bartholdy. He prevailed on Macfarren to arrange a meeting with the Master, that he might have an opportunity of expounding the theory, and indoctrinating Mendelssohn therewith. The meeting took place at Macfarren's residence; but, he told me, before Dr. Day had proceeded far with his argumentative exposition, the face of Mendelssohn assumed an expression so suggestive of his having taken a dose of nauseous medicine, that, to avoid a scene, Macfarren was compelled to bring the discussion to an abrupt, if not untimely, end. His explanation was that Mendelssohn was so opposed to theorizing about the beautiful art which he so enriched by his productions, not that he rejected Dr. Day's theories in themselves. Anyhow, Day had evidently reckoned – not, indeed, without his host – but without calculating the temper of his host's distinguished guest. As Macfarren remarks, in his biographical sketch in the 'Imperial Dictionary of Biography': '[Mendelssohn] had the strongest aversion to pedantry, and detested theoretical discussions, as being the cause, if not the result, of pedantic feeling.'

H.C. Banister: *Life of Sir George Macfarren* (London, 1891), pp. 80–81, 117–18

VII

IN BRITAIN
1829–1844

HENRY HEINKE

Mendelssohn was twenty when, in 1829, he visited England for the first time. Strangely enough he arrived in a steamer named the 'Attwood,' and 'dear old Mr. Attwood' was to be one of his earliest and most attached English friends. Moscheles had found him lodgings in the house of Mr. Heinke, a German ironmonger, at the above address. His sitting-room was on the first floor, with a side window looking down the street. The house remains practically unaltered. Mr. Heinke is dead; but his son, Mr. Henry Heinke, who was a boy at the time of Mendelssohn's first visit, and who was born and has lived in this same house all his life, tells the story of Mendelssohn's doings. Mr. H. Heinke – 'Henry,' as Mendelssohn used to call him – speaks of Mendelssohn with that strength of affection characteristic of all those who came under the influence of his fascinating personality. Mrs. Heinke (Mendelssohn's landlady) was *au fait* at making bread-and-butter puddings, and Mendelssohn was so fond of them that he asked her to keep a reserve of cold pudding in the cupboard in his sitting-room, to which he might help himself on his return from a late concert or social evening. The cup supporting a pie crust was a novelty to the young musician, and he was always much amused when it was lifted and the juice bubbled out. He used to give very select dinner-parties, covers being laid for four – Mr. and Mrs. Moscheles, Dr. Rosen, Professor of Oriental Languages at University College, and himself. Mrs. Moscheles presided; 'no one could carve a fowl like Mrs. Moscheles,' Mr. Heinke observes. Mendelssohn had two grand pianofortes in his room. He was constantly practising, and often after returning home late at night he would sit down to play; moreover, he used to practise on a dumb keyboard while sitting up in bed! The London street musicians disturbed him as they did Wagner. In those days there was an institution known as 'The Marylebone Band,' which rejoiced in the possession of a big drum. No sooner had Mendelssohn begun his morning's practice than the band would commence its lusty operations. Rushing to the top of the stairs, and putting both hands to his ears, Mendelssohn would scream out 'Henry! Henry! send

them away: here is a shilling!' Another similar infliction was a street
performer on the bag-pipes.

Henry Heinke: recalled in F.G. Edwards: *Musical Haunts in London* (London, 1895),
pp. 42–3

MISS TAYLOR

> In July 1829, Mendelssohn and Karl Klingemann left
> London for Edinburgh. After visiting the Hebrides, they
> came south through Glasgow and the Lake District to
> Liverpool. From there, Klingemann returned to London
> and Felix went on down to Wales. Miss Taylor recorded
> these memories fifty years later:

It was in the year 1829 that we first became acquainted with Mr.
Mendelssohn. He was introduced to us by my aunt Mrs. Austin,
who had well known his cousin Professor Mendelssohn at Bonn. He
visited us early in the season in Bedford Row, but our real friendship
began at Coed Du, which was a house near Mold in Flintshire,
rented for many years by my father, Mr. John Taylor.

Mr. Mendelssohn came down there to spend a little time with us,
in the course of a tour in England and Scotland. Soon we began to
find that a most accomplished mind had come among us, quick to
observe, delicate to distinguish. We knew little about his music, but
the wonder of it grew upon us; and I remember one night, when my
two sisters and I went to our room, how we began saying to each
other: 'Surely this must be a man of genius . . . we can't be mistaken
about the music; never did we hear any one play so before. Yet we
know the best London musicians. Surely by-and-by we shall hear
that Felix Mendelssohn Bartholdy is a great name in the world.'

My father's birthday happened while Mr. Mendelssohn was with
us. There was a grand expedition to a distant mine, up among the
hills; a tent carried up there, a dinner to the miners. We had
speeches and health-drinkings, and Mendelssohn threw himself into
the whole thing as if he had been one of us. He interested himself in
hearing about the condition and way of life of the Welsh miners.
Nothing was lost upon him. A letter that he wrote to my brother
John just after he left Coed Du charmingly describes the impres-

sions he carried away of that country. Sometimes he would go out sketching with us girls, sitting down very seriously to draw, but making the greatest fun of attempts which he considered to be unsuccessful. One figure of a Welsh girl he imagined to be like a camel, and she was called 'the camel' accordingly. Though he scorned his own drawings, he had the genuine artist-feeling, and great love for pictures. I need not say how deeply he entered into the beauty of the hills and the woods. His way of representing them was not with the pencil; but in the evening his improvised music would show what he had observed or felt in the past day. The piece called 'The Rivulet,' which he wrote at that time for my sister Susan, will show what I mean: it was a recollection of a real actual 'rivulet.'

We observe how natural objects seemed to suggest music to him. There was in my sister Honora's garden a pretty creeping plant, new at the time, covered with little trumpet-like flowers. He was struck with it, and played for her the music which (he said) the fairies might play on those trumpets. When he wrote out the piece (called a capriccio in E minor) he drew a little branch of that flower all up the margin of the paper.

The piece (an Andante and Allegro) which Mr. Mendelssohn wrote for me was suggested by the sight of a bunch of carnations and roses. The carnations that year were very fine with us. He liked them best of all the flowers, would have one often in his button-hole. We found he intended the arpeggio-passages in that composition as a reminder of the sweet scent of the flower rising up.

Mr. Mendelssohn was not a bit 'sentimental,' though he had so much sentiment. Nobody enjoyed fun more than he, and his laughing was the most joyous that could be. One evening in hot summer we stayed in the wood above our house later than usual. We had been building a house of fir branches in Susan's garden up in the wood. We made a fire a little way off it in a thicket among the trees, Mendelssohn helping with the utmost zeal, dragging up more and more wood; we tired ourselves with our merry work; we sat down round our fire, the smoke went off, the ashes were glowing, it began to get dark, but we could not like to leave our bonfire. 'If we had but some music.' Mendelssohn said, 'Could anybody get something to play on?' Then my brother recollected that we were near the gardener's cottage, and that the gardener had a fiddle. Off rushed our boys to get the fiddle. When it came it was the wretchedest thing in the world, and it had but one string. Mendelssohn took the instrument into his hands, and fell into fits of laughter over it when he heard the sounds it made. His laughter was very catching, he put us all into peals of merriment. But he somehow afterwards brought beautiful music out of the poor old fiddle, and we sat listening to one strain after another, till the darkness sent us home.

My cousin John Edward Taylor was staying with us at that time. He had composed an imitation Welsh air, and he was before breakfast playing this over, all unconscious that Mr. Mendelssohn (whose bedroom was next the drawing-room) was hearing every note. That night, when we had music as usual, Mr. Mendelssohn sat down to play. After an elegant prelude, and with all possible advantage, John Edward heard his poor little air introduced as the subject of the evening. And having dwelt upon it, and adorned it in every graceful manner, Mendelssohn in his pretty playful way, bowing to the *composer*, gave all the praise to him.

I suppose some of the charm of his speech might lie in the unusual choice of words which he, as a German, made in speaking English. He lisped a little. He used an action of nodding his head quickly, till the long locks of hair would fall over his high forehead with the vehemence of his assent to anything he liked.

Sometimes he used to talk very seriously with my mother. Seeing that we brothers and sisters lived lovingly together and with our parents, he spoke about this to my mother, told her how he had known families where it was not so, and used the words, 'You know not how happy you are.'

He was so far away from any sort of pretension, or from making a favour of giving his music to us, that one evening when the family from a neighbouring house came to dinner, and we had dancing afterwards, he took his turn in playing quadrilles and waltzes with the others. He was the first person who taught us gallopades, and he first played us Weber's last waltz. He enjoyed dancing like any other young man of his age. He was then twenty years old. He had written his 'Midsummer-night's Dream' (Overture) before that time. I well remember his playing it. He left Coed Du early in September 1829.

Miss Taylor, quoted in Sebastian Hensel: *The Mendelssohn Family 1729–1847* (London, 1881), I, pp. 225–8

REVIEWS

The performance of Mozart's concerto by M. Mendelssohn was perfect. The scrupulous exactness with which he gave the author's text, without a single addition or *new reading* of his own, the precision in his time, together with the extraordinary accuracy of his execution, excited the admiration of all present; and this was increased, almost to rapture, by his two extemporaneous cadences, in which he *adverted* with great address to the subjects of the concerto, and wrought up his audience almost to the same pitch of enthusiasm which he himself had arrived at. The whole of this concerto he played from memory.

Review in *The Harmonicon*, June 1833, p. 135, of the sixth Philharmonic Concert, 13 May 1833

M. Moscheles gave the septetto written for the Philharmonic Society, with exceedingly good effect. He also, with M. Mendelssohn, played Weber's Gipsies' March with concertante variations, as a duet for two piano-fortes, which excited the most lively interest – these two highly distinguished musicians having each contributed his share of variations, and, in friendly conflict, put forth all their powers in the performance of them. Their cadences were of the most masterly kind, and excited the admiration of a crowded room, in which were most of the connoisseurs in town.

Review in *The Harmonicon*, July 1833, p. 155, of concert given in the Opera Concert Room, 1 May 1833, including Mendelssohn's First Symphony

FANNY & SOPHY
HORSLEY
(1815–1849) (1819–1894)

Fanny and Sophy were the daughters of William Horsley, a London organist who wrote a large number of glees, much admired by Mendelssohn. He was one of the founders of the Philharmonic Society in 1813. His eldest daughter, Mary, married Isambard Kingdom Brunel. The following letters are written to their aunt Lucy, barely older than themselves:

Sophy, 23 June 1833
They did come on Friday with the exception of Mr Mendelssohn; he was seized with histerics in the morning and therefore was too unwell to come out in the evening. Mama however sent this morning to know whether he was better, and he is quite well. Mendelssohn said on Friday even that he should not go (as he had before intended) on Saturday to Cambridge to the meeting of Philosophers which is to be held there next Tuesday. Mr K. told Mama he should endeavour to persuade him to go, for that Mr Mendelssohn was subject to these fits of illness, and if he became worse it is so short a distance from Cambridge to London that he could hear of it and be up to town in a day.

Fanny, 27 June 1833
Mendelssohn was in great spirits and very agreeable. He was very funny and pretended to cry, and imitated a drunk person for my edification with great success.

Sophy, undated
Mendelssohn called there in the morning to tell Mrs Moscheles that he could not dine at her house that day as his father had made a previous engagement for him. She begged him if he could to come during the evening and bring his father with him. I really did not in the least regret his absence for he was very cross and sulky and sat at the drawingroom table looking over the score of the oratorio taking no notice of anyone, not even of his little god-child* (he is really a very fine boy according to Mama and Mary; very much improved since I last saw him and his complexion has almost entirely dropped acquaintance with the walnut-jar) who was seated on Mary's lap. At last Mrs M. said 'I do not think you care a bit about your god-child' upon which he turned round and made a horrid noise at it, partaking both of the nose as well as the throat, which frightened the poor little thing so that unless Mary had not tossed it up nearly to the ceiling for the following five minutes we should have had a regular squall from Felix Junior, for which Felix Senior would richly

* Felix Moscheles [RN]

have deserved, not to be hung, but to be well reproved as it would have been entirely his fault.

> Friedrich Rosen, for whom Fanny was feeling a danger-
> ous attraction, was Professor of Oriental Languages at
> University College, London from 1828 until his early
> death in 1837:

Fanny, 7 July 1833
Mendelssohn talked to me the other night about Dr. Rosen in such affectionate terms that he was quite touching. The tears came quite into his eyes as he said that he was not only great but good, and that though still so young no one knew him without revering and respecting him. It was difficult which most to admire, the praised or the praiser. Mendelssohn is a generous high-minded creature, but, to descend from these heights, he was dressed very badly, and looked in sad want of the piece of soap and the nail brush which I have so often threatened to offer him, Oh dear, Oh dear——

Fanny, 15 July 1833
Our middle dish at dessert was Anna's and Julia Prince's wedding Cakes in the papers and white satin ribbon ornamented with sprigs of myrtle. It was very good, and Felix stuffed down a great and surprising quantity. After tea we went into the garden and all played at Ghost except old Mendelssohn and I. We walked round and talked, very pleasant. Mendelssohn runs the quickest, but Dr. Rosen the most gracefully. They all looked very droll. Mary's hair came down and they tore about in fine style. Mendelssohn and Sophy at my desire played the beautiful lovely Ottetto; and the bass, though perhaps you won't believe it, was quite as good as the treble. Afterwards we had a quadrille, and now for the wonder, Dr. Rosen *danced*, danced on my word. He would not consent for a long time but at last he did with Sophy and he *performed extremely well* as they say in Sir Charles. Mendelssohn engaged me before tea. He was very droll, in the highest spirits I ever saw, laughing at his own jokes, whirling round in pirouettes and all sorts of 'folies'.

Fanny, 25 July 1833
Mary and I went to call on Mrs John Buckley. Whilst we were there
Mamma sent for us home and on entering the room we found seated K[lingemann] and M[endelssohn] looking very cross. He sat in
deep glumps and sighs all the time till he went, and then went on
apologising in a mumbling tone for nearly ten minutes when he
took his leave, Klingemann in high spirits as a matter of course, for
with them it is a rule that when one rises the other falls. They did
not stay long as they had a cab waiting at the door to take them to
Vauxhall to bathe, nasty indecent creatures I think to mention a
word about it, but men are sad dirty pigs after all. Felix was very
lachrimose and rushed four times in and out of the room in a very
phrenzied manner. I gazed at him for some time in such deep amaze
that I am sure at last he perceived it. What an odd tempered creature
he is. But most geniuses are the same they say, and at any rate he is
always delightful for he is always original.

Fanny, 28 August 1833
Mama happily soon sent for us by Anne who came in with (she is by
the way a great oddity) 'Miss Fanny, your Mama says you and Miss
Sophy is to go up, as Mr. Mendishlum and Mr. Liggimum is there'.
We just stopped to correct her pronunciation, and then proceeded
to the drawing-room where sat Felix and K. They stayed a full half
hour and it was a very merry visit and we all talked and laughed a
great deal. F. sank once or twice behind a cloud, but I stirred him up
with such a very long pole the instant that I saw the attack coming
on, that his spirits rose and he went off quite elate.

Mendelssohn showed us on a panorama of Düsseldorf, which is in a
book of the Rhine which the Langs lent us, the place where he is to live,
the Belgrave Square of the town he says, and also the fashionable walk
where he pretends he shall promenade every day from 1 to 3, dressed
in a short coat, and with large moustachios and a small riding whip in
his hand. Fancy him! He wants to compose a great deal I believe, and I
think he had better at the same time compose himself, for his mind
wants a little settling in my opinion. He is looking much handsomer
than he has yet, for his hair is long again like it was last year, which is so
very becoming. I don't think you ever saw him with his Spanish crop.

*

A little after 9 the two worthies arrived, looking rather small about the eyes, and boasting of their great punctuality, which did not strike me as very wonderful. I sat by Felix at breakfast, and we had great fun being very polite to each other. The ball of conversation was brilliantly kept up by Mama, Papa and the two gentlemen, interluded by the occasional observations of your three nieces and eldest nephew. It turned principally on Mozart and his son who lives at Milan, a favourite friend of Felix's, and on Shakespeare, with of course a few invectives against Berlin. We sat at the table till 1/2 past 10, and then Papa and Felix went into the study to look at Clementi's manuscripts, one of which Papa presented him with. Felix Mendelssohn then played his new Rondo and the Philharmonic overture* and Popey† one of Clementi's Exercises, which led to our forming a contract together. It is that at Christmas we are to send him over a box full of presents, in return for which he is going to arrange for Mary and Sophy the overture. He is to write, at the end of September or beginning of October, an exact inventory of all his room contains, and we are to gather from thence what he wants and to fill the box accordingly. Klingemann belongs to the Association so he will help us.

Mendelssohn drew up the contract which we have in our possession and which we shall always have. It is such a valuable memorial of him. He begins it in a flourishing hand with 'Know all men that we' etc etc and at the end he drew a great seal with our house and Düsseldorf on it. We also drew up one which he took away, so that we have a check upon one another.

Sophy, 28 August 1833 (enclosed with Fanny's)

I do not know whether you saw in my garden before you left Kensington a plum, the sole and only produce of a tree on the other side. As the branch however which bare it, had strayed over to my wall, it became my property, and when Mendelssohn was at Düsseldorf I had shown it to Mr. Klingemann, and we agreed it should be eaten the day they were to spend at our house; that day you know never came, but my plum in the mean time had become

---

* To Melusina
† Sophy

so very ripe that on Wednesday morning Fanny and I agreed that it would be much better to wait no longer; so I ran into the yard, mounted on one of the back parlour chairs, tho' as sure as papa sees me on one of them, he predicts my sinking through it, and Anne who was standing by said 'La! miss, it looks very ricketty, had I not better hold it steady?' and, in spite of papa's prophecy, pulled off the plum, and reached the ground in a more agreable manner than bursting through the cane-work. I determined not to eat it however, as I thought I would give them still another chance till the evening, and I am very glad I did not, for they came that very afternoon and I had to divide into 7 parts, this unfortunate plum, as Mama, Fanny, Mary, Charles, Klingemann, Mendelssohn and myself were each to have a share. It was very difficult, and what made it worse, Mendelssohn and Klingemann quite poked into me whilst I was cutting it, the former saying 'Cut it into two fourteenths', which made me feel very like an enraged cat, and much inclined, if I had done as I liked, to give him a hard knock with the knife, but good-breeding got the better of my ill-temper.

Fanny and Sophy Horsley, quoted in R.B. Gotch: *Mendelssohn and his Friends in Kensington* (London, 1934), pp. 19, 23, 26–7, 36–7, 40–41, 44–6, 66–70, 74–5 (with cuts)

SIR WILLIAM STERNDALE BENNETT

Letter to J. W. Davison, February 1837
Thank you for conducting it [his overture *The Naiads*] ... I have shown it to Mendelssohn, who said he liked it very much, and particularly a passage which is rather a favourite of mine:

Mendelssohn's bride is here, one of the handsomest girls I ever saw; he will (be) married at Frankfurt in about two months. He is quite happiness itself ... I must tell you that there is here a very nice fellow, who is named *Schumann*, and whom I like very much. He is very clever; plays pianoforte beautifully when he likes, composes a great deal, although his music is rather too eccentric.

Sir William Sterndale Bennett, quoted in Henry Davison: *Music during the Victorian Era* (London, 1912), pp. 25–6, 30–31

September 1837
A few days later, he started for Birmingham; but, the coach losing four hours on the road, he reached the Town Hall just as the performance of 'St Paul' was concluding. Two special attractions of the Festival still remained. Mendelssohn was to introduce his new P.F. concerto in D minor, and to give a solo-performance on the organ. To those who heard such organ-playing for the first time, as Bennett probably did on this occasion, the revelation was astonishing. Mendelssohn played on the last day of the Festival, and, when he had finished, hurried away to catch the coach for London. Bennett went to see him off, and unable to restrain his curiosity, asked, 'How ever did you come to play like that?' It was an old story; there had been no royal road; and Mendelssohn replied rather sharply, 'By working like a horse.'

Sir William Sterndale Bennett, quoted in James Robert Sterndale Bennett: *The Life of William Sterndale Bennett* (Cambridge, 1907), p. 65

F.[REDERICK] G.[EORGE] EDWARDS
(1853–1909)

Two events greatly furthered the cause of Bach's organ music in England. First, the introduction of the CC compass, which was largely due to the advocacy of Dr. Gauntlett. One of the earliest CC instruments was Hill's organ in St. Peter's, Cornhill. Secondly, the visits to London of Mendelssohn, whose zeal for Bach in the great Cantor's own country is so well known. In spite of much opposition Mendelssohn revived the 'St. Matthew' Passion in Berlin, in 1829, exactly one hundred years after it had been produced in Leipzig. Bach suffered shameful neglect in Germany. It will hardly be credited that not a note of his music was heard at the famous Leipzig Gewandhaus Concerts till Mendelssohn assumed the directorship in 1835.

An interesting reference to Mendelssohn's playing of Bach's organ music is contained in the following extract from a letter written by Dr. Gauntlett to Miss Elizabeth Mounsey, formerly organist of St. Peter's, Cornhill, who retains such pleasant recollections of Mendelssohn's organ performances there in 1840 and 1842. Gauntlett, writing on January 23, 1875, says:

We knew the six Grand Fugues and the Exercises. But what Mendelssohn did was this: He brought out what Marx called the 'not well-known' Pedal organ music. He was the first to play the G minor, the D major, the E major, and the short E minor, of which he gave a copy to Novello, who printed it with a note. And he taught us how to play the *slow* fugue, for Adams had played all fugues fast. I recollect Mendelssohn's saying: 'Your organists think Bach did not write a slow fugue for the organ.'

In 1832 Mendelssohn paid his second visit to London, when he was for a time the guest of Thomas Attwood – 'dear old Mr. Attwood,' as he affectionately called him – at his villa, Beulah Hill, Norwood. One Sunday morning during Mendelssohn's visit, Attwood wrote the following hurried note to his friend, Vincent Novello, then residing at Frith Street, Soho:

'Sunday, May 27 [1832] 8 o'c
'Dear Novello, — Mendelssohn has just rec^d. some Manuscripts of Sebastian Bach, which he purposes trying this Morn^g: hope you will meet him — 11 o'c.

'Yours truly,
'THOS. ATTWOOD.'

The place of meeting was St. Paul's Cathedral, where Attwood was then organist. Here and elsewhere Mendelssohn played, from memory, his favourite Organ Fugue by Bach – the 'little E minor.' Novello also took a fancy to it, and asked Mendelssohn for a copy. In reply to this request Mendelssohn wrote to Novello (in English) as follows:

As soon as I have a free moment, I will try to write for you the Fugue in E [minor]; but I cannot promise whether I shall succeed, as I fear I do not recollect exactly the distribution of parts in some passages. However, I will try it, and if I do not recollect it, get you a copy from Germany.

Novello did not receive the transcript from Mendelssohn till the following year (1833). He was then issuing his 'Select Organ Pieces,' and, as usual, was keenly eager for novelties. He lost no time in publishing the 'little E minor,' which Mendelssohn had procured for him in MS. After a good deal of research, I am able to state the interesting fact that this well-beloved Fugue of Bach's was *first printed and published in England*. To the house of Novello doth this honour belong.

F.G. Edwards: 'Bach's music in England', *The Musical Times*, 1 November 1896, p. 724

IGNAZ MOSCHELES

Letter to unknown addressee, Birmingham, 23 September 1840
Mendelssohn's appearance here has given me fresh enjoyment of life. After my own family, he ranks next in my affections. I see him in various characters, as a brother, son, lover; but chiefly as a fiery musical enthusiast, who appears but dimly conscious to what a height he has already attained. He knows so well how to adapt himself to this commonplace world, although his genius soars so high above it. Whilst Birmingham prided herself on bringing out his newest work, he still found time to make a pen-and-ink drawing of Birmingham for our children. We have a view of the town with its chimneys, warehouses, Town Hall, and the railway carriage in which he and I sat – the perspective is throughout remarkably good, and there are some witty explanations added. In the evening I walked home with him; our chat was so delightful that he insisted on walking back with me two good English miles, but I would only allow him to go part of the way. The night was coldish; he had only just recovered from an illness, and with so much work before him, I knew he wanted rest. Yesterday at an early hour the Town Hall again looked very imposing. The second part of the performance was devoted to Mendelssohn; he was heartily received with ringing cheers, but seemed all anxiety to make his bow to the public, and get the thing over. Of course this was sheer modesty. His conducting of the band in his performance of the 'Lobgesang' effected a marvellous unity and precision, and one of the chorales of this glorious work told so powerfully that the whole audience rose involuntarily

from their seats – a custom usually confined in England to the performance of the Hallelujah Chorus.

Ignaz Moscheles, quoted in Charlotte Moscheles: *Aus Moscheles Leben* (Leipzig, 1872;
Eng. tr. A.D. Coleridge, London, 1873), II, 69–70

ELIZABETH MOUNSEY

Mendelssohn first visited St. Peter's Cornhill on Wednesday
September 30 1840; Dr. Gauntlett (the designer of the organ)
prevailed on him to come. That was the first occasion on which I
had the honour of having any communication with him. Dr.
Gauntlett informed me and the churchwarden of his coming.
Although this visit was not announced publicly, it became known –
and the church was crowded. He came once more on 12 June 1842
– playing as morning service ended. Close upon its conclusion, I
played Haydn's well-known *Hymn to the Emperor* as a dismissal
hymn; then, as he commenced, he took that melody, and extemporised on it with wonderful variety, learning and beauty – as all
accounts tell. Yet this was *indeed* an extempore performance, as he
only came up to the organ loft while I was playing the hymn – and
he could not have previously known that I should play it.

It was Gauntlett who prevailed on him to come on both occasions
– and who chiefly assisted him respecting the stops. At both of these
visits, Gauntlett was on one side of Mendelssohn, and I on the other
side – Gauntlett appearing to me to understand so well what stops
he would like, that I presumed they must have had some previous
consultation. I of course only endeavoured to carry out any hint
from one or the other.

Elizabeth Mounsey, recollections noted not earlier than 1886, Bodleian MS. M. Deneke
Mendelssohn c. 51/1. fol. 10

WILLIAM SMITH ROCKSTRO

He played on the organ at St. Peter's, Cornhill, and Christ Church,
Newgate Street. On the former occasion – Sunday, the 12th of June
[1842] – the congregation had been singing a Hymn to Haydn's
well-known tune, *Gott erhalte Franz den Kaiser*, and on this theme

he extemporised the concluding voluntary. At Christ Church, four days afterwards, he again treated the same theme, but in a wholly different manner, terminating with a long and elaborately-developed Fugue. During the course of the Fantasia by which this Fugue was introduced, a long treble A began to sound on the swell. Mendelssohn accompanied it in the form of an inverted organ-point of prodigious length, treating it with the most ingenious and delightful harmonies, his invention of which seemed to be inexhaustible. We were very young in those days; but we well remember whispering to our kind old friend, Mr. Vincent Novello, who was sitting next to us at the east end of the Church: 'It must be a cypher;' and he quite agreed with us. After harmonising the note in an infinity of different ways, with ever-varying passages which would probably have filled some pages of music-paper, he at last confirmed our impression by leaving it to sound, for some considerable time, alone. By this time, all present were convinced that during the remainder of the performance, that particular manual would be useless; when to our astonishment, the A quietly glided through G sharp and G natural to F sharp; and the organ-point came to the most natural conclusion imaginable. While he was amusing himself with this little *plaisanterie*, a number of inconsiderate persons had the bad taste to crowd so closely round the unusually confined and inconvenient organ-loft, that, to save himself from fainting, Mendelssohn was compelled to leave off in the middle of an unfinished passage, and make his way to the staircase. He was so ghastly pale, that it was feared he really would faint, but after breathing the fresh air, he speedily revived, and as he passed down the stairs, he laughed and said, 'You thought it was a cypher, I know you did.'

Leaving his family quietly settled at Frankfurt, he arrived in London for the eighth time on the 10th of May, once more became the guest of his old friend, Klingemann, and, on the 13th of the month, assumed command of the famous orchestra. The season was a brilliant one, and in addition to the interest it derived from his presence, was rendered memorable by the first appearance in London of Ernst, Joachim, and Piatti. The chief attractions of its varied programmes were the *Walpurgis-Nacht*, the *Midsummer Night's Dream*, the Overtures to *Leonora* (No. 1), *Egmont*, and *The Ruins of Athens*, Bach's *Orchestral Suite in D major*, and Schubert's Overture to *Fierabras*. At the last concert of the season (June 24th), Mendelssohn astounded the orchestra by his powerful rendering of the overture to *Egmont*, the *sforzandi* in the last movement of which had never before been correctly played in our English orchestras. It was at this concert, also, that he played, for the first time in England, Beethoven's Pianoforte Concerto in G major.

At the rehearsal, on Saturday the 22nd, he enriched the first movement with a magnificent extempore *cadenza*, in which he worked up the varied subjects of the piece with the skill which never failed him when he gave the reins to his exuberant fancy. On reaching the shake at its close he found the orchestra a little uncertain in taking up its point. In order to remove all fear of misunderstanding, he again extemporised a *cadenza* entirely different from the first, though not a whit less beautiful. The orchestra again missed its point so decidedly that he found it necessary to make a third trial. This last *cadenza* was by far the longest and most interesting of the three, and totally different, both in matter and in style, from its predecessors. It had, moreover, the effect of rendering the orchestral point so safe that no fear whatever was anticipated with regard to the Monday performance.

It will be readily understood that all present looked forward to this performance with intensest excitement; feeling certain that another new *cadenza* would be improvised at the concert. And it really was so. The same subjects were placed in so different a light, that their treatment bore not the slightest shade of resemblance to the Saturday performance, until the approach of the final shake, which was so arranged as to enable the orchestra to take up its point with the most perfect accuracy.

William Smith Rockstro: *Felix Mendelssohn Bartholdy* (London, 1884), pp. 81–3, 95–7

QUEEN VICTORIA
(1819–1901)

16 June 1842, Buckingham Palace
After dinner came Mendelssohn Bartholdy, whose acquaintance I was so anxious to make. Albert had already seen him the other

Sketches by Wilhelm Hensel:
1 Mendelssohn's mother, Lea, 1823. 2 Mendelssohn's father, Abraham, 1823.
3 Mendelssohn at thirteen, c. 1822. 4 Fanny Mendelssohn Bartholdy, 1829.

5 First page of Mendelssohn's autograph of a fugue in E flat, *c.* 1826.
6 Residence of the Moscheles family, 3 Chester Place, drawn by Mendelssohn,
1835.

7 Portrait of Mendelssohn by Joseph Schmeller, 1830.
8 Oak tree at Interlaken drawn by Mendelssohn, 1842.

9 Portrait of Cecile Jeanrenaud by Eduard Magnus;
Mendelssohn married her in 1837.

10 Ignaz Moscheles.
11 Karl Klingemann. Sketch by Wilhem Hensel.
12 Eduard Devrient.

13 A *Punch* cartoon of an 1845 London performance of Sophocles's *Antigone* with choruses by Mendelssohn. 'The choir leader,' he wrote, 'with his tartan trews showing, is a masterpiece.'

14 Leipzig Gewandhaus Orchestra, with first violins Ferdinand David, Klengel and Joachim, rehearsing presto passage in Beethoven's *Leonora Overture no. 3*. After sketches by violoncellist Riemers, *c.* 1850.

15 Portrait of Mendelssohn by Eduard Magnus, 1845/6.

morning. He is short, dark, & Jewish looking, delicate, with a fine intellectual forehead. I should say he must be about 35 or 6. He is very pleasing & modest, & is greatly protected by the King of Prussia. He played first of all some of his 'Lieder ohne Worte', after which his Serenade & then, he asked us to give him a theme, upon which he could improvise. We gave him 2, 'Rule Britannia', & the Austrian National Anthem. He began immediately, & really I have never heard anything so beautiful, the way in which he blended them both together & changed over from one to the other, was quite wonderful as well as the exquisite harmony & feeling he puts into the variations, & the powerful rich chords, & modulations, which reminded me of all his beautiful compositions. At one moment he played the Austrian National Anthem with the right hand, he played 'Rule Britannia' as the bass, with his left! He made some further improvisations on well known tunes & songs. We were all filled with the greatest admiration. Poor Mendelssohn was quite exhausted, when he had done playing.

9 July 1842, Buckingham Palace
Mendelssohn came to take leave of Albert, previous to his returning to Germany & he was good enough to play for us, on Albert's organ, which he did beautifully. As he wished to hear me sing, we took him over to our large room, where, with some trepidation, I sang, accompanied by him, 1st a song which I thought was his composition, but which he said was his sister's, & then one of his beautiful ones, after which he played to us a little. We thanked him very much, & I gave him a handsome ring as a remembrance.

30 May 1844, Buckingham Palace
We went over to the Drawingroom to see Mendelssohn & talked to him for some time, then he played to us beautifully, some of the fine compositions he has written lately, amongst them music for the 'Midsummer Night's Dream', 2 of his 'Lieder ohne Worte', & improvised wonderfully on Gluck's beautiful chorus 'Que de grâces, que de Majesté'* bringing in besides a song by his sister, which I often sing. He is such an agreeable, clever man & his countenance beams with intelligence & genius.

* 'Que d'attraits, que de majesté', from *Iphigénie en Aulide* (Act I scene 5) [RN]

1 May 1847, Buckingham Palace
We had the great treat of hearing Mendelssohn play, & he stayed an hour with us, playing some new compositions, with that indescribably beautiful touch of his. I also sang 3 of his songs, which seemed to please him. He is so amiable & clever. For some time he has been engaged in composing an Opera & an Oratorio, but has lost courage about them. The subject for his Opera is a Rhine Legend, & that for the Oratorio,* a very beautiful one, depicting Earth, Hell & Heaven, & he played one of the Choruses out of this to us, which was very fine.

Queen Victoria: unpublished journal

IGNAZ MOSCHELES

Diary entry, 9 October 1847
Charlotte said, 'You have never told us all about your last stay in London' and this remark elicited from him much about our common friends that interested us. Then he gave us an account of his visit to the Queen. She had received him very graciously, and he was much pleased with her rendering of some of his songs, which he had accompanied; he had also played to the Queen and the Prince. She must have been pleased, for, when he rose to depart, she thanked him, and said, 'You have given me so much pleasure, now what can I do to give you pleasure?' Mendelssohn deprecating, she insisted; so he candidly admitted that he had a wish that only her Majesty could fulfil. He, himself the head of a household, felt mightily interested in the Queen's domestic arrangements; in short, might he see the Royal children in their Royal nurseries? The Queen at once entered into the spirit of his request, and in her most winning way conducted him herself through the nurseries, all the while comparing notes with him on the homely subjects that had a special attraction for both.

Ignaz Moscheles, quoted in Charlotte Moscheles: *Aus Moscheles Leben* (Leipzig, 1872; Eng. tr. A.D. Coleridge, London, 1873), II, pp. 179–80

---

* *Lorelei* and *Christus*, both unfinished [RN]

ANON

Not very much has been recorded of Mendelssohn's viola playing, doubtless because of its private nature. At the house of Mr. Alsager, of the *Times*, in Queen Square, he used to play the viola in his Quintet in A (Op. 18), having as his colleague the late Mr. J.H.B. Dando, who communicated to the present writer the following affectionate tribute to the composer: 'When dear Mendelssohn,' writes Mr. Dando, 'played tenor with me, I used to play *first* tenor; but if difficulties arose which he thought I could execute better, he used quietly to *change the books*, and I knew my duty. It was always so. He knew quite well how I loved him and his music.'

At a musical party given by Dr. Billing, a practitioner well known in musical circles, Mendelssohn once played in concerted music with Paganini. The event is recorded in the *Morning Post* of May 16, 1833:

PAGANINI.—It has been frequently said that this extraordinary performer could not take part in a quartet with any effect. This is far from being correct. At a *soirée* given by Dr. Billing, the other evening, Paganini, Mendelssohn, and Lindley performed a trio for viola, guitar, and violoncello (composed by Paganini), Mendelssohn playing the guitar part on the pianoforte, adding a bass in the most ingenious manner. Paganini's performance on the tenor was of the true school; there were no tricks, no jumping and skipping, but all the passages were legitimately and beautifully played, as were those given to the violoncello by Lindley. As a composition it reflected credit on the Signor; it was well conceived, scientifically written, and remarkably pleasing and effective.

Mendelssohn read Dickens, whom he once met in London. Mr. Arthur O'Leary remembers that when he entered the Leipzig Conservatorium (in 1847) Mendelssohn offered to lend him the 'Pickwick Papers.' Taking the volume down from his bookcase, he said to young O'Leary: 'You must take great care of this copy, as it was given to me by my mother.' In this connection Miss Sabilla Novello writes from Genoa: 'I remember Mendelssohn sitting down by me on one occasion and, knowing that I was conversant with German, asking me in his lisping manner – "What ith a thtump?" This somewhat peculiar word I translated into German for him. He then told me that he had been reading Dickens, and found the words "Magpie and Stump" rather difficult to understand, so I explained to him that they were the sign of a certain well-known inn.' Here is the Pickwickian 'stump' passage over which Mendelssohn stumbled:

When we add, that a weather-beaten sign-board bore the half-obliterated semblance of a magpie intently eyeing a crooked streak of brown paint, which the neighbours had been taught from infancy to consider as the 'stump,' we have said all that need he said, of the exterior of the edifice. – ('Pickwick Papers,' Chap. xx.)

The Musical Times, 1 November 1897 (with cuts)

GEORGE HOGARTH
(1783–1870)

Hogarth was a London journalist from 1830 and secretary to the London Philharmonic Society from 1850 to 1864.

The history of this magnificent overture [*Ruy Blas*], in connection with the Philharmonic Society, is interesting and characteristic of the author. During the season 1844, when Mendelssohn conducted the Society's Concerto, this overture (in manuscript), was tried at a morning trial-performance, when, it would appear, it did not 'go' to the composer's satisfaction. When Mr. Anderson, after the performance, expressed his admiration of the new work, he was surprised to hear Mendelssohn say, with some heat, that he was much displeased with it – so much, that he would burn it. Mr. Anderson said something deprecating such a resolution, but Mendelssohn repeated his determination that it should never be heard in public. Mr. Anderson then said: 'You have often expressed your admiration of my good master, Prince Albert; I am sure it would gratify him to hear a new composition of yours, so pray let me give him that pleasure by means of the Queen's private band.' Mendelssohn consented, on condition that the overture should never be publicly performed, and gave Mr. Anderson the original orchestral parts. The overture was frequently performed at Buckingham Palace and Windsor Castle, to the admiration of Her Majesty and the Prince. Some time after the composer's lamented death, Mr. Anderson wrote to Madame Mendelssohn, informing her of all that had passed with respect to this overture, and requesting her permission to perform it at Mrs. Anderson's next annual concert. The permission was kindly given, and the overture was performed at that lady's concert in the season 1849; this being the first time it was ever publicly heard in England.

George Hogarth: *The Philharmonic Society of London* (London, 1862), pp. 100–01

KARL KLINGEMANN
(1798–1862)

He was secretary to the Hanoverian Legation in Berlin and, from 1828, a diplomat in London. He accompanied Felix on his Scottish tour in 1829. He was also a lyrical poet, and Felix set nine of his poems to music.

Letter to Fanny (this postscript to Rebecka), London, 18 May 1844
I am indebted to London for a great deal of Felix, who from time to time, and always at the right moment, sends a delightful breeze of recollections ruffling my hair – which is getting gray – and in every way does me more good than I can express. Why do not you come over like a gentle zephyr? You would find something here to suit you, for it is not all Babbage and 'Rule Britannia,' and you would enjoy yourself, I am certain. Felix fortunately feels the spell as well as exercises it. Although his wife is not with him, and we miss her sorely, he looks well and cheerful, and enjoys the lobster and the pies and the English ladies, and is just as much astonished as ever at the number of Englishmen he meets, and the amount of English he hears spoken, and is altogether in good spirits. If he does not compose the finest works, it is only because of the incessant bustle, for such a 'lion' has no time to himself except early in the morning and late at night. Those hours I have him entirely, and we lead the life of common human beings, and talk of our friends. I profit most, of course. As an artist, no stranger ever held the position here that

Felix does; his strong, calm disposition elevates him far above all the smoke and hubbub, and even the Philistines feel this and respect and appreciate, each in his own way, the power all acknowledge. We, John Bulls though we be, are altogether more childlike and candid in this respect than the scribbling Continent. Shrewder too than your lazy maccaroni-eaters, we possess the organ of veneration, and can admire honestly and gladly.

Karl Klingemann, quoted in Sebastian Hensel: *The Mendelssohn Family 1729–1847* (London, 1881), II, pp. 279–80

'MAESTRO'

> ... the pen name of a Mr Grüneisen, who had, among other things, been a newspaper correspondent in Spain during the Carlist Wars. Davison describes him as having had 'very little technical knowledge of music, but a great deal of energy'.

The 'Maestro' gives a vivid description of a visit by Mendelssohn on June 15, 1844, to Erat's music rooms where the Society of British Musicians were giving a concert in his honour. The programme included a trio for pianoforte, violin and 'cello by Horsley and a vocal piece by Macfarren, and when it had been gone through: 'Mr. Calkin requested Dr. Mendelssohn in the name of the company, to sit down to the pianoforte, and favour them with an extemporaneous performance, a requisition instantly complied with by the great master. Wonderful was the inspiration which followed. With the most extraordinary readiness of memory and invention he, after a rich and elaborate introduction, seized the quaint scherzo in Horsley's trio, and reproduced it under the most novel and picturesque aspects. Presently the ear caught the sentimental phraseologies of Macfarren's canzonet, which, in its turn, came out invested with the most delicate and ingenious imageries – the efflorescent produce of the moment. By and by the subject came out in droll alternation – the merriment of the one, the languor of the other, peeping through a framework of sweeping arpeggios, in a way of which it is impossible to give the faintest notion. The subjects, antagonising as they were in form and character, were now heard conjointly – treated with wonderful flexibility and skill – displaying an ingenuity in fitting them harmonically, either in fragment or in entirety, perfectly astonishing. This great exhibition of art and genius ended with a fugue based on the canzonet, which the player worked in the most masterly manner reaching at length a climax of exalted grandeur which served as a contrasting preparation to the "dying fall" with which the performance closed, wherein the scherzo and the song were faintly heard, mocking each other as it were, and retroceding delicately and deliberately into silence.'

'Maestro', quoted in Henry Davison: *Music during the Victorian Era* (London, 1912), pp. 56–7

FOURTH PHILHARMONIC CONCERT

Felix Mendelssohn Bartholdy is at last among us, wielding the sceptre of art, and ruling us with the might of his genius. His first appearance in the midst of our artists was at the rehearsal for the fourth Philharmonic concert, on Saturday morning. He was hailed, on his stepping into the orchestra, with acclamations, which he acknowledged by a short address, characterised equally by dignity and unpretence. He said how glad he was again to be in England – how he felt certain that the good feeling hitherto exercised towards him by Englishmen would be continued – and other things appropriate for the occasion, but scarcely worth relating now. The presence of Mendelssohn was soon felt; – the severity of his discipline, tinctured though it be by kindness and gentlemanly bearing, is still something wholly different from what the band had been accustomed to. Three quarters of an hour over Mozart's well known symphony in E flat, was something quite unlooked for. However, the Philharmonic orchestra is, in a great measure, composed of true artists, and the influence of a man like Mendelssohn is felt and acknowledged. Every word he has to say is listened to with eager attention, and the consequent benefit of his counsel is immense. The result of his first rehearsal was manifested on Monday evening, in the splendid interpretation of the following magnificent programme:—

PART I

SINFONIA, in E flat . . . . MOZART.
ROMANCE, 'Va dit elle,' (*Robert le Diable*) Madame
    Castellan . . . . MEYERBEER.
CONCERTO in C minor, Piano-forte, Mr. W.S. Bennett. . BENNETT.
SCENA, 'Wo'berg ich mich,' (*Euryanthe*) Herr Staudigl. . WEBER.
OVERTURE, No. 1, (*Leonora*) first time of performance in
    this country . . . . BEETHOVEN.

PART II

SINFONIA, No. 3, A minor. . . . . MENDELSSOHN BARTHOLDY.
CAVATINA ED ARIA, 'Ah non credea,' (*La Sonnambula*)
    Madame Castellan . . . . BELLINI.
CONCERTO, Violin, M.A. Pott . . . . POTT.
ARIA, 'O wie will ich triumphiren.' (*Die Entführung aus
    dem Serail*) Herr Staudigl . . . . MOZART.
OVERTURE, (*Der Berggeist*) . . . . SPOHR.
    Leader MR. T. COOKE.
    Conductor, DR. F. MENDELSSOHN BARTHOLDY.

The crowded condition of the room, which shewed not one empty place, testified to the wisdom of the directors in engaging Dr. Mendelssohn. Doubtless this season will have been the most brilliant which the Philharmonic Society has seen for many a year.

The Musical Examiner, 18 May 1844, pp. 585–6

ANON

We have elsewhere inserted a sensible article, from a cotemporary, in defence of the great composer, Mendelssohn, against the virulent and unseemly attacks of a certain *clique* in the profession. What we should have said on the subject is there expressed, more effectively than we could have expressed it. But we cannot let the matter pass without giving vent to our sincere displeasure at the unworthy treatment of the most illustrious living musician. We could not have dared to imagine that England contained the artist, who would so disgrace his honorable calling as to offer insult to a man, who is no less esteemed for his liberality and gentlemanly bearing than for his wonderful and unparalleled genius. We can scarcely believe that we are perusing the columns of an English musical journal, while reading an attack upon MENDELSSOHN – upon MENDELSSOHN, who has raised the art of music and its followers to a position which even Beethoven and Mozart, because unappreciated, failed to attain. And, how silly and meaningless are the charges brought against the illustrious German! We shall but allude to one of them – the rest are beneath our notice. It has been insinuated that Mendelssohn made unfair use of his position as conductor of the Philharmonic concerts, to advance his own interests, and to injure those of Englishmen. This is *untrue*, malicious, and absurd. It was expected by every one that Mendelssohn would have played at three or four of the concerts which took place under his direction. Nothing would have been more reasonable or fair. But how often did he play? – *Once, and only once* – and that once, even, at the earnest solicitation of the authorities of the society. Moreover, it was anticipated *and desired*, by the subscribers (the main support of the Philharmonic) that two or three of the compositions of Mendelssohn should be given at each concert. Yet, reasonable and just as was the expectation, only one of his works was given at each of four concerts, and at the seventh concert *not even one!* Did he put aside the claims of English composers? – The fact that at no previous season have so many English compositions been performed at once refutes this calumny. The concerto of Sterndale Bennett in C minor (*executed by the composer*) – the overture to the '*Naiades*' of the same composer – a duet from '*Pascal Bruno*' of Mr. Hatton – and a choral composition of Henry Smart, were performed under the conduct of Mendelssohn, *and at his suggestion*. Besides which, he strongly recommended the symphony in C sharp minor of Macfarren for performance at the last concert – *but was strenuously opposed by the English directors!* We say it without hesitation – Mendelssohn has shown a more liberal feeling, and has proved himself a warmer friend to English artists and English art than can be found among their own ranks – be he who he may. Who helped to make the European reputation of Sterndale Bennett? – MENDELSSOHN! Who pronounced Mrs. Alfred Shaw and Miss Clara Novello the best singers in Germany? – MENDELSSOHN! Who has on all occasions spoken with enthusiasm of English musicians, and enforced a respect for them in Germany, which but for him would perhaps *never* have existed in that prejudiced country? – MENDELSSOHN! And yet this same Mendelssohn is the first German musician who comes to England to be insulted and mistaken – while other bigoted foreigners without a tithe of his genius are exalted to the seventh heaven! Shame – shame on English artists! We blush to think that you so little appreciate the immense benefits conferred *upon you all*, by this amiable man and unrivalled artist.

Time presses now – but we shall resume the subject. Would that occasion had not called us to the rescue of genius misunderstood and maltreated!

'From a cotemporary'

The question has been asked of us – 'Will Mendelssohn come to England next year, to conduct the Philharmonic Concerts?' We feel a difficulty in replying in the affirmative, and a great distaste to answering in the negative. Yet we have our qualms on the subject. It appears that there is a strong party in London against the greatest living composer, and one of the finest spirits that ever shed lustre on the art of music! Why is this? Let a musical cotemporary speak for the party which it represents:—

'As we cannot afford to be the parasites of any man, even though he be as eminent as Dr. Mendelssohn, we shall not attempt to join in the unqualified eulogies pronounced upon him by some of our cotemporaries. We have as little hesitation in canvassing the public acts of Dr. Mendelssohn as in commenting upon the career of the most humble member of the profession; and we feel constrained to admit that Dr. Mendelssohn has not appreciated the generous reception with which he was met in this country. *His arbitrary demand for the dismissal of a member of the band who ventured to express his disapprobation at waiting nearly an hour for the arrival of the conductor at the rehearsal; and his attempt to supplant an efficient instrumental performer at Exeter Hall, to make way for a protégé of his own, which the Sacred Harmonic Society indignantly refused to entertain, are not the only instances of his modest reliance upon the extent to which his vagaries would be permitted in this country.* It may be very acceptable to receive the adulatory applause of an orchestra; but it is not so pleasant to be reminded that he who enforces such rigid punctuality ought also to offer an example of it in his own person. The instrumental performer in England is ill able to bear the loss of giving a single lesson, and cannot afford to have his time trifled with by one who, however high in rank, is equally the servant of the public. *The firmness of the directors of the Philharmonic Society alone rescued Maurer's quartet for four violins from suppression by Dr. Mendelssohn, who so far lent himself to the absurd pretensions of Ernst and Joachim as to declare that unless these violinists took part in the quartet it should not be done.* He was, however, reminded that he was the paid servant of the directors, who insisted upon the performance of the quartet, for which two eminent vocalists were forthwith engaged: – Willy and Sainton, whose efforts, in conjunction with Sivori and Blagrove, fully bore out the directors in their determination. THE PLACING OF THE WEAK OVERTURES OF SCHUBERT IMMEDIATELY BEFORE THE COMPOSITIONS OF MENDELSSOHN, BY WHICH THE EFFECT OF THE LATTER WAS SO GREATLY ENHANCED, IS A PARDONABLE WEAKNESS WHICH WE CAN MANAGE TO LOOK OVER; *not so, however, the glaring neglect to allow English composers an opportunity of trying their works, whilst facility was readily afforded to the trial of two very indifferent symphonies by German Composers.* We hear that Dr. Mendelssohn threatens not to return to this country, but we cannot give him so little credit for studying his own interests as to believe this rumour. At all events, we shall be glad to see him amongst us again, and to record an improvement in his private bearing towards his brother professors. We cannot close these observations without contrasting the demeanour of Sir G. Smart, who took his farewell as conductor at the first Philharmonic Concert, amidst the unanimous and hearty expressions of respect and esteem of every member of the orchestra.'

Reader – observe the sentences printed in italics, and the sentence displayed in capitals – for on what they imply is founded the strong feeling in certain quarters against Dr. Mendelssohn. We have not the least hesitation in denouncing them as utterly devoid of truth. On the morning of the eighth and last Philharmonic Concert, a rehearsal was called at eleven o'clock, for the instrumental portion of the *First Walpurgis Night*, which at the ordinary rehearsal was merely read through by the band, owing to the presence of His Royal Highness Prince Albert. Mendelssohn, who is known to be a model of punctuality, was engaged on the same morning at a meeting of the council of the 'Handel Society,' which was called at half-past ten. Owing to some important matters in which he was chiefly concerned, Mendelssohn, against his inclination, was detained till a quarter past eleven, when he directly started for Hanover Square, to arrive at which place, as the 'Handel Society' holds its meetings at Messrs. Cramers', could not have taken him five minutes. Thus, at the utmost, he was twenty minutes behind the time appointed. At the moment of his entering the orchestra, a *gentleman* (!) who professes to play the viola, began to offer him gross insults, by hissing him, and using vulgar and commonplace language deprecatory of the delay, to which he, the important viola-holder, had been forced to submit. Mendelssohn naturally taken by surprise, asked the *gentleman* (!) who was thus proving his right to the appellation, whether it was to him (Mendelssohn) that these noisy and gross insults were addressed. Upon being insolently answered in the affirmative, Mendelssohn, *very properly*, said that either he, Mendelssohn, or he, the viola-holder, must resign, for the nonce, the situation which each was respectively holding in the orchestra. After which, very properly and *very justifiably*, the illustrious composer complained to the directors of the insult offered him, and insisted upon some notice being taken of it, but *did not* demand the dismissal of the viola-holder. The directors, *very properly and very justly*, upon considering the affair, sent the offending individual *his dismissal*. Had they done less than this, they would have taken part, necessarily, in the gross and unwarrantable liberty taken with Dr. Mendelssohn, by a person utterly unknown and obscure. The plea of *losing a lesson* goes for nothing in this case – as, in the first place, only *twenty minutes* were lost – in the second place, the offending party is a man of property sufficient to render him independent of the profession – and, in the third place, the members of the Philharmonic orchestra are amply, and more than amply paid, all things considered, for their services. But granting all the premises of our cotemporary, we have too much respect for the members of the English orchestra (of whom his journal is the avowed organ) to suppose that they would not unanimously approve of the dismissal of a person who proved himself so wanting in all the best feelings of an English artist, as to insult, grossly and stupidly, the greatest representative of the art and its followers now existing. *We pity* the man who could have the heart, or rather the want of it, to utter a disrespectful word to so great and good a man, so thorough an artist in every respect, and so wonderful a genius as Mendelssohn, whose name should be a talisman throughout the musical world. We say boldly that GENIUS is, or ought to be, *despotic* – it is so rare a thing, it is so absolutely the presence of GOD in humanity, it is so supremely above all else that the inhabitants of earth possess, that he who reverences it not, obeys it not, appreciates it not, is little better than *an animal* without reason, a creature without SOUL.

The Exeter Hall affair is ludicrous. Dr. Mendelssohn requested, as a favour, that a gentleman who plays the trumpet, would permit another gentleman who plays the trumpet *to read out of his book for one night*, in place of a third gentleman who plays the trumpet!! This was ridiculously and insultingly refused him. What supreme nonsense, to throw this at the head of the great composer, as a scheme to supplant an Englishman by a foreigner! But really we waste our ink in bestowing a moment's consideration on such *twaddle!* The assertion that Schubert's overtures were placed *as foils* to the compositions of Mendelssohn is a thoroughly *dishonest fabrication*, with not a shadow of truth to sanction it – a fabrication unworthy the journal in which it appears, and the party which it so zealously represents. *One only overture* of Schubert's was performed throughout the whole of the five concerts which Dr. Mendelssohn directed – that to *Fierabras* – and instead of being placed *'immediately before'* any composition of the great musician, *it was played at the end of the concert* which was honored by the presence of royalty, and was only performed at all BECAUSE HIS ROYAL HIGHNESS PRINCE ALBERT HAD COMMANDED IT. What can be said to such flagrant dishonesty as is comprised in the accusation we thus triumphantly and contemptuously overthrow! In respect of the power which was at Mendelssohn's disposal to essay the works of English composers: – *there was no such power awarded him.* He desired and advised the directors, not merely to try, but to *play at the last concert*, a symphony by an English composer which he admired and strongly recommended – *but he was refused by the directors* – who perhaps, (as the journalist well remarks) told him 'that he was but the paid servant of the Society' – and not a director. This too then falls to the ground – and what remains against the illustrious composer? – NOTHING. The concluding sentence about Sir George Smart, *is in bad taste*, to say the least of it – and that said, we have said all we intend to say on the subject. We quote the following remarks as containing much truth, and more worthy than the rest of the article of the pen and the feelings of an artist:—

'There can be no doubt that the engagement of a distinguished musician to direct a series of performances, instead of confounding the orchestra with different conductors, each with a varied conception of his duties, was a step in the right direction; and to this circumstance the band owes much of its increased efficiency and power. *As the Mendelssohn mania has partially subsided, we will venture to pronounce a dispassionate opinion that a like successful result would attend the efforts of any distinguished musician, of whatever country, placed in the advantageous position which Dr. Mendelssohn was allowed to assume.* The great German composer was met with a welcome as cordial as his eminent abilities entitled him to; audience and orchestra alike vied in their zeal to support the career of the new conductor, to whom the post was conceded with a cheerfulness highly honourable to the feelings of the well qualified professors of our country; for it is absurd to argue that no English musician is capable of directing the concerts of the Philharmonic Society at the present day: we forbear naming several whose genius and profound musical knowledge eminently qualify them for the post; but the tone of feeling in musical circles, the jealousy and pitiful rivalry of individual members of the profession, rendered the task of selection a hazardous experiment, more especially as the old absurdity of engaging different conductors for each concert was universally condemned in all quarters. Under these circumstances the appointment of Dr. Mendelssohn was, on the whole, a judicious one.'

With the paragraph displayed in Italics we wholly disagree. The 'Mendelssohn *mania*,' as it is termed, will only die with music itself; and no musician now living, foreign or native, could produce the same results, by constant superintendence of an orchestra, as Dr. Mendelssohn, because no one else has the transcendant abilities, which he possesses, to enforce attention and command respect. If Mendelssohn had said he would not again visit England, as conductor of the Philharmonic, he would assuredly hold to his word; – and whom should we have to thank for this lamentable deprivation? – *But we know that he has said no such thing.* On the contrary – he loves England – respects English artists – and is on the best possible terms with all the Philharmonic directors, who are by far too wise to dispense with services *vitally necessary to the continued prosperity of the society.*   Q.

The Musical Examiner, 10 August 1844, pp. 721–2, 725–7

VIII

THE SCHUMANNS

ROBERT SCHUMANN
(1810–1856)

Letter, date and addressee unknown
Mendelssohn has a bride and, his thoughts entirely taken up with
her, still gains in charm and greatness of soul; not a day goes by
without him coming up with at least a pair of thoughts that could be
instantly engraved in gold.

Robert Schumann, quoted in Hans Gerhard Weiss: *Felix Mendelssohn-Bartholdy: ein
Lebensbild . . .* (Berlin, 1947), p. 147

Mendelssohn on his own compositions
Later on he didn't want to talk about his character pieces. He had
still been possessed by Bach and Handel in those days.

Also in later years his Capriccio in F♯ minor (Opus 5) no longer
pleased him. Only when I drew his attention to the powerful
momentum of the last two pages did he again seem to remember the
piece with fondness.

His favourite piece from his youth was certainly the Octet; he
spoke with delight of the wonderful time when he wrote it.

According to him, he wrote the G minor Piano Concerto in
Munich in a few days ('three', I think he said). As to Delphine von
Schauroth, who was an excellent and very beautiful pianist, he
thought of her as someone who might be dangerous for him. He
described her personality with great charm.

The first *Song without Words* is not the one in E major, but the
one in A (in common time) in the same volume. The one in E major
was the second to be written.

Once, as I was looking through the collected *Songs without Words*,
I said: 'That was a good idea of yours.' He replied: 'Well, at least it
was well meant.'

About various of the *Songs without Words*:

As he was playing the E major one from the third volume (No. 3)
from the manuscript, I asked him why he had not yet allowed it to
be published, and he said it was 'not musical enough'. (We do, by

the way, have the autograph of this piece, as of most of those in the fifth volume, which show numerous variants) (also No. 2 in the fourth volume) –

The E minor one from the fifth volume, which was played as a funeral march at his burial service.

Of C.P.E. Bach by comparison with his father: 'It was like a dwarf in the company of giants.'

On the G minor Concerto and the Studies of Moscheles 'he thought that these were the point at which Moscheles first began to be a real composer'.

He found male partsongs hard to write. On the favourite second inversion triad.

On Field, and how he never thought it beneath him that, even as an old man, he should practise the most thorough-going mechanical exercises. – (In London)

That he had never written occasional pieces, Fantasies on themes from, etc. – only once had he been in danger of this, in the presence of Malibran in London, who gave him the silly notion of writing such a piece. He was intending to write a *Requiem* for Malibran (November 1836).

He owned the original score of Beethoven's Seventh Symphony. To my question as to who had given it to him, he laughed 'an ass'!

If he was not asked, he would not say what he thought (about musical compositions).

The founding of the Conservatory and his behaviour in the matter, that he wished to be considered only as Director.

He couldn't stand it when people, especially musicians, looked up music afterwards in the *score*. After all, a musician has ears.

After he'd played an awful piece by Czerny and I'd made fun of it, he said good-naturedly 'yes, that was stupid of me!'

He doesn't often play modern works. Only once did he have the urge to play Chopin's F minor Concerto.

To consider the notion of 'always being first'. Ambition in the noblest sense.

His delicacy in the gifts he offered to those he liked: as he did to Clara (*Hermann and Dorothea*) – and especially in the gift of Immermann's *Tristan and Isolde*.

He very much liked the saying: 'Tell me where you live and I'll tell you what kind of a composer you are.'

On Meyerbeer: the idea that a composition was simply a piece of the artist's life, a necessity, was something he had no inkling of.

There was deep meaning in everything he did or said, from the smallest to the greatest.

On the [Beethoven] Ninth Symphony and its critics; the wonderful end of the first movement and, come to that, the wonderful character of the whole of the first movement. The Adagio especially one of the things he most admired.

On the Eighth Symphony – that people should see it as a lesser or weaker work, how wrong that is.

His judgment of musical matters, for example on compositions – the most penetrating thing imaginable, going right to the heart of the matter.

He spotted the mistake and the cause and effect immediately and without fail.

Of the Bach E flat chorale prelude 'Schmücke dich, o liebe Seele' [Deck thyself, my soul, with gladness, BWV 654] he said with the deepest feeling: 'If life had taken everything from me, this piece would comfort me again.'

He was the fiercest, most conscientious critic of his own work of any artist I have ever met. He revised some passages five and six times. (In particular in *Elijah*; his wonderful remark about it that 'he thought there were quite a few things he could improve'.)

His face on his deathbed. He looked like a priest, like some champion of God who had won the battle – 6 November 1847.

The letter about Melusine and Mendelssohn's reply that I should write that the overture was a 'Mésalliance'.

On old Italian church music, that 'it seemed to him like incense'.

In 1845, when I was complaining to him about my nervous illness, 'but, Heavens above, look at the works you've dug out of yourself in the last few years!'

If, on the path of Art, old friends begin to leave us and talk of 'false directions' – how sad that was.

His painstaking corrections to the proofs – and the engraver's sarcastic remark that 'it's like a game of chess' and Mendelssohn's unbending attitude in this.

If he offended anyone without a cause – speaking disapprovingly of a third party – he could not rest until he had put the matter right (the story of Hofmeister).

His attitude towards the arrogance of virtuosos – as with Ole Bull.

When I told him about the large telescope and one of the remarks, which I'd read somewhere, that if the inhabitants of the sun gazed at us through a telescope, we should look something like worms in a cheese – 'Yes, but *The Well-Tempered Clavier* would still command their respect' (or something similar).

He has never kept a journal or anything like that, he told me.

His behaviour towards other living composers, an entirely unfair judgment about this which was frequently made. Where he could find nothing to praise, he kept silent; but where he found unmistakable talent, he was the first to proclaim it ([Sterndale] Bennett, Gade, Rietz)

By Henselt's Concerto 'he was very deceived – had turned into a real old sourpuss' – he described it as 'passagework with a tune stuck over the top'.

1836. We were talking about composers growing old, how 'sad to think that inspiration *dried up*', how distressing this thought was to him.

His enormously wide reading: the Bible, Shakespeare, Goethe, Jean Paul, (also Homer), certainly the main passages of these he knew pretty well off by heart.

And then the amount of music he knew . . .

To my question as to 'whether, in his youth, he had ever thought of *not* becoming a *musician*', he replied: 'Just once, on a gloomy, rainy day – he had wanted to become a lawyer.'

His requirement for the most sensitive musical ear. 'That, as a child, one must guess the pitch of the windowpane' he seems to take this for granted in everyone.

The last music we heard him play was pieces from *A Midsummer Night's Dream*, which he played as a piano duet with Clara, at one of Bendeman's matinees, on 29 March 1846.

The last piece I saw him conduct was my C major Symphony and his G minor Piano Concerto.

If all his close friends were writers, they would all have something utterly different and extraordinary to say about him, they would all be able to fill whole volumes. Every day he was as though born anew.

Did he feel that his mission was fulfilled? I believe so.

The melancholy which is often to be found in the works after the *Lobgesang*.

His conversation with children, so kind and thoughtful.

The strictest observation of his duty towards God and men.

He very much enjoyed drinking Rhenish wine, though always in moderation. Once (on Clara's birthday in 1842) he was unwell when he came to us and so was reluctant to taste the very good Rhenish wine we were offering him. But in the end he did taste some, saying 'Just a little of a wine like this can't do any harm', and drank with the best.

The opposition to him in Berlin kindled his artistic ambition in the highest degree. This was a cause of his early death.

His incredible memory.

Every artist paid him homage. The most important compositions of the young generation of composers are dedicated to him: Gade (Symphony), [Sterndale] Bennett (Sonata), Verhulst (   ), Rietz (   ), Hiller (Destruction), Spohr (Sonata)

His mission was fulfilled. He knew this better than anyone:

'Lord, now lettest Thou Thy servant depart in peace'!

How sad.

His handwriting also a picture of his inner harmony.

When Truhn brought him an overture, supposedly for *Romeo and Juliet*, he said: 'It's more like one for *King Lear*.'

He rarely read the musical papers – he would like to have someone get him some if he was unwell and had to stay in bed; then he would read a year's output at a time. But he knew about all the most important compositions that appeared. When he read through a new work, you could plainly see from his face what he was thinking.

Or occasionally one would hear him say 'Heavens above!'

About critics of the last movement of the Ninth Symphony, he would say 'I can understand it'.

On Rellstab: 'One could not deny that he had common sense.'

Mendelssohn was *true* in everything (Goethe).

He was not susceptible to flattery, nor capable of it.

He said that 'once he had laid aside his pen, he stopped thinking about music'. He very often composed surrounded by the noise of children.

He was free from all the weaknesses of vanity.

On his relationship with Meyerbeer, 'they had never got on with one another; even if one of them had said "Good day" to the other, the other would certainly have suspected an ulterior motive.'

I first saw him in August 1835 in the hall of the Gewandhaus. The orchestra was playing his overture *Calm Sea and Prosperous Voyage*. I told him that I knew all his works well; he made some very modest reply. The first impression that of an unforgettable man.

Conversations with Mendelssohn in the years 1835, 1836, 1837,
15 March 1837

On 14 March 1837. To him early, at 9.30. The day before, Beethoven's Ninth Symphony. Mendelssohn took the first movement unbelievably fast; it was so distressing for me that I walked out on the spot. I told him so, expressing myself bluntly and to the point. He was astonished, 'he would never have imagined the movement otherwise'. Then 'the first three movements were *excessively* beautiful'. Earlier he had felt that 'the momentum of the first movement did not have its equal in music, that perhaps the end of the first movement of the Bach D minor Concerto was some long way behind it'. 'He would have liked perhaps a few touches of instrumentation to be otherwise, in the Scherzo (I know the spot), and one in the Adagio (where the violins answer the strong idea in the middle section [?bars 65–82]): in the first, the theme was inaudible and in the second the violins were too weak.' 'As for the last movement, he didn't *understand* it.' Meaning 'it was the one he liked least'.

A fortnight from now he is to be married. 'Wasn't it terrible of him: he stood so near the goal of his happiness and, even so, a wrong note caused him as much pain as ever, but when he was with his bride everything was forgotten.' She was a *child*. A few days earlier he said wistfully 'Schumann, how sad it would have been if I were to have passed this house by.'

When we'd finished with the Beethoven symphony, he took my hand: 'Schumann, don't be offended by what I'm about to say; I find myself so at ease in your company; but I've had such sad experiences, especially with people connected to the public press that a certain inhibition has remained,' even towards those he knew there was no need to be afraid of. He was keen to write to me, and very often, about what he had on his mind. Would I promise him discretion? That was the gist; some embarrassment on my side; but it was smoothed over quickly.

I asked him about his setting of Goethe's *Walpurgis Night*, which he had made quite some time ago. 'Nowadays he couldn't stand the first part, on the other hand he liked the second very much.' 'He looked forward to a time when he could compose another version of the first part.'

Of the Bach B minor Mass: 'some of it was dry, but most of it was incomparably beautiful: just look at the notes'.

He very much liked Cherubini's Requiem.

Then a long discussion about *St Paul*. I showed him the places which, for me, had not gone well at the rehearsal. He said I must 'tell him straight whether the oratorio hadn't begun to strike me as dry or monotonous, he'd already taken out one aria'. I replied that 'I'd never had any such thought'.

On Chopin (before 1840): 'he's a distinct talent. His second ideas (his second themes) are always weaker than his first. Chopin had played him a piece (the G major Nocturne before the Andante spianato) [?] which Mendelssohn described in very poetical terms: you felt as though you were gazing into a garden with people silently walking up and down, with fountains in between and strange birds – an image, Mendelssohn thought, of music's own enchanted life.

To my question as to who among living composers wrote the best fugues, he replied without thinking 'Spohr'. He hadn't thought of Cherubini who, in 1836, was still alive.

On Gade (1843). Mendelssohn very much liked his First Symphony, but was less happy with the Second. But there was something else about the latter, in that if you compared it with the work of a man like Lindpaintner, every now and then there were passages of four or eight bars which would never have occurred to someone like Lindpaintner in their lives. He liked Gade, both when he spoke and when he was silent.

[Sterndale] Bennett he called sweet-natured; Bennett plays his three water pieces (The Millstream, The Fountain, The Lake) inimitably.

On Clara. The smoothness of her playing. He admires her enormously. 'She understands how to play the piano.' He always liked taking really fast tempi when playing piano duets with her, and especially when sightreading.

He always spoke of Bach, Gluck, Handel, Mozart, Haydn and Beethoven with the deepest respect. On one occasion he criticized Mozart's choral writing in the cantata *Davidde penitente*, in the handling of the vocal lines; this was the only reproach against Mozart I ever heard him make.

He doesn't remember ever having done mechanical exercises.

He knew everything that was going on in the world. You couldn't tell him anything new.

His motto: 'You must compose something every day.'

The last weeks of his life. That he might see England again. That he might breathe the Swiss mountain air once more.

The highest moral and artistic maxims: as a result, he could seem implacable, and at times apparently brusque and inhuman.

Robert Schumann: *Erinnerungen an Felix Mendelssohn Bartholdy*; *nachgelassene Aufzeichungen von Robert Schumann*, ed. G. Eismann (Zwickau, 1948), pp. 28, 31, 32, 35, 36, 39, 40, 43, 44, 47, 48, 51, 55, 58, 61, 62, 64, 67, 68, 71, 74, 77 (with cuts)

ROBERT & CLARA
SCHUMANN

Diary entry, 3 May 1832 (Robert)
Mendelssohn got off lightly; he was, it seems, making an enormous impact in Paris; his tone and touch were poor; for the rest he plays furiously, but only Beethoven and Mozart.

Diary entry, 23 September 1836
Meal with Mendelssohn and a happy reunion. 'He was engaged to be married'; thought 'he was bewitched by . . .' On his right,

Lipinski and Nowakowsky, who did not have much speech on their left. Mendelssohn light-hearted, rosy-cheeked.

Diary entry, 27 September 1836
Evening in the hotel pretty drunk, told Mendelssohn bits from the Rahel book.* His sister looked on calmly.

Diary entry, 9 October 1836
Mendelssohn stamping: in a furious rage.

Diary entry, 25 February 1837
After the performance of [Spohr's] *Faust* with Bennett, Frank and Goethe in Auerbach's cellar. Mendelssohn introduces his fiancée to me; a blooming, tall foreign rose.

Diary entry, 4 October 1837
I met Mendelssohn yesterday in the street and walked with him for a while. What a refreshing man! With him everything abounds with riches. 'He's not sincere with me,' said Clara this evening. In the afternoon Mendelssohn on your arm, in the evening Clara next to your heart – do you deserve it?

Diary entry, 14 November 1840
Clara (asked me) said to me that my attitude to Mendelssohn seems to have changed; certainly not towards him as an artist – you know that – for years I have contributed more to his elevation than almost anyone else. However – let us not forget ourselves too much over this. Jews remain Jews; they take their place at table ten times before it's the Christian's turn. The stones we supply to build their temple of fame, they then use to throw at us. So what I'm saying is, moderation in all things. We must act and work for ourselves too. Above all, let us approach ever closer to the beautiful and the true in art.

---

* Rahel Varnhagen, about whose blue-stocking activities Mendelssohn had mixed feelings. The book in question might have been *Rahel, ein Buch des Andenkens für ihre Freunde* (1833) or *Gallerie von Bildnissen aus Rahels Umgang* (1836), both edited by Karl August Varnhagen von Ense. [RN]

Diary entry, 15 November 1840 (Clara)
Firstly I must say to you, dear husband, with reference to the above words, that I entirely agree with you, and that in secret I have often felt the same way, but that out of deep admiration for Mendelssohn's art I have yet again treated him with the old excessive courtesy. I shall follow your advice and not abase myself too much before him, as I have so often done.

Robert and Clara Schumann: *Tagebuch 7*, ed. G. Eismann (Leipzig, 1971), I, p. 383; *Tagebuch 8*, ed. G. Neuhaus (Leipzig, 1987), II, pp. 26–7, 32, 36; *Tagebuch 9*, ed. G. Neuhaus (Leipzig, 1987), II, pp. 122–3

HENRY SCOTT HOLLAND
& WILLIAM SMITH ROCKSTRO

The concert described below was given in the Leipzig Gewandhaus on 12 April 1846.

Madame Clara Schumann (*née* Wieck), who was then residing in Dresden, came to Leipzig in the course of the afternoon, with the intention of taking a seat among the audience. On arriving at the railway-station, after her four hours' journey, she drove at once to Mendelssohn's house, for the purpose of paying him a visit. She found him a little anxious about his share in the duties of the evening, which was exceedingly onerous, since, beside his own solos, he had accepted the responsibility of accompanying every piece in the programme. Thus circumstanced, he begged Madame Schumann to add to the interest of the performance by taking part in it herself. She was tired with her journey; quite unprepared to play, and not even provided with a suitable toilette for the evening; but she unhesitatingly consented; and Mendelssohn well knew that she would prove more than equal to the occasion, when the moment for the fulfilment of her promise arrived.

Long before the appointed time, the room was crowded, to its remotest corner. The *bénéficiaire* sang – as she always did, when supported by Mendelssohn's matchless accompaniment – her very best. Mendelssohn played Beethoven's 'Sonata in C♯ minor,' as no one but he could play it; and, when the point in the programme was reached, at which he was expected to play his own '*Lieder ohne Worte*,' he came down to the place in which Madame Schumann was seated among the audience, and led her, in her travelling dress, to the piano. She was received with an ovation; and played two of the '*Lieder*' – Nos. I. and IV. in the Sixth Book – and a 'scherzo' of her own, with an effect which could scarcely have been surpassed. The performance concluded, in accordance with the previous announcement, with a selection of songs, by Mdlle. Lind, accompanied by Mendelssohn, in his own inimitable manner; and the audience departed in raptures.

Henry Scott Holland and William Smith Rockstro: *Memoir of Mme. Jenny Lind-Goldschmidt* (London, 1891), pp. 375–6

FERDINAND HILLER

A large number of friends had been invited to hear Mendelssohn, Clara Schumann amongst them. He played Beethoven's great F minor Sonata 'Appassionata'; at the end of the Andante he let the final chord of the diminished seventh ring on for a long time, as if he wanted to impress it very forcibly on all present; then he quietly got up, and turning to Madame Schumann, said 'You must play the Finale.' She strongly protested. Meanwhile all were awaiting the issue with the utmost tension, the chord of the diminished seventh hovering over our heads all the time like the sword of Damocles. I think it was chiefly the nervous, uncomfortable feeling of this unresolved discord which at last moved Madame Schumann to yield to Mendelssohn's entreaties and give us the Finale. The end was worthy of the beginning, and if the order had been reversed it would no doubt have been just as fine.

Ferdinand Hiller: *Felix Mendelssohn-Bartholdy* (Cologne, 1874; Eng. tr. M.E. von Glehn, London, 1874), pp. 214–5

IX

BERLIOZ AND
OTHER COMPOSERS

HECTOR BERLIOZ
(1803–1869)

To Gounet, Girard, Hiller, Desmarest, Richard, Sichel, Nizza,
6 May 1831
I've met Mendelssohn; Montfort knew him already. We took to each other at once. He's an excellent lad, his playing abilities are as great as his musical genius, and that's saying a lot. I've been delighted with all the music of his I've heard; I firmly believe he is one of the greatest musical talents of the age. He has been acting as my guide. I've been going to see him every morning and he's played me a Beethoven sonata or we've sung Gluck's *Armide,* then he's taken me to see all the famous ruins which, I must confess, haven't made much of an impression on me. Mendelssohn is one of those open characters you don't find often; he believes firmly in his Lutheran religion and several times I've seriously shocked him by laughing at the Bible. He has been responsible for the only tolerable moments I've had during my stay in Rome.

To Ferdinand Hiller, Rome, 17 September 1831
Has Mendelssohn arrived? He is enormously, extraordinarily, superbly, prodigiously talented. I can't be suspected of friendly bias when I say this, because he's told me frankly he found my music utterly incomprehensible. Give him all my best. His is a virginal character, he still has his beliefs. He's slightly cool in his dealings with people but, although he may not realize it, I'm very fond of him.

To Ferdinand Hiller, 1 January 1832
All best wishes to Mendelssohn; we often talk about him at the Villa Medici. At Mme Fould's the other day I heard the symphony he had performed in London [First Symphony], which he has *deranged* for violin, double bass and piano duet. The first movement is superb, I don't remember the adagio in every detail, the intermezzo is fresh and pungent; as for the finale, combined with a fugue, I detest it. I can't understand how such a talented man can turn himself at times

into a note-weaver as he has done, but it must make sense to him. It's always the same story: there is no absolute beauty.

Hector Berlioz: *Correspondence générale*, I (Paris, 1972, ed. Pierre Citron), pp. 441, 486–7, 517

> The following excerpts suggest that, even if there was an attraction of opposites between Mendelssohn and Berlioz, it was nonetheless a fairly prickly friendship. In 1834 Mendelssohn inveighed against Berlioz's orchestration, with the recommendation that after perusing a Berlioz score one should wash one's hands.

My acquaintance with Mendelssohn had begun in Rome [in May 1831] in a rather bizarre way. At our first meeting he talked about my cantata *Sardanapale* which had been awarded first prize by the Institute in Paris and parts of which my fellow-prizewinner Montfort had introduced him to. When I myself made it clear that I had a real aversion against the cantata's opening allegro he cheerfully exclaimed: 'Good for you! I congratulate you . . . on your taste! I was afraid you might be happy with that allegro; frankly, it's pretty awful!'

One day I started to talk about the metronome and its usefulness:

'Why bother with a metronome?' protested Mendelssohn vigorously. 'It's an utterly useless invention. A musician who can't work out the right tempo for a piece just by looking at it is a blockhead.'

I could have replied that there were a lot of blockheads around; but I held my tongue.

I'd written hardly anything at that time.

Mendelssohn knew only my *Irish Melodies*, in the version with piano accompaniment. One day he asked to see the score of my *King Lear* overture, which I'd just written in Nice, and just as he was about to put his fingers to the keys to play it (which he did with incomparable skill), he asked:

'Give me the right tempo!'

'Why?' said I. 'Didn't you tell me yesterday that any musician who couldn't tell the right tempo for a piece just by looking at it was a blockhead?'

He didn't want me to know it, but these ripostes, or rather these unexpected thrusts annoyed him considerably.

He would never mention the name Johann Sebastian Bach without adding ironically 'your little pupil'. In short, he was a real hedgehog as long as music was the topic under discussion; you never knew where to get hold of him without getting pricked. But he had an excellent character and a sweet and charming disposition. He willingly accepted being contradicted on any other subject and I in my turn traded on his tolerance during the discussions we sometimes had about philosophy and religion.

One evening we were exploring the baths of Caracalla together and debating the question of the merit or demerit of human actions and their reward during this earthly life. As I was replying with some outrageous remark or other to his statement of his absolutely religious, orthodox opinion, his foot slipped and there he was rolling about, with a mass of cuts and bruises, in the ruins of a very uneven stairway.

'You have to admire divine justice,' I said as I helped him up, 'I'm the one who blasphemes and you're the one who falls over.'

This impious response, accompanied by loud bursts of laughter, seemed to strike him as going too far and from then on discussions of religion were always avoided.

It was in Rome that I had my first experience of that delicate, pretty, richly coloured substance known as the *Fingal's Cave* overture. Mendelssohn had just completed it and gave me a fairly accurate idea of the piece, such was his prodigious ability to play the most complicated scores on the piano. On days when the enervating sirocco was blowing, I often used to go and interrupt his labours (he is an indefatigable worker). Then he would put down his pen with a very good grace and, seeing me swollen with spleen, would try and calm me by playing whatever I chose from the works of those masters we both loved. How many times, sitting peevishly on his sofa, have I sung the aria 'D'une image, hélas! trop chérie' from *Iphigénie en Tauride*, while he accompanied me, sitting correctly at the piano. And he would exclaim: 'That's beautiful! Beautiful! I could listen to it from morning to night without getting tired of it, endlessly, endlessly!' And we'd begin again. He also liked to get me, as I lay horizontal, to apply my irritated voice to two or three of the songs I had written on verses by Thomas Moore, and which he liked. Mendelssohn has always felt a certain esteem for my . . . lighter songs.

After a month of these meetings, which I had ended up by finding extremely interesting, Mendelssohn disappeared without saying goodbye to me and I didn't see him again. So his letter came, really, as a very pleasant surprise. It seemed to reveal in him a kindliness and polished manners that I had not found in him before, and I was soon to find, when I reached Leipzig, that these excellent qualities had indeed become his. Not that he has lost any of his inflexible rigidity over artistic principles, but he doesn't try and impose them violently on people. When exercising his duties as *Kapellmeister*, he confines himself to bringing out what he considers beautiful and letting what he regards as bad or harmful remain in the shadows. Only he is still rather too keen on composers who are dead.

Just as Mendelssohn was coming down off the podium, radiant with the joy of conducting his work, I went forward to meet him, thrilled to have heard it. The moment could not have been chosen better for such a meeting. And yet, after the first exchange of words, the same sad thought struck us both simultaneously:

'Can it be twelve years ago, twelve years ago that we dreamt together on the Roman plain!'

'Yes, and in the baths of Caracalla!'

'Still a tease, still ready to laugh at me!'

'No, no, I'm not mocking in the slightest; I was testing your memory and seeing whether you'd pardoned me for my irreligious remarks. So far am I from mocking that I want you (and I ask this in all seriousness) to mark our first meeting by giving me something I value extremely highly.'

'Which is?'

'The baton with which you've just conducted the rehearsal of your new work.'

'Of course, on condition you'll send me yours.'

'I'll be trading brass for gold; but never mind, I agree.'

And immediately Mendelssohn's musical sceptre was brought to me. The next day, I sent him my heavy lump of oak with the following letter which, I trust, The Last of the Mohicans would not have been ashamed of:

'To Chief Mendelssohn!

Great chief! We promised to exchange our tomahawks; here's mine! It is rough, yours is simple. Only squaws and palefaces like ornamented weapons. Be my brother! and when the great Spirit has sent us hunting in the land of souls, may our warriors hang our tomahawks together over the door of the meeting-house.'

Hector Berlioz: *Mémoires* (Paris, 1870; R/1969), Premier voyage en Allemagne, 4e lettre, 'Leipzig', II, pp. 85–90 (with cuts)

LUIGI CHERUBINI
(1760–1842)

Cherubini lived in Paris from 1786 and wrote a number of sacred choral works and operas, the most successful of the latter being *Lodoïska* (1791), *Médée* (1797) and *Les deux journées* (1800). Beethoven had a high opinion of his music. He was connected with the Paris Conservatoire from its foundation and was its Director from 1822 until his death.

In 1825, he had this to say about Felix's F minor Piano Quartet of 1823:

'*Ce garçon est riche; il fera bien; il fait même déjà bien, mais il dépense trop de son argent, il met trop d'étoffe dans son habit.*'

[This boy is rich [in talent]; he will do well; he is already doing well, but he spends too much of his money, he puts too much material into his coat.]

Luigi Cherubini, quoted in Carl Mendelssohn-Bartholdy: *Goethe and Felix Mendelssohn-Bartholdy* (Leipzig, 1871; Eng. tr. M.E. von Glehn, London, 1872), p. 43

FERDINAND HILLER

December 1831 – April 1832
On the whole, as is evident from his published letters, Mendelssohn led a pleasant easy-going life in Paris, and gave himself up to the enjoyment of the moment without hesitation. A large part of his time was devoted to chess; he was a capital player, and his usual antagonists, Michael Beer, the poet, a brother of Meyerbeer's, and

Dr. Herman Franck, only occasionally succeeded in beating him. Franck would not allow that he was inferior, and upon this Mendelssohn invented a phrase which he relentlessly repeated after every victory: 'We play quite equally well – *quite equally* – only I play a very little better.'

Meyerbeer, who was certainly a sincere admirer of his talent, Mendelssohn saw but seldom. A funny little incident occurred shortly after his arrival in Paris. Mendelssohn was often told that he was very like the composer of 'Robert;' and at first sight his figure and general appearance did perhaps give some ground for the idea, especially as they wore their hair in the same style. I sometimes teased Mendelssohn about it, to his great annoyance, and at last one morning he appeared with his hair absolutely cropt. The affair excited much amusement in our set, especially when Meyerbeer heard of it; but he took it up with his usual invincible good-nature, and in the nicest way.

Chopin had been at Munich at the same time with Mendelssohn, and had given concerts there, and otherwise exhibited his remarkable abilities. When he arrived in Paris, as a complete stranger, he met with a very kind reception from Kalkbrenner, who, indeed, deserved all praise as a most polished, clever, and agreeable host. Kalkbrenner fully recognized Chopin's talent, though in rather a patronizing way. For instance, he thought his *technique* not sufficiently developed, and advised him to attend a class which he had formed for advanced pupils. Chopin, always good-natured, was unwilling to refuse outright, and went a few times to see what it was like. When Mendelssohn heard of this he was furious, for he had a great opinion of Chopin's talent, while, on the other hand, he had been annoyed at Berlin by Kalkbrenner's charlatanry. One evening at the Mendelssohns' house there, Kalkbrenner played a grand Fantasia, and when Fanny asked him if it was an improvisation, he answered that it was. The next morning, however, they discovered the improvised Fantasia, published note for note under the title of 'Effusio musica.' That Chopin, therefore, should submit to pass for a pupil of Kalkbrenner's seemed to Mendelssohn, and with justice, to be a perfect absurdity, and he freely expressed his opinion on the matter. Meantime, the thing soon came to its natural conclusion. Chopin gave a soirée at the Pleyel Rooms; all the musical celebrities were there; he played his E minor Concerto, some of his Mazurkas and Notturnos, and took everybody by storm. After this no more was heard of want of *technique*, and Mendelssohn had applauded triumphantly.

The relations between Kalkbrenner and Mendelssohn were always somewhat insecure, but Kalkbrenner's advances were such that Mendelssohn could not altogether decline them. We dined there together a few times, and everything went quite smoothly, though no entreaties could ever persuade Felix to touch the keys of Kalkbrenner's piano. Indeed, we were none of us very grateful for Kalkbrenner's civilities, and took a wicked pleasure in worrying him. I remember that one day, Mendelssohn, Chopin, Liszt, and I, had established ourselves in front of a café on the Boulevard des Italiens, at a season and an hour when our presence there was very exceptional. Suddenly we saw Kalkbrenner coming along. It was his great ambition always to represent the perfect gentleman, and knowing how extremely disagreeable it would be to him to meet such a noisy company, we surrounded him in the friendliest manner, and assailed him with such a volley of talk that he was nearly driven to despair, which of course delighted us. Youth has no mercy.

I must here tell a little story, if indeed it deserves the name, to show what mad spirits Mendelssohn was capable of at that time. One night as we were coming home across the deserted boulevard at a late hour, in earnest conversation, Mendelssohn suddenly stops and calls out: – 'We *must* do some of our jumps in Paris! our jumps, I tell you! Now for it! one! – two! – three! –' I don't think my jumps were very brilliant, for I was rather taken aback by the suggestion, but I shall never forget the moment.

Mendelssohn went occasionally to see Cherubini. 'What an extraordinary creature he is!' he said to me one day. 'You would fancy that a man could not be a great composer without sentiment, heart, feeling, or whatever else you call it; but I declare I believe that Cherubini makes everything out of his head alone.' On another occasion he told me that he had been showing him an eight-part composition, *a capella* (I think it was his 'Tu es Petrus' [op. III, posthumous work for voices and orchestra]), and added, 'The old fellow is really too pedantic: in one place I had a suspended third in two parts, and he wouldn't pass it on any condition.' Some years later, happening to speak of this incident, Mendelssohn said: 'The old man was right after all; one ought not to write them.'

Felix's wonderful musical memory was a great source of enjoyment to us all as well as to himself. It was not learning by heart, so much as retention – and to what an extent! When we were together, a small party of musical people, and the conversation flagged, he would sit down to the piano, play some out-of-the-way piece, and make us guess the composer. On one occasion he played an air from Haydn's 'Seasons.'

> 'The trav'ller stands perplexed,
> Uncertain and forlorn – '

in which not a note of the elaborate violin accompaniment was wanting. It sounded like a regular pianoforte piece, and we stood there a long time as 'perplexed' as the traveller himself.

The Abbé Bardin, a great musical amateur, used to get together a number of musicians and amateurs at his house once a week in the afternoons, and a great deal of music was gone through very seriously and thoroughly, even without rehearsals. I had just been playing Beethoven's E flat Concerto in public, and they asked for it again on one of these afternoons. The parts were all there, and the string quartet too, but no players for the wind. 'I will do the wind,' said Mendelssohn, and sitting down to a small piano which stood near the grand one, he filled in the wind parts from memory, so completely, that I don't believe even a note of the second horn was wanting, and all as simply and naturally done as if it were nothing.

Frankfurt, 1836

When Felix appeared, Rossini received him with marked respect, and yet in such a friendly manner, that in a few minutes the conversation resumed its flow and became quite animated. He wanted Mendelssohn to play to him, and after a little resistance on Mendelssohn's side, they arranged to meet at our house again next morning. These meetings were often repeated in the course of the next few days, and it was quite charming to see how Felix, though inwardly resisting, was each time afresh obliged to yield to the overwhelming amiability of the Maestro, as he stood at the piano listening with the utmost interest, and expressing his satisfaction more or less openly. I cannot deny the fact – and indeed it was perfectly natural – but Felix, with his juvenile looks, playing his compositions to a composer whose melodies just then ruled the whole world of song, was, in a certain measure, ostensibly acting an inferior part – as must always be the case when one artist introduces himself to another without any corresponding return. Mendelssohn soon began to rebel a little. 'If your Rossini,' said he to me one morning when we met at our bath in the Main, 'goes on muttering such things as he did yesterday, I won't play him anything more.'

'What did he mutter? I did not hear anything.'

'But I did: when I was playing my F sharp minor Caprice, he muttered between his teeth, "*Ça sent la sonate de Scarlatti.*"'

'Well, that's nothing so very dreadful.'

'Ah – bah!'

However, on the following day he played to him again. I must add that Rossini always looked back to this meeting with Mendelssohn with heartfelt pleasure, and expressed the strongest admiration for his talent.

1839

Towards the spring Liszt arrived in Leipzig fresh from his triumphs at Vienna and Prague, and revolutionized our quiet town. It will be remembered that in Paris he had excited Mendelssohn's highest admiration. At his first concert, as he glided along the platform of the orchestra to the piano, dressed in the most elegant style, and as lithe and slender as a tiger-cat, Mendelssohn said to me: 'There's a novel apparition, the virtuoso of the 19th century.' I need hardly describe the impression made by his playing. When he played Schubert's 'Erlkönig' half the people stood on their chairs. The Lucia fantasia turned everybody's head. With some others pieces, however, he was less successful – for instance, with Mendelssohn's D minor concerto, which had just appeared, and which he could neither read at sight nor find time to study with any care, so that people thought that the composer played it better himself. His performance of a part of the Pastoral Symphony, in the same room where it had so often been heard with all its orchestral effects, also did not meet with general approval. In the preface to his arrangement of the Beethoven Symphonies Liszt boldly declares that every effect can be reproduced on the modern piano. When Mendelssohn read this, he said: 'Well, if I could only hear the first eight bars of Mozart's G minor Symphony, with the delicate figure in the tenors, rendered on the piano as it sounds in the orchestra, – I would believe it.'

Ferdinand Hiller: *Felix Mendelssohn-Bartholdy* (Cologne, 1874; Eng. tr. M.E. von Glehn, London, 1874), pp. 23–9, 57–8, 164–5 (with cuts)

F. MAX MÜLLER

In March 1840 Mendelssohn gave a *matinée musicale* for Liszt in Leipzig:

Liszt appeared in his Hungarian costume, wild and magnificent. He told Mendelssohn that he had written something special for him. He sat down, and swaying right and left on his music-stool, played first a Hungarian melody, and then three or four variations, one more incredible than the other.

We stood amazed, and after everybody had paid his compliments to the hero of the day, some of Mendelssohn's friends gathered round him, and said: 'Ah, Felix, now we can pack up (jetzt können wir einpacken). No one can do that; it is over with us!' Mendelssohn smiled; and when Liszt came up to him asking him to play something in turn, he laughed and said that he never played now; and this, to a certain extent, was true. He did not give much time to practising then, but worked chiefly at composing and directing his concerts. However, Liszt would take no refusal, and so at last little Mendelssohn, with his own charming playfulness, said: 'Well, I'll play, but you must promise me not to be angry.' And what did he play? He sat down and played first all of Liszt's Hungarian Melody, and then one variation after another, so that no one but Liszt himself could have told the difference. We all trembled lest Liszt should be offended, for Mendelssohn could not keep himself from slightly imitating Liszt's movements and raptures. However, Mendelssohn managed never to offend man, woman, or child. Liszt

laughed and applauded, and admitted that no one, not he himself,
could have performed such a *bravura* . . .

F. Max Müller: *Auld Lang Syne* (New York, 1898), pp. 1–33; reprinted in *Mendelssohn and his World*, ed. R. Larry Todd (Princeton, 1991), p. 253

FANNY MENDELSSOHN

On 21 February 1843, the Henzels went to Leipzig,
where they spent a very pleasant week. Fanny writes in
her diary:

We had a great deal of music, and heard Gade's first work, a symphony in C minor, which is full of promise. Felix was quite
enchanted with it, and directed the rehearsals with a care and attention which might almost have been called affectionate. Berlioz was
at Leipzig at the same time with us, and his odd manners gave so
much offence that Felix was continually being called upon to
smoothe somebody's ruffled feathers. When the parting came,
Berlioz offered to exchange batons, 'as the ancient warriors
exchanged their armour,' and in return for Felix's pretty light stick of
whalebone covered with white leather sent an enormous cudgel of
lime-tree with the bark on, and an open letter, beginning, 'Le mien est
grossier, le tien est simple.' A friend of Berlioz who brought the two
translated this sentence, 'I am coarse and you are simple,' and was in
great perplexity how to conceal the apparent rudeness from Felix.

Fanny Mendelssohn, quoted in Sebastian Hensel: *The Mendelssohn Family 1729–1847* (London, 1881), II, pp. 184–5

CHARLES GOUNOD
(1818–1893)

Gounod won the Prix de Rome in 1839, and it was in
that city that he met Felix's sister Fanny and her
husband. The following memoir belongs to May 1843:

I left for Leipzig. This was where Mendelssohn was living, and his
sister Madame Hensel had given me a letter of introduction to him.

My reception at his hands was wonderful – I use this word deliberately to describe the condescension with which a man of his standing welcomed a lad who must have seemed to him to be no more
than a schoolboy. I can truly say that, during the four days I spent in
Leipzig, Mendelssohn turned his attention solely upon me. He ques-
tioned me about my studies and my compositions with the liveliest
and most sincere interest; he asked to hear my latest pieces on the
piano and was full of the most valuable words of approval and
encouragement. I shall mention only one, which made me so proud
that I have never forgotten it. I had just played him the 'Dies irae' of
my Vienna *Requiem*. He pointed to a movement for five-part
unaccompanied chorus and said: 'My dear Gounod, that movement
could be by Cherubini!' Words like those, coming from such a master, are truly decorations and one wears them more proudly than
many a ribbon.

Mendelssohn was the Director of the Gewandhaus Orchestra.
Although the orchestra was not meeting at that time of year, the
concert season being over, he was kind and thoughtful enough to
bring it together for me and allowed me to hear his fine Scottish
Symphony in A minor. He made me a present of the score and wrote
a few friendly words in it.

He did not confine himself just to directing the Gewandhaus. He
was also a first-class organist and wanted to introduce me to some
of the numerous and splendid works the great Johann Sebastian
Bach wrote for the instrument of which he was the supreme master.
With this in mind, he had the old organ at St Thomas's, which Bach
himself had once played, restored to serviceable condition and
there, for more than two hours, he revealed to me marvels I had not
dreamt of. Then, to set the seal on the favours he had done me, he
presented me with a volume of motets by that Bach for whom he
had a religious veneration.

Even the most amiable of geniuses is not immune to the tricks of
Fate. So it was that those delightful works which today are the
favourites of subscribers to the Conservatoire concerts required the
death of their composer before they could find favour with those
same ears which had once rejected them.

Charles Gounod: *Mémoires d'un artiste* (Paris, 1895; repr. 1991), pp. 123–5 (with cuts)

X

MANNERS, APPEARANCE, CHARACTER

SIR GEORGE GROVE

In person Mendelssohn was short, not so much as 5 ft. 6 ins. high, and slight of build; in figure lithe, and very light and mercurial. His look was dark and very Jewish; the face unusually mobile, and ever varying in expression, full of brightness and animation, and with a most unmistakeable look of genius. His complexion was fresh, and shewed a good deal of colour. His hair was black, thick, and abundant, but very fine, with a natural wave in it, and was kept back from his forehead, which was high and much developed. By the end of his life, however, it showed a good deal of gray and he began to be bald. His mouth was unusually delicate and expressive, and had generally a pleasant smile at the corners. His whiskers were very dark, and his closely-shaven chin and upper lip were blue from the strength of his beard. His teeth were beautifully white and regular; but the most striking part of his face were the large dark brown eyes. When at rest he often lowered the eyelids as if he were slightly short-sighted – which indeed he was; but when animated they gave an extraordinary brightness and fire to his face, and 'were as expressive a pair of eyes as were ever set in a human being's head.' When he was playing extempore, or was otherwise much excited, they would dilate and become nearly twice their ordinary size, the brown pupil changing to a vivid black. His laugh was hearty, and frequent; and when especially amused he would quite double up with laughter and shake his hand from the wrist to emphasize his merriment. He would nod his head violently when thoroughly agreeing, so that the hair came down over his face. In fact his body was almost as expressive as his face. His hands were small, with taper fingers. On the keys they behaved almost like 'living and intelligent creatures, full of life and sympathy.' His action at the piano was as free from affectation as everything else that he did, and very interesting. At times, especially at the organ, he leant very much over the keys, as if watching for the strains which came out of his finger tips. He sometimes swayed from side to side, but usually his whole performance was quiet and absorbed.

*

No musician – unless perhaps it were Leonardo da Vinci, and he was only a musician in a limited sense – certainly no great composer, ever had so many pursuits as Mendelssohn. Mozart drew, and wrote capital letters, Berlioz and Weber also both wrote good letters, Beethoven was a great walker and intense lover of nature, Cherubini was a botanist and a passionate card-player, but none of them approach Mendelssohn in the number and variety of his occupations. Both billiards and chess he played with ardour to the end of his life, and in both he excelled. When a lad he was devoted to gymnastics; later on he rode much, swam more, and danced whenever he had the opportunity. Cards and skating were almost the only diversions he did not care for.

Sir George Grove: *Dictionary of Music and Musicians*, first edition (London, 1880), pp. 294, 296 (article on Mendelssohn)

WILHELM ADOLPH LAMPADIUS

He was a man rather under the ordinary stature and size, somewhat neglectful of his personal appearance, yet graceful in his walk and bearing. His head was covered with glossy black hair, curling in light locks; his forehead, as befitted the head which teemed with such a burden of thought and feeling, was high and arched; his features sharply cut, but noble. His eyes were unspeakably expressive: when they glowed with indignation, or looked at you with estrangement, too much to bear; but, in his general friendly mood, indescribably charming; his nose, noble, and inclined to the Roman type; his mouth, firm, fine, in his serious moods more than dignified, authoritative, I might say, yet capable of the sweetest smile and the most winning expression. In this graceful, finely-moulded form, was hidden not only a royal spirit, but a most kindly heart. To speak out in a single word what was the most salient feature of his character, he was a Christian in the fullest sense. He knew and he loved the Bible as few do in our time: out of his familiarity with it grew his unshaken faith, and that profound spiritual-mindedness without which it would have been impossible for him to produce those deep-felt sacred compositions; and, besides this, the other principle of the genuine Christian life, love, was powerful in him. God had blessed him with a large measure of this world's goods; but he made a noble use of them. He carried the biblical injunction into effect, to 'visit the widow and the fatherless in their affliction;' and he knew that to feed the hungry and to clothe the naked is a fast acceptable to the Lord. His threshold was always besieged by the needy of all sorts, but his kindness knew no bounds; and the delicacy and consideration with which he treated the recipients of his bounty largely increased the worth of his gifts, valuable as they were, even in a merely material sense. Since he died, deed upon deed has come to light, which I am not at liberty here to relate, out of courtesy to the receiver, out of consideration to the giver, which only shows how literally he fulfilled the Savour's injunction, not to let the left hand know what the right hand doeth.

But what is to be reckoned largely to his credit is, that, with his worldly advantages, he cherished such a love of work; that he was a man of such restless activity. Many successful wooers of the German Muse have been the children of poverty, and without the stimulus of necessity, would have always been unknown: in many a man of genius, the sad experience has been repeated, that, so soon as Fortune smiled, his genius has been soothed to easy slumbers; but Mendelssohn, born in the lap of luxury, never gave himself with easy resignation to a life of contentment with worldly comforts: he only used his wealth as a means of giving his talents the more exclusively to his art; he did not compose in order to live, but he lived in order to compose. I must grant that this impulse to labour was the law of his nature. To be idle was for him to die. Sometimes, while his pupils in the Conservatorium were engaged on their tasks, he would execute charming little landscapes with his pen, which he used to gather up, and carry home. No little thing was able to disturb him when he composed. The place was indifferent. Sometimes, on his journeys, he would set himself at a table as soon as he had reached an inn, and had established himself for a tarry, long or short, for dinner or for the night, 'to write his notes,' as he used to say. What he was to his wife and his children, despite this ceaseless activity, I need not try to tell. Enough to say, that he was the most devoted of husbands, the most affectionate of fathers. Whoever did not know him intimately, and perceive how careful he was to shield himself from over-excitement, and every kind of influence which should jar upon him, would hardly suspect that his heart was framed for friendship, and that he was a very approachable man. But the large number of his intimate correspondents; the openness with which he revealed himself to them; the hearty interests in their work and welfare; and especially the close bonds which bound him to his friends in Düsseldorf, London, and Leipzig; the rich store of communications which his friends still hold, – declare the very opposite. Of course, a man like him could not open his nature to every one who approached: this was sheerly impossible. He was in much the same position as Goethe, though with a far warmer and more communicative nature than he. But Mendelssohn carried to an almost morbid extent an unwillingness to allude to anything pertaining to himself. From principle, he almost never read what was written about himself; and he was very unwilling that anything, musical criticism excepted, should be published about him.

Wilhelm Adolph Lampadius: *Felix Mendelssohn-Bartholdy: ein Denkmal für seine Freunde* (Leipzig, 1849; Eng. tr. W.L. Gage, New York, 1866), pp. 145–8 (with cuts)

JULIUS SCHUBRING

Leaving out of consideration Music, as the central point of his life, his natural gifts were exhibited in the most various ways, without any vain parade of them on his part. He was, for instance, a vigorous and skillful gymnast. The horizontal pole and the bars stood under the trees in the garden, and, shortly before the concerts which used to be given at home every fortnight, at twelve o'clock on Sunday morning, even when he had to play the piano, Felix thought nothing of having a half hour's good turn at gymnastics. On one occasion, he was summoned straight from the horizontal pole to the piano; but he had just run a small splinter into his finger, and the consequence was that he left marks of blood upon the keys during Beethoven's E-flat-major concerto, and I carefully wiped them away while he was playing. – He was a very good swimmer. During all one hot summer, we used to bathe nearly every day at Pfuel's Baths, and I was annoyed because, when struggling against one another in the water, he always got the better of me, and sent me under, though I was the taller and stronger of the two. On account of the great distance of the baths, at the Silesian Gate, Mama provided a carriage, and the consequence was that I drove home with him nearly every evening that summer. After tea we regularly had music, which was best, perhaps, when we were alone. At that time, he never extemporised as he subsequently did. His own compositions he never played, as a rule, unless especially requested to do so. After tea was, in so far, an unfortunate time, because we generally went on till nine o'clock, and then the drummers of the guard passed under the windows beating the retreat from the Leipzig Gate to the offices of the Minister of War. It was by no means rare for this to come precisely in the *Adagio*, disturbing us, of course, in a very disagreeable manner. Even when the drummers were at a distance we could hear them gradually advancing, the nearer they approached the greater being the hubbub, until, when it reached its highest point, the window-panes rattled again. Any one who ever heard the melting tones of Mendelssohn's playing, and saw how his soul was absorbed by the magnificent creations of art – how he entered into them, and how his feeling for them was expressed on the gradually drooping lids of his beautiful eyes – will comprehend how such discordant sounds jarred upon our reverential feelings. When we got over the interruption, too, we knew we had to expect it on the march back. On one occasion, Mendelssohn jumped up in the midst of the movement, exclaiming angrily: 'What stupid, monstrous, childishness!' It is true that we never thought of exercising ordinary precaution and going out of the way of the evil spirits.

Mendelssohn was, likewise, a good horseman. On the sole occasion I rode with him, we went to Pankow, walking thence to the Schönhauser Garden. It was about that time when he was busy with the overture to *A Midsummer Night's Dream*. The weather was beautiful, and we were engaged in animated conversation, as we lay in the shade on the grass when, all of a sudden, he seized me firmly by the arm, and whispered: 'Hush!' He afterwards informed me that a large fly had just then gone buzzing by, and he wanted to hear the sound it produced gradually die away. When the Overture was completed, he showed me the passage in the progression, where the violoncello modulates in the chord of the seventh of the descending scale from B minor to F sharp minor, and said: 'There, that's the fly that buzzed past us at Schönhauser!' He was also an elegant dancer, a circumstance which, when he was a youth, procured him many friends. In consequence of this, his birthday was once celebrated, to please him, by a masquerade. Skating was the only thing at which he was not a good hand. On the one solitary occasion that I succeeded in prevailing on him to try it, he suffered so much from the cold, despite his large fur gloves, that he probably never repeated the experiment.

As in such pleasing exercises, so also in the sphere of the intellect, his natural gifts were variously exhibited. He played chess admirably, a game, by the way, of which his Father, also, was very fond. That he surprised his mother on her birthday with a translation which he had himself made of Terence's *Andria*, and which his tutor had sent to the printer's, is a fact with which I only became acquainted outside the house. He never boasted of such things, Rösel was his drawing-master; and, though I am not qualified to give an opinion of productions of this description, yet may I state that Mendelssohn possessed a feeling for the artistic conception of Nature as well as for plastic art: he was capable of appreciating with intelligence and enthusiastic admiration the masterpieces of both ancient and modern times. Anything connected with mathematics, however appeared to be less in his way. In vain did I once attempt to make him understand why the Polar Star, which happened just then to be shining beautifully clear and bright, was alone sufficient to guide us over the four quarters of the globe. He could not master the line to be let fall, in his mind, perpendicularly on the horizon, the extension of the line of sight backwards through the eye, and its intersection at right angles with the side-line.

Mendelssohn's character had a deep feeling of religion for its basis. That this wanted the specifically church colouring is a fact on which we disputed a great deal in our earlier years. As an unconditional Schleiermacherite, I was then almost incapable of recognising Christianity in any other shape, and, consequently, wronged Felix. Wilmsen, who had instructed and confirmed Mendelssohn, and his brothers and sisters, struck me as a man of no great capacity, and I let fall some hint or other to the effect that it would have been better had they gone to Schleiermacher. Felix was seriously angry, and gave me to understand he would not allow anyone to attack his spiritual adviser, for whom he entertained a feeling of affectionate reverence. It is true that he did not go very often to hear him perform Divine Service. When I recollect, however, with what a serious religious feeling he pursued his art, the exercise of it always being, as it were, a sacred duty; how the first page of everyone of his compositions bears impressed on it the initial letter of a prayer; how he devoted the time, as he watched through the night by the bed of his dying friend, Hanstein, to marking in the first fugue, composed here, of the six he afterwards published – in E minor – the progress of the disease as it gradually destroyed the sufferer, until he made it culminate in the chorale of release in E major; how the very best touches in his oratorios result from his delicate tact – for instance, the words for the air of Paul during the three days of his blindness, when he had just been converted before Damascus, for which Mendelssohn, dissatisfied with everything proposed to him, himself hit upon the 51st Psalm, that seems as though it had been written on purpose, moreover, when I call to mind everything connected with my beloved friend, as regards his views and opinions on art and artists – whether he was standing at the conductor's desk, sitting at the piano, or taking the tenor-part in a quartet – religion and veneration were enthroned in his countenance; this was why his music possessed such a magic charm. On one occasion, he expressly said that sacred music, as such, did not stand higher in his estimation than any other, because every kind of music ought, in its peculiar way, to tend to the glory of God.

Julius Schubring: 'Reminiscences of Felix Mendelssohn-Bartholdy', *Musical World*, 31 (12 and 19 May 1866); reprinted in *Mendelssohn and his World*, ed. R. Larry Todd (Princeton, 1991), pp. 221–7 (with cuts)

HENRY FOTHERGILL CHORLEY

I had already made myself aware that he was not in the least like any portrait I have seen, and that he is a capital conductor, though in quite a different *genre* from Moscheles – as different as their two musics ... He is very handsome, with a particularly sweet laugh, and a slight cloud (not to call it thickness) upon his utterance, which seemed like the voice of some friend . . . Nothing could be kinder than he was.

Henry Fothergill Chorley: *Autobiography, Memoir and Letters* (London, 1873), I, p. 307

RICHARD STORRS WILLIS

Mendelssohn was a man of small frame, delicate and fragile looking; yet possessing a sinewy elasticity, and a power of endurance, which you would hardly suppose possible. His head appeared to have been set upon the wrong shoulders, – it seemed, in a certain sense, to contradict his body. Not that the head was disproportionately large; but its striking nobility was a standing reproof to the pedestal on which it rested. His eye possessed a peculiarity which has been ascribed to the eye of Sir Walter Scott, – a ray of light seemed often to proceed from its pupil to your own, as from a star. But yet, in the eyes of Mendelssohn, there was none of that rapt dreaminess so often seen among men of genius in art. The gaze was rather external than internal: the eye had more outwardness than inwardness of expression. In his gait, he was somewhat loose and shambling: he had a flinging motion of the limbs and a supple-jointedness, which, coupled with other little peculiarities of carriage, determined him – according to popular German tradition – as of Oriental origin. But this listlessness of bearing seemed to disappear entirely the moment he sat down to a pianoforte or organ, and came into artistic action. Then, like a full-blooded Arabian courser, he showed his points: you had before you a noble creature. All awkwardness disappeared: he was Mendelssohn, and no longer a son of Mendel. His wife was as beautiful as she was high-bred and refined. She bore him children of remarkable personal charms. One boy, particularly, I was never weary of gazing at, for his extreme comeliness. He had his father's eye, and his mother's elegance and grace of figure.

Richard Storrs Willis, quoted in Wilhelm Adolph Lampadius: *Felix Mendelssohn-Bartholdy: ein Denkmal für seine Freunde* (Leipzig, 1849; Eng. tr. W.L. Gage, New York, 1866), pp. 213–4

EDUARD DEVRIENT

The habit of constant occupation, instilled by his mother, made rest intolerable to him. To spend any time in mere talk caused him to look frequently at his watch, by which he often gave offence; his impatience was only pacified when something was being done, such as music, reading, chess, &c. He was fond of having a leaf of paper and pen at hand when he was conversing, to sketch down whatever occurred to him.

His manners were most pleasing. His features, of the Oriental type, were handsome; a high, thoughtful forehead, much depressed at the temples; large, expressive dark eyes, with drooping lids, and a peculiar veiled glance through the lashes; this, however, sometimes flashed distrust or anger, sometimes happy dreaming and expectancy. His nose was arched and of delicate form, still more so the mouth, with its short upper and full under lip, which was slightly protruded and hid his teeth, when, with a slight lisp, he pronounced the hissing consonants. An extreme mobility about his mouth betrayed every emotion that passed within.

His bearing retained from his boyhood the slight rocking of the head and upper part of the body, and shifting from foot to foot; his head was much thrown back, especially when playing; it was always easy to see whether he was pleased or otherwise when any new music was going on, by his nods and shakes of the head. In society his manners were even then felt to be distinguished. The shyness that he still retained left him entirely during his subsequent travels, but even now, when he wished to propitiate, he could be most fascinating, and his attentions to young ladies were not without effect. In his affections filial love still held the foremost place; the veneration with which he regarded his father had in it something religious and patriarchal; with his sisters the fondest intimacy prevailed; from his brother disparity of age still somewhat divided him. His elder sister, Fanny, stood musically most related to him; through her excellent nature, clear sense, and rich fund of sensibility (not perceptible to every one), many things were made clear to him. For his youngest sister, Rebecka, now in the bloom of her girlhood, he had an unbounded admiration, sensitive as he was to all that was fair and lovely.

Felix's nature fitted him particularly for friendship; he possessed already then a rich store of intimates, which increased as he advanced in life. To his friends he was frankly devoted, exquisitely tender; it was indeed felicity to be beloved by Felix. At the same time it must be confessed that his affection was exclusive to the utmost; he loved only in the measure as he was loved. This was the solitary dark speck in his sunny disposition. He was the spoilt child of fortune, unused to hardship or opposition; it remains a marvel that egotism did not prevail more than it did over his inborn nobleness and straightforwardness.

The atmosphere of love and appreciation in which he had been nurtured was a condition of life to him; to receive his music with coldness or aversion was to be his enemy, and he was capable of denying genuine merit in any one who did so. A blunder in manners, or an expression that displeased him, could alienate him altogether; he could then be disagreeable, indeed quite intolerable. The capital musician, Bernhard Klein, he never could bear, and simply because – as he himself confessed to me – Klein, sitting beside Felix in a box at the opera when Felix was yet a boy, whose feet when sitting on a chair did not reach the ground, impatiently muttered, 'Cannot that boy keep his feet from dangling?' About such small things he could be unforgiving, for he could not use himself to hear what displeased him, and he never had been compelled to conform cheerfully to the whims of any one. I often took him to task about this, and suggested that, like the Venetian, he should keep a book of vengeance, in which to enter a debtor and creditor account for offences. I could venture to speak thus jokingly to him, for he knew that I could never have believed him capable of retaliation, even for unkindness and spite.

But his irritability, his distrustfulness even towards his most intimate friends, were sometimes quite incredible. A casual remark, a stupid jest, that he often accepted from me with perfect good temper, would sometimes suddenly cause him to drop his lids, look at me askance, and ask doubtfully, 'What do you mean by that? Now I want to know what you wish me to understand by this?' &c., and it was difficult to restore his good humour. These peculiarities in Mendelssohn caused him, though much beloved, to be often judged unfavourably; but those who knew him intimately accepted these few faults, the natural growth of his exceptional position, and prized none the less all that was excellent in him.

He was exquisitely kind-hearted and benevolent, even towards dumb animals. I recollect him, when a boy of thirteen, ardently pleading for the life and liberty of a small fish which had been given to his brother Paul, who wished to have it fried for himself. Felix in anger said, 'If you were anything of a boy, you would put it back in the water directly.' Although the mother took the part of her nestling, the father decided the point with, 'Paul, put the fish back into the water. You are no fisher, and are not entitled to his life; for pleasure or for daintiness' sake we are not to take the life of any creature.' Felix joyfully seized the little fellow's hand, ran with him to the pond, and threw in the struggling fish. I have often since thought of that fish when I have seen Felix take the part of those who were in trouble.

This considerateness guided him too in judging of others' performance; he could not bear to find fault, and when his opinion was asked by a composer of his own works, he knew how first to commend every point that was at all commendable, and then with the greatest delicacy and firmness point out the defects. Above all he never assumed to criticise on matters of taste, every kind of pretension being foreign to his nature. He hated all unrealness, affectation, and frivolity, as so much want of principle. This conscientiousness unmistakably ruled his musical faculty; he was thoroughly in earnest about all he did; the sense of duty was ever present to him, and forbade his offering to the world anything void of purpose, or for the mere sake of pleasing, anything immature or frivolous, much less anything vulgar, for the artist is bound to advance good taste and pure perception in his art. On this account – as even the cavillers against his genius must admit – in the whole range of his works there is not to be found a vulgar or trivial thought; and for this reason, he was so very careful in publishing. 'I have a tremendous reverence for print,' he often said to me, and could he have foreseen his premature death, he would have taken means to make the publication of his immature works impossible. On this account, too, his fortunate social position was an additional incentive to create according to his highest conviction, to work unceasingly like the very poorest, and to give only his best to the world.

One might conclude that so moral and æsthetic a creed would imply a very grave disposition, some amount of pedantry might be suspected; but it was quite the reverse with Felix, he was of a most happy temperament. His deep convictions were never uttered in ordinary intercourse with the world; only in rare and intimate moments did they ever appear, and then only in the slightest and mostly funny allusions.*

Eduard Devrient: *Meine Erinnerungen an Felix Mendelssohn-Bartholdy* (Leipzig, 1869; Eng. tr. Natalia Macfarren, London, 1869), pp. 65–73 (with cuts)

FELIX MOSCHELES

He had strong likes and dislikes, and would not always take the trouble to conceal them; as on one occasion, when he very pointedly showed his dislike to Miss F., an Irish girl, who was studying at the Conservatorio in Leipzig. I think he was prejudiced against her because she had a mass of fluffy reddish hair, which would break away from the rule of the hairpin and escape in a spirit of rebellion; just the sort of thing we admire nowadays, but that was thought positively improper then.

There were tears shed on the evening of the Pupils' concert at the Gewandhaus. When Miss F.'s turn came, it was found she had forgotten her music, and Mendelssohn, behind the scenes, was in a rage. There was an awkward pause whilst the music was being fetched and the audience was waiting, but my father called up the tuner to officiate and fill the gap, and so appearances were saved. But Mendelssohn never forgave poor Miss F.

Felix Moscheles: *Fragments of an Autobiography* (New York, 1899), pp. 98–9

---

* Amongst many little words peculiar to him was the word 'plaisir,' which he mostly used for the highest kind of satisfaction. This has been found fault with as frivolous.

F. MAX MÜLLER

It was at Bunsen's* house, at a *matinée musicale*, that I saw him last. He took the liveliest interest in my work, the edition of the Rig Veda, the Sacred Hymns of the Brâhmans. A great friend of his, Friedrich Rosen, had begun the same work, but had died before the first volume was finished. He was a brother of the wife of Mendelssohn's great friend, Klingemann, then Hanoverian Chargé d'Affaires in London, a poet many of whose poems were set to music by Mendelssohn. So Mendelssohn knew all about the Sacred Hymns of the Brâhmans, and talked very intelligently about the Veda. He was, however, subjected to a very severe trial of patience soon after. The room was crowded with what is called the best society of London, and Mendelssohn being asked to play, never refused. He played several things, and at last Beethoven's so-called 'Moonlight Sonata.' All was silence and delight; no one moved, no one breathed aloud. Suddenly in the middle of the Adagio, a stately dowager sitting in the front row was so carried away by the rhythm, rather than by anything else, of Beethoven's music, that she began to play with her fan, and accompanied the music by letting it open and shut with each bar. Everybody stared at her, but it took time before she perceived her atrocity, and at last allowed her fan to collapse. Mendelssohn in the meantime kept perfectly quiet, and played on; but, when he could stand it no longer, he simply repeated the last bar in arpeggios again and again, following the movements of her fan; and when at last the fan stopped, he went on playing as if nothing had happened.

F. Max Müller: *Auld Lang Syne* (New York, 1898), pp. 1–33; reprinted in *Mendelssohn and his World*, ed. R. Larry Todd (Princeton, 1991), p. 257

HEINRICH DORN

(1804–1892)

Dorn became a pupil of Zelter and was subsequently both a composer and a conductor. He was chief opera

---

* Baron Christian von Bunsen was a German diplomat and orientalist. [RN]

conductor in Berlin from 1849 to 1869 and thereafter
worked as a teacher and critic. In fact, when he was
twenty-three (1827) Mendelssohn would have been
eighteen.

I was a young man of three-and-twenty, prosecuting my legal
studies in Berlin, when I first knew Felix Mendelssohn.

One Friday, at the 'at home' evening of my old countryman
Abraham Friedländer, as I was in the midst of the well-known duet of
Spohr's between Faust and Röschen, with a talented young singer,
a commotion arose in the anteroom, which was most unusual,
for a profound silence always prevailed when anything was going
on. During the pathetic air, 'Fort von hier auf schönere Augen
[Hence from here to lovelier eyes],' my partner whispered to me,
'Felix is come;' and when the duet was finished, I made the
acquaintance of Felix Mendelssohn, then a lad of twelve years old,
residing with his parents on the Neue Promenade, only a few steps
from Friedländer's house. He apologised for having interrupted
our song by his entrance, and offered to play the accompaniments
for me; 'or shall we play them alternately?' he said – a regular
Mendelssohn way of putting the question, which, even twenty years
later, he made use of to a stranger in a similar position. At that time
it would have been difficult to picture a more prepossessing exterior
than that of Felix Mendelssohn; though every one made use of the
familiar 'Du' in addressing him, yet it was very evident that even his
most intimate acquaintances set a great value on his presence
amongst them. He was rarely allowed to go to such large parties,
but when he did do so, the music, and the *con amore* spirit with
which it was carried on, seemed to afford him real pleasure, and he,
in his turn, contributed largely to the enjoyment. People made a
great deal of him, and Johanna Zimmermann, Friedländer's niece,
who had lost her husband while bathing in the Tyrol, regularly
persecuted the young fellow, so that he could scarcely escape from
her attentions. Young as he was, he even then accompanied singing
in a manner only to be met with amongst the older and more
thorough musicians who possessed that especial gift. At Königsberg
the orchestral management of the piano was an unknown thing,
and even in Berlin I had as yet had no opportunity of admiring this
skill and facility in any one. That man was considered a very

respectable musician who played from the printed copy *con amore*, and thus helped the singer now and then; but he who was able to enrich the slender pianoforte accompaniment with octave basses and full chords, of course stood in a much higher position. Such a gifted being was Felix even at that time, and in the duet between Florestan and Leonora, which he accompanied, he astonished me in the passage 'Du wieder nun in meinen Armen, o Gott [You again now in my arms, O God!]!' by the way in which he represented the violoncello and the contre-basso parts on the piano, playing them two octaves apart.

Professor Zelter, with whom Felix had studied counterpoint, was his most eager auditor, and at the same time his most severe censor. More than once after the performance, I myself have heard Zelter call out in a loud voice to his pupil that several alterations were necessary, whereupon, without saying a word, Felix would quietly fold up the score, and before the next Sunday he would go over it, and then play the composition with the desired corrections. In these rooms also, before the family removed to Leipziger Strasse, a three-act comic opera was performed, all the characters being apportioned and the dialogue read out at the piano. The *libretto* for 'The Uncle from Boston' was written by a young physician, Dr. Caspar, who afterwards became a famous man.

Although the musical compositions of this 'American Uncle' pleased all the parties connected with it extremely, the subject of it was nevertheless very weak. Dévrient, and his *fiancée*, Therese Schlesinger, Johanna Zimmermann, the Doctors Andriessen and Dittmar, all took part in this opera. I was also a chorus-singer in it, and from one circumstance this evening will never be forgotten by me. When the opera was finished, there were the regular slices of bread-and-butter, with the usual addition of anchovies, cold meat, cheese, &c. Edward Rietz and myself were enjoying our portion, when Felix, who was going the round of the room to thank all the singers personally, stopped before us to ask how we were faring in the way of refreshment. I showed him my share of the spoil.

'And which do you consider your *dux*?' (the leading, principal subject), he asked; 'and which is your *comes*?' (the secondary theme).

'Well, of course I consider my bread-and-butter my *dux*.'

'Oh, no,' said he, 'a guest must always regard his bread-and-butter as only the *comes*.'

Just as he had uttered this little sally, Zelter's voice resounded through the room:

'Felix, come here.'

The old gentleman stood in the middle of the room with a brimming glass in his hand, and whilst every one was listening intently, he said: 'Felix, you have hitherto only been an apprentice; from today you are an assistant, and now work on till you become a master.'

Therewith he gave him a tap on the cheek, as if he were dubbing him a knight, and then the whole party pressed forward to congratulate the affected and astonished parents, as well as Felix, who pressed his old master's hand warmly more than once.

I had frequent opportunities of meeting Mendelssohn at the rooms of Johanna Zimmermann, the young widow previously mentioned, who, although somewhat eccentric, possessed a thoroughly musical nature; so that Felix felt himself completely at his ease in that unconstrained artistic atmosphere. His own home was, of course, much frequented by interesting and celebrated people, but the greater portion of them were not musicians. Foreign musical celebrities were, indeed, always hospitably received, but native talent was very weakly represented. Although Felix was by no means insensible to praise, he was not at all blind as to whether it was given with discrimination or the reverse. Marx and he were at Dehn's rooms on one occasion I remember, and the first part of the evening we employed ourselves in all sorts of fools' tricks, such as cutting out figures with paper and apple-parings, until Felix got up and, unasked, played on the old piano till long after midnight a number of his own and other compositions. This gave him more real satisfaction than on many an occasion at his parents' house, where, with a first-rate Broadwood at his command, he had a large but very mixed audience. I well recollect a lady (Rahel Varnhagen) asking him for the A Minor fugue of Bach's. 'If I had played some variations of Czerny's, it would have been all the same to her,' he remarked to me afterwards. Such an uncongenial assembly was never to be found at Madame Zimmermann's; there all participated equally, listening and performing; and I have never heard Felix extemporise better than at this house, where he was conscious of being thoroughly understood.

On the 13th of September, 1843, Robert Schumann celebrated the birthday of his wife Clara. I appeared as an unexpected guest at the breakfast table, where, besides David and Grützmacher, I met Mendelssohn again after thirteen years. When we had partaken of a bountiful repast, we had a succession of musical enjoyments. Schumann surprised his wife with a new trio, which was instantly tried, and Felix produced as his present 'The Spring Song,' and played it for the first time. This beautiful piece is the pearl of the fifth book of his 'Lieder ohne Worte' which, as is well known, is dedicated to Madame Schumann. The little company was so enraptured with it that the composer had to repeat it twice. It was a worthy conclusion to the celebration of the day.

The next day I dined at Councillor Frege's, and again had the pleasure of meeting Mendelssohn, who even during the dessert placed himself at the piano and gave us some of his beautiful songs, which were sung with full appreciation by Livia Gerhardt, the celebrated singer. My third and last day at Leipzig was devoted to my friend Petschke, who had assembled a little party in honour of Mendelssohn, who seemed to be as much as his ease as he had formerly been as a young man in the house of Johanna Zimmermann. Petschke had asked me to bring some of my own compositions with me, and I found some attentive listeners to my 'Schöffen von Paris.' Mendelssohn, however, greatly surprised me by declaring he already knew one of the airs I had played, and seating himself at the piano, went through ten or twelve bars, where certainly the harmonies of my air occurred, although I failed to recognise where I had heard them before. 'Why, you do not know your own composition again?' said Mendelssohn; 'that is the final chorus to "The Magician and Monster."' That was a melodrama for which I had written the music, and which Mendelssohn had liked at the time, and of which now, sixteen years later, he could remember chords, that had long since passed from my mind. When I expressed astonishment at his memory, he said, in a very gratifying manner, 'It is only good melodies we should endeavour to retain.'

Heinrich Dorn: 'Recollections of Felix Mendelssohn and his friends', *Temple Bar*, February 1872, pp. 397–9, 402, 404 (with cuts)

EDUARD DEVRIENT

In the summer of 1833, Mendelssohn accepted the post of Musical Director in Düsseldorf, to run from the following October. This involved organizing both church and theatre performances:

Meanwhile I had been prosecuting my search after available talents for the Düsseldorf stage; and when, on the 29th August [1834], Felix came to Berlin, he had only to test and engage his principal and chorus singers. The task was most distasteful to him, as we know from letters written to his family. This coolly considering people and effects, as fitted or not for a special purpose, was foreign to his nature; to him all was personal. The usual wretched manœuvres revolted him; that a chorister should twice abate his charge, and, after bargaining like a huckster, accept what was offered him at first, he took as a personal affront, as though the man expected by such shuffling tricks to attain a greater advantage. He was quite beaten down and full of bitter feelings towards all mankind after these bargainings. How would he preserve his equanimity amid similar wranglings that are every-day occurrences in a theatre? Such things were opposed to his nature.

His stay in Berlin was extended till past September. On his return to Düsseldorf in October the theatre was opened under Immermann's direction; the month was not over before Felix's testy excitability exploded, and he threw up his entire responsibilities.

Eduard Devrient: *Meine Erinnerungen an Felix Mendelssohn-Bartholdy* (Leipzig, 1869; Eng. tr. Natalia Macfarren, London, 1869), pp. 183–4

WILLIAM STERNDALE BENNETT

Once more the Concerto was played in the Hanover Square Rooms, at the Midsummer concert of the Academy on June 26, 1833.

By the side of Lord Burghersh, at this concert, sat a young foreigner whom the Ambassador, adopting a then usual precaution of British diplomacy, addressed by the title of Count. When Bennett had finished the slow movement of his Concerto, the *Count*, being short of stature, stood up, saying, 'I want to have a good look at him.' Later he asked to be made acquainted with the boy, and was accordingly taken by Lord Burghersh to the greenroom. Thus was Bennett introduced to Mendelssohn, the lad of seventeen to the young man of twenty-four. Mendelssohn forthwith invited him to Germany. 'If I come,' said Bennett, 'may I come to be your pupil?' 'No, no,' was the reply, 'you must come to be my friend.'

In the diary of this first visit to Leipzig, there is one name not so continually mentioned as might be expected. Bennett met Mendelssohn in general society; dined most days at the same table with him; and attended the concerts conducted by him; but of close personal association there is not much trace for some time. He noticed the quiet deference shown by Schumann and others to the leader of the musical circle, and was himself impressed with the distinction of Mendelssohn's personality. 'I cannot describe what I mean,' he would afterwards say, 'but Mendelssohn's entrance into a room caused a check, and everything seemed different.' So Bennett, at first, modestly kept at a little distance. He would naturally be unwilling to encroach upon the private time of a great man busily occupied. Then, again, in these months, the thoughts of Mendelssohn's spare moments were not so free as to be given exclusively to his Leipzig entourage. The rehearsing and performing at the Gewandhaus under Mendelssohn's direction, and the successful result, would help to dissipate Bennett's shyness; so between the parts of the next concert he went into the orchestra to have a chat with the conductor, and the few minutes thus spent prepared the way to more intimate friendship. Miss Jeanrenaud, to whom Mendelssohn was soon to be married, had just arrived in the town on a visit to some friends, and was seated in the concert-room. She was now pointed out to Bennett, who, after expressing his own admiration for the young lady, began to teaze her betrothed about the impending sacrifice of liberty. Mendelssohn, who was (according to the diary) 'mad with happiness' broke out in singing the words, '*Hang* the liberty;' and this phrase thenceforward became a friendly watchword which passed between himself and Bennett when they met or corresponded.

Bennett also spoke of 'the gain to English art by the never-too-often repeated visits of this great man,' and of the *love* which, to his own knowledge, Mendelssohn had entertained for England; a love that so distinguished him (as Bennett well knew, though this he did not publicly say) from many other foreign visitors who showed their aversion to everything pertaining to this country except its money. Prince Albert, who was well-placed to observe, and well-qualified to comment on existing musical conditions, called Mendelssohn, in 1847, 'a second Elijah . . . encompassed by idolaters of Baal.' No wonder that the few musicians in England on the classical side valued the actual presence in their midst of this great prophet of their own creed. There are full records of his Birmingham and Phil- harmonic triumphs; he has himself described his gracious reception by Queen Victoria and her Consort; but it must also be remembered that this much-fêted man, in what he called a 'time-eating country,' spent hours in humbler places giving a helping hand to musicians who were striving to do good, though little noticed, work. Dando, the violinist, treasured to a ripe old age the memory of this noble yet lowly minister of Music having played for him at his little Quartet- concerts in the city; and a study of Mendelssohn's doings during the nine weeks he spent here in 1844 reveals other like acts of encouraging support, many more of which, done privately, have passed into oblivion. Bennett could not speak at length on such matters, while thinking of his own connection with them. He drew his pen through the words, 'ever ready to cheer and encourage the young artist,' and wrote instead, 'Had I not known him so intim- ately, I might have trusted myself to talk more of his vast claims upon our affections.'

In course of time he saw with disapproval that the English idea of Mendelssohn was being corrupted by sentimentality and romance, and he wrote in 1858, 'One would greatly welcome a faithful biog- raphy of Mendelssohn.' Shortly after his own death in 1875, a lady gave the following reminiscence. 'He (Bennett) was not an enthusiastic man. In speaking not long ago to the writer of these pages* of his friend Mendelssohn and all that had been written of him, he said, "I knew and loved the man himself too well to like to see him so absurdly idealized."' Some of Bennett's little stories about Mendelssohn seemed to be told with the express object of reducing him to a reality. Two of them, though he told them as against himself, he often repeated, because he admired the sharp decisive manner in which Mendelssohn answered questions which he deemed needless. On first going to Leipzig, being under the impression (which was probably, in general, a correct one) that Handel was less familiar to the Germans than to the English, he asked Mendelssohn whether he knew a great deal of his music, and Mendelssohn snapped at him with the reply, 'Every note.' Then he would talk of Mendelssohn's manly vigour, as *e.g.* of his strength as a swimmer, without mentioning the more feminine graces which rhapsodists had attributed to their ideal musician. He said, again, that he had often been struck with Mendelssohn's practical business qualities, which he could not understand his possessing. He would sometimes qualify his statements, in the one direction or the other, in order to give the real Mendelssohn. Of this Mr W. Crowther Alwyn, who, in Bennett's later days, studied composition under him at the Academy, records the following instances: – 'On discussing one morning, during the Composition class, an impromptu characterization of Mendelssohn's pianoforte-playing, with which he was in profound disagreement, he said, speaking very earnestly and with deep feeling: "It was not playing that *could* be criticized. At times it seemed to send a thrill through every fibre of my body – but he did not always play alike, for, after all, he was human." Again, he said that Mendelssohn's personal appearance was often insignificant, not such as would attract passers-by in the street – but that, at other times, he had the appearance of an *angel*.'

Although Bennett's musical tastes, and principles as an artist were determined quite early in life, and were causes rather than effects of his congenial association with Mendelssohn, yet it is certain that he was much strengthened, at the outset of a career which his conscience made a hard one, by the fellow-feeling and approbation of this elder brother. When he wanted counsel, Mendelssohn, who was not only older but who had been surrounded from his youth up with a greater variety of educational and social advantages, was able and ready to give it. Bennett acknowledged his debt, when he wrote in 1844: 'How much all my professional life has been influenced by your friendship;' but the friendship, as their letters have shown, was no mere professional alliance. They shared, as Mendelssohn wrote, 'not only musical pleasures and sorrows, but also the domestic ones on which life and happiness depend.' Bennett would sometimes quote adages and maxims which Mendelssohn had received from his father for the guidance of life, and which the son had recommended to the use of another; and when doing this he would reproduce the pious reverence of tone in which the son had uttered his father's sayings. This gave the impression to his hearers that his conversations with Mendelssohn must often have taken a very serious turn, and that music was not, perhaps, the greatest thing that bound them together. When Bennett, after hearing of Mendelssohn's death, wrote to David and Kistner, he expressed himself mindful of the many valued friendships, including their own, which still remained to him; but, without fear of being misunderstood or of hurting feelings which were sure to agree with his own, he could write of Mendelssohn, 'I have lost the dearest and kindest friend I ever had in my life.'

William Sterndale Bennett, quoted in James Robert Sterndale Bennett: *The Life of William Sterndale Bennett* (Cambridge, 1907), pp. 30, 57, 178–80 (with cuts)

JAMES WILLIAM DAVISON
(1813–1885)

Davison founded *The Musical Examiner* in 1842 and was music critic of *The Times* from 1846 to 1879.

Had Davison wavered at all in his allegiance to music, an event which occurred in 1836 probably restored and confirmed him. On the Whit Sunday and Monday of that year was held the eighteenth Lower Rhenish Musical Festival, at Düsseldorf. Thither was sent Sterndale Bennett by the firm of Broadwood, who took an interest in native talent, and especially in Bennett. Davison, probably with his friend's assistance, accompanied him. Coming one morning to see the young Englishman, Mendelssohn was told by Bennett that his friend had been deprived of rest by a severe headache. Mendelssohn looked all compassion, stroked Davison's head, and said, with his German accent, 'Poor fallow, poor fallow,' an incident which, fifty or sixty years after, Davison would feelingly relate. Such a slight touch of nature from the genius to his particular admirer, from the player of the 'Kreutzer,' the conductor of the Ninth Symphony, the composer of 'Paulus,' from music's then hero, in short, put a seal on the admirer's devotion.

James William Davison, quoted in Henry Davison: *Music during the Victorian Era* (London, 1912), pp. 49–50 (with cuts)

FERDINAND HILLER

Hiller visited Mendelssohn in Leipzig in 1839:

Our way of life was regular and simple. At about eight we break-fasted on coffee and bread and butter. Butter Felix never ate, but broke his bread into his coffee like any schoolboy, 'as he had been accustomed to do.' We dined at one, and though he despised butter he always liked a glass of good wine, and we often had to try some special sort, which he would produce with great delight, and swallow with immense satisfaction. We generally made quick work with our dinner, but in the evenings after supper we used often to sit round the table for hours chatting (not smoking), unless we moved to the pianino which had been presented to Madame Mendelssohn by the directors of the Gewandhaus.

The first few days were taken up with paying and receiving visits, and passed quickly enough. My next thought was to resume my work. I had a performance of my oratorio in prospect, and there was still a great deal to be done towards it. 'We must sit and compose at the same table together,' said Mendelssohn, one morning; 'and let's begin at once to-day.'

The following day was the Liedertafel, by which I must not be supposed to mean one of those huge societies formed in the last forty years to assist the love of the Vaterland and of 'wine and woman.' This one consisted of a dozen thorough musicians, some of them still representing the most zealous supporters of music in Leipzig, who used to meet from time to time, and did all honour to their title, for their *table* was no less excellent than their songs. Mendelssohn thought it would be great fun if we set the same words to music, and let the singers guess which was which. No sooner said than done. We looked through several volumes of poetry, and soon agreed in the choice of a song of Eichendorff's. I can still see us sitting opposite one another, dipping our pens into the same ink-stand, the silence only broken at rare intervals by some joke or other, and the piano not once touched. In writing out the parts, each copied half of his own composition and half of the other's. The scores were not to appear, and above all the secret was on no account to be betrayed to the members of the Liedertafel.

The evening arrived, and the thing was a complete success. The songs were sung at sight in capital style, and only one of the singers, Dr. Schleinitz, one of the most accomplished of living amateurs, gave his opinion, with thorough conviction – and was right. None of the others could make up their minds. We laughed and – held our tongues.

Though I had felt no difficulty in throwing off a simple song in my friend's presence, it was quite different with more serious work. It was impossible to feel at ease at the piano, with the consciousness that every idea had a listener, and such a one! Besides, I afterwards discovered, by chance, that Mendelssohn equally disliked his com-munings with his genius to be overheard. How could it have been otherwise? Still, I found it extremely difficult, in the midst of much kindness and affection to come forward with the announcement, that, delightful as was our way of life, it must come to a stop. After many discussions, I at last got permission to look out for a lodging close by, on the condition that I should only work and sleep there; and to our general satisfaction we found one within a few steps. They were the same rooms in Reichel's garden which Mendelssohn had inhabited in his bachelor days. So, after about a fortnight at my friend's house, I moved into my new quarters.

We had had a tolerable quantity of music, however, during this time. Mendelssohn had just finished his great D minor trio, and played it to me. I was tremendously impressed by the fire and spirit, the flow, and, in short, the masterly character of the whole thing. But I had one small misgiving. Certain pianoforte passages in it, constructed on broken chords, seemed to me – to speak candidly – somewhat old-fashioned. I had lived many years in Paris, seeing Liszt frequently, and Chopin every day, so that I was thoroughly accustomed to the richness of passages which marked the new pianoforte school. I made some observations to Mendelssohn on this point, suggesting certain alterations, but at first he would not listen to me. 'Do you think that that would make the thing any better?' he said. 'The piece would be the same, and so it may remain as it is.' 'But,' I answered, 'you have often told me, and proved to me by your actions, that the smallest touch of the brush, which might conduce to the perfection of the whole, must not be despised. An unusual form of arpeggio may not improve the harmony, but neither does it spoil it – and it becomes more interesting to the player.' We discussed it and tried it on the piano over and over again, and I enjoyed the small triumph of at last getting Mendelssohn over to my view. With his usual conscientious earnestness when once he had made up his mind about a thing, he now undertook the lengthy, not to say wearisome, task of rewriting the whole pianoforte part. One day, when I found him working at it, he played me a bit which he had worked out *exactly* as I had suggested to him on the piano, and called out to me, 'That is to remain as a remembrance of you.' Afterwards, when he had been playing it at a chamber concert with all his wonderful fire, and had carried away the whole public, he said, 'I really enjoy that piece; it is honest music after all, and the players will like it, because they can show off with it.' And so it proved.

In the course of that winter I witnessed a curious example of Mendelssohn's almost morbid conscientiousness with regard to the possible perfection of his compositions. One evening I came into his room, and found him looking so heated, and in such a feverish state of excitement, that I was frightened. 'What's the matter with you?' I called out. 'There I have been sitting for the last four hours,' he said, 'trying to alter a few bars in a song (it was a quartet for men's voices) and can't do it.'

He had made twenty different versions, the greater number of which would have satisfied most people. 'What you could not do to-day in four hours,' said I, 'you will be able to do to-morrow in as many minutes.' He calmed down by degrees, and we fell into such earnest conversation that I stayed with him till very late. Next day I found him in unusually good spirits, and he said to me, 'Yesterday evening when you were gone I was so excited that it was no use thinking of sleep, so at last I composed a little hunting-song, which I must play you at once.' He sat down to the piano, and I heard the song, which has since delighted hundreds and thousands of people, namely Eichendorff's, 'Sei gegrüsst du schöner Wald!' I hailed it with joyful surprise.

Leipzig, 1840
One day, speaking of his adherents and his opponents, he said that he could perfectly understand that certain musicians who took up the very strict line considered him half a deserter, because many of those of his compositions which met with most favour must appear to them frivolous compared to former ones, and therefore they might say he had forsaken his better style.

With his earnest character, it was especially disagreeable to him when people treated serious things with exaggeration. 'I had a visit from a Belgian author this morning,' he told me, a few hours later; 'the man really has an astounding flow of talk, and said several good things. But when he was gone, and I began to think it over, I found that it might have been expressed much better in the very simplest way: therefore why use such big words? why want to appear so deep?' It is this simplicity, always exemplified in his works, which makes them appear shallow to those people who take bombastic nonsense for depth. There is no shallowness to be found in Mendelssohn's works, but rather in those which are too shallow to contain the beauty of simplicity.

He sometimes talked to me about his studies with Zelter, and of the peripatetic way in which they were usually carried on in the garden behind his father's house. What he told me of them confirmed me in the opinion which Marx expressed when he said that 'when Zelter became Mendelssohn's master, he merely put the fish into the water, and let it swim away as it liked.' With all his love for his old teacher, the remembrance of the following fact always made him angry. Some years before Felix's birth, his father, who was a friend of Zelter's, gave the latter a great quantity of Bach's Cantatas in the original manuscripts; and when Felix became his pupil, Zelter used sometimes to take him to the closet where these treasures were stored up, and show them to him, saying, 'There they are; just think of all that is hidden there!' But poor Felix, though he thirsted for these costly treasures, was never once allowed to look inside them, and taste them. They would certainly have been better cared for in Mendelssohn's hands than in Zelter's.

Ferdinand Hiller: *Felix Mendelssohn-Bartholdy* (Cologne, 1874; Eng. tr. M.E. von Glehn, London, 1874), pp. 150–56, 175–8 (with cuts)

EDUARD DEVRIENT

In May 1841, Mendelssohn came to Berlin to discuss the possibility of taking up the post of Director of Music there:

But the very first great conference quite upset him again. The matter was not treated simply and with directness, but wrapped in formalities and generalities; the Council of Education, also, who were to hold the distribution of funds for his department, held ominously aloof. Two long hours did we debate after this occasion in the shady walks of the garden, trying to allay his rising and growing dislike to the whole affair. I endeavoured to impress upon him that the view he took of the matter was not a just one, in so far as he expected too much from others and not enough from himself; that he accepted the task of founding a conservatorium, and at the same time expected it to be handed over to him spick and span, before he could make up his mind to accept the direction of it; that he required immunity from all unavoidable trials and troubles in bringing means and ends together, from the animosity and uncongeniality of persons and circumstances, etc.; in a word, that he would only do just what was sympathetic to him, and nought besides. I maintained that he had no right to expect practical arrangements from persons unversed in the subject, and exhorted him for once to overcome his nature and go into a matter not congenial to him; to take upon himself 'odiosa,' to have patience with ceremoniousness and pedantry, and to put forth all his energy to bring about the result. I said how he was the only man in all Germany who could accomplish the happy plan of the king; that this great chance for the progress of German music, once lost, might never occur again, and that the great responsibility rested on him. To all these fine things Felix wanted not for replies, and I silently agreed with him that it was hard to fight against the dominant conditions; that to do so required peculiar powers, which Felix did not possess in the least. However, he promised that he would do his utmost.

He handed in his memorandum for a music school to be instituted in Berlin, and told me that he had bound himself towards Herr von Massow (who acted in the matter from the most noble and sincere motives) to remain one year, in order to bring matters to a clear issue; this was a hopeful prospect.

In ten days, however, I again found him, after a second official conference, quite beside himself. He told me that 'he would not stay here, but from Leipzig, whither he was called immediately for the adjustment of sundry affairs, he would send in his resignation. He felt he was not the man for Berlin, for people who wanted to have him without being able to make use of him.' Of the honours and rewards offered him he spoke with the utmost disdain, longed only to escape from the official atmosphere, to live again amongst people who had some soul, some enthusiasm for music, away from this narrowness of dominion and mediocrity.

I knew that nothing could be done with him whilst this storm lasted; I knew he was not in the wrong, so I could do nothing but try to soothe him with generalities. I went to him the following day to renew my homily; that he should not, spite of all his suffering, think of leaving before the termination of his promised twelvemonth, and that he would for ever repent if he left a great service to art unperformed. I could have spared my wisdom, for Herr von Massow, against whom Felix had already taken the field, held him down to his given promise; and so he departed, to return in August for a twelvemonth.

Eduard Devrient: *Meine Erinnerungen an Felix Mendelssohn-Bartholdy* (Leipzig, 1869; Eng. tr. Natalia Macfarren, London, 1869), pp. 219–23 (with cuts)

WILLIAM SMITH ROCKSTRO

After our first interview with Mendelssohn, in 1842, we had never ceased to hope for the privilege of being, some day, brought into more intimate relations with him, in his own country. We knew that he never forgot: and, at the season of Pentecost, in the year 1845, we visited Germany, for the first time, well assured that he would not fail to give us the good counsel he had promised. Reaching Frankfurt, at the beginning of the bright spring weather, we found him living out of doors, and welcoming the sunshine, and the flowers, with a delight as unaffected as that of the youngest of his children. On the evening of our arrival, after taking us to see Thorwaldsen's lately-finished statue of Goethe, and the poet's birth-place in the Hirschgraben, he playfully proposed that we should go to an 'open-air concert,' and led the way to a lonely little corner of the public gardens, where a nightingale was singing with all its heart.

'He sings here every evening,' said Mendelssohn, 'and I often come to hear him. I sit here, sometimes, when I want to compose. Not that I am writing much, now; but, sometimes, I have a feeling like this' – and he twisted his hands rapidly, and nervously, in front of his breast – 'and when that comes, I know that I must write. I have just finished some Sonatas for the Organ; and, if you will meet me at the Catherinenkirche, at ten o'clock to-morrow, I will play them to you.'

He played them, exquisitely – the whole six, straight through, from the neatly-written MS. We remember noticing the wonderfully delicate staccato of the pedal quavers in the second movement of the Fifth Sonata, which he played upon a single 8-ft. stop, with all the crispness of Dragonetti's most highly-finished *pizzicato*.

There was only one other auditor, besides ourselves. He parted from us, at the Church door; and then Mendelssohn took us home with him, to his early dinner, with Madame Mendelssohn and the children – Karl, then seven years old, Marie, and Paul. He was full of fun, with a joke for each of the little ones; and made us all cover up the lower part of our faces, to see what animals we were like. '*Ich bin ein Adler*,'* he said, placing his hand in a position which

* 'I am an eagle.'

made the likeness absurdly striking. Madame Mendelssohn was pronounced to be a hare; Karl, a roebuck; Paul, a bull-finch; and we ourselves a setter. Having some business to attend to, after dinner, he left us for half an hour in his study; giving us the choice of amusing ourselves with looking through Félicien David's *Le Désert*, which had just been sent to him from Paris; or his own Pianoforte Trio in C minor, as yet unpublished, and untried. We chose the Trio; but had not found time to trace out half its beauties, before he returned, to advise with us concerning our future proceedings. 'There is only one thing for you do,' he said. 'Ferdinand David will be here, to-morrow, on his way back to Leipzig, from the Lower Rhine Festival, where he has been playing. I will ask him to let you travel with him. He will introduce you to all the people you will care to know. Enter yourself immediately at the Conservatorium; and get into training as soon as you possibly can. My own plans are so undecided, that I should be able to do nothing for you, here; but I am almost certain to return to Leipzig, before the end of the year, and I shall then hope to see a great deal of you.'

David arrived, late that night; and, on the next evening, Mendelssohn gave a delightful little party, at which the two friends, assisted by an excellent violoncellist, played the C minor Trio, for the first time, with scarcely less effect than they afterwards produced when introducing it to the general public at the Gewandhaus. It was our last pleasant meeting in the Bockenheimer Gasse. David had arranged to start, on the next evening, for Leipzig. We met him, at the office of the Schnell-post; and, a few moments later, Mendelssohn joined us, to say, as he was careful to express it in mixed German and English, 'Not *Leben Sie wohl*, but *Auf Wieder-sehn*.' He had thought of everything that could help to make the dreary diligence journey comfortable. A little basket of early fruit, for refreshment during the night; a packet of choice cigars for David; and, for ourselves, a quite paternal scolding for insufficient defences against cold night-air. There were many last words to be said; but so much confusion had been caused by the hurried arrival of a party of outside passengers, that, at the moment of starting, our kind friend, who had wisely retired from the scuffle, was missing. The conductor declared that he could wait no longer, and we were just giving up Mendelssohn for lost, when he suddenly reappeared, rushing round the corner of the street, with a thick woollen scarf in his hand. 'Let me wrap this round your throat,' he gasped, quite out of breath with his run; 'it will keep you warm in the night; and, when you get to Leipzig, you can leave it in the coach.'

We need scarcely say that we did *not* 'leave it in the coach.' It has not been worn for many a long year; but it lies before us, on the table, as we write its history – the dear remembrance of a very happy time.

William Smith Rockstro: *Felix Mendelssohn-Bartholdy* (London, 1884), pp. 99–102 (with cuts)

FERDINAND HILLER

First performance of *A Midsummer Night's Dream* with Mendelssohn's music, Potsdam, 14 October 1843:

It is characteristic of Mendelssohn's views of things that he should have been very much excited after the performance, and this from a twofold cause. It had been arranged, according to his wish, that the whole thing, with the entr'actes, should be played without any pause whatsoever, as in his opinion this was indispensable for the proper effect. Nevertheless, not only was a long pause introduced, but it was made use of to offer all kinds of refreshments to the people in the front rows belonging to the Court, so that a full half-hour was taken up with loud talking and moving about, whilst the rest of the audience, who were quite as much invited, though per-haps only tolerated, were sitting in discomfort, and had to beguile the time as best they could. This disregard of artistic considerations, as well as common civility, so enraged Mendelssohn that he hardly took any notice of all the fine things that we had to say to him.

Ferdinand Hiller: *Felix Mendelssohn-Bartholdy* (Cologne, 1874; Eng. tr. M.E. von Glehn, London, 1874), pp. 213–4

RICHARD WAGNER

But just as the Jews have stood aloof from our manual work, so our newer musical conductors have none of them risen from the ranks of musical craftsmen, for sheer reason of their dislike of real hard labour. No: this new style of Conductor forthwith planted himself atop of the musical confraternity, somewhat as the Banker on top of our world of work. For this he had to bring something ready in his pocket, something the step-by-step musician did not own, or found most hard to come by, and seldom in sufficience: as the banker his Capital, this gentleman brought his Polish (*Gebildetheit*). Advisedly I say *polish*, not culture (*Bildung*); for whoso owns this last in truth, can be no target for our scoffs: he towers above all others. But the possessor of Polish is fair enough game.

No instance has come to my knowledge in which the fruit of veritable culture, freedom of spirit, Freedom in general, had crowned the happiest cultivation of this Polish. Mendelssohn himself, for all his manifold and diligently-tended gifts, shewed plainly he had never reached that freedom; he never overcame that peculiar sense of constraint which, in the eyes of the earnest observer, kept him outside our German art-life in spite of all his merited successes, nay, perchance became a gnawing inward pain that led to his so incomprehensibly early death. And the reason is just this: there is no spontaneousness at bottom of such a thirst for culture, but it issues rather from the obligation to cloak a part of one's own nature than from any impulse to unfold it. The resultant culture can therefore only be a pseudo-culture: in certain directions the brain may acquire a high degree of keenness; but the point where all directions meet, can never be the true clear-seeing Intellect itself.

At the time when I came into closer contact with a young musician who had been in Mendelssohn's company, I was perpetually told of the master's one piece of advice: In composing never think of making a sensation or effect, and avoid everything likely to lead to it. That sounded beautiful and right enough, and in fact not a single faithful pupil of the master's has ever chanced to produce a sensation or effect. Only, there seemed to me a deal too much negation in the doctrine, and its positive results were not particularly ample. I fancy all the teachings of the Leipzig Conservatorium are founded on that negative maxim, for I have heard that the young folk there are plagued to death with its warning, whilst the most promising talents can gain them no favour with their teachers unless they forswear all taste for music not in strict accordance with the Psalms.

Richard Wagner: 'On conducting', *Collected Writings*, ed. Ashton Ellis (London, 1895), IV, pp. 340–41, 344

BAYARD TAYLOR

My first winter in Europe (that of 1844–5) was passed in Frankfurt-on-the-Maine. During the great Annual Fair, I was walking, one afternoon, with my friend Willis, along the northern bank of the Maine. It was a deliciously warm, sunny day, at the close of March; and the long stone quay was thronged with thousands of strangers from all parts of Europe.

As we pushed through the crowd, my eyes, which had been wandering idly over the picturesque faces and costumes around us, were suddenly arrested by the face of a man, a little distance in front, approaching us. His head was thrown back; and his eyes, large, dark, and of wonderful brilliancy, were fixed upon the western sky. Long, thin locks of black hair, with here and there a silver streak, fell around his ears. His beard, of two or three days' growth, and his cravat, loosely and awkwardly tied, added to the air of absorption, of self-forgetfulness, which marked his whole appearance. He made his way through the crowd mechanically, evidently but half conscious of its presence.

As he drew nearer, I saw that his lips were moving, and presently heard the undertone of a deep, rich voice, chanting what appeared to be a choral; judging from the few bars which reached me in passing. It was evidently – as I felt immediately – a soliloquy in music. I have not yet lost, and never shall lose, the impression it produced upon me, though I can no longer recall the notes. My companion grasped my arm, and whispered, 'Mendelssohn!' as he slowly brushed past me; and, for a single moment, the voice of his inspiration sang at my very ear. I stopped instantly, and turned; yet, so long as I could follow him with my eye, he was still pressing slowly onward, with the same fixed, uplifted gaze, lost to every thing but his art.

I was twenty years old, and as enthusiastic and sentimental as youth of that age are prone to be. So I wrote, the next day, an eloquent letter to the composer, concluding with the request, that he would send me a line as a souvenir of the place and the season in which I first became acquainted with his works. (If there was any indiscretion in this, I have since received ample punishment for it.) He replied immediately in a very kind note, enclosing the score of a chorus in the 'Walpurgisnacht,' in his own manuscript:

'Still shines the day,
Whene'er we may
A pure heart bring to thee.'

Something kindly and cordial in his words inspired me with confidence to venture farther. I had written several poems on musical subjects during the winter; and it entered my mind, that I might use them as a means of introducing myself to his acquaintance. On second thoughts, I selected the best, – a lyric, entitled 'Beethoven' (which, I am now glad to say, was never published), – and set out for Mendelssohn's residence. He was then occupying modest apartments in the Bockenheimer Gasse, not far from the gate of that name. The servant ushered me into a plainly furnished room, containing a grand piano, and a few pictures and books, in addition to the ordinary articles. A moment afterwards, the door of an adjoining chamber opened, and Mendelssohn appeared. I explained, in rather an embarrassed manner, that I was the person who had written to him two days before, and begged pardon for the additional liberty I had taken. He at once gave me his hand, asked me to be seated, and drew another chair for himself to the little round table near the window.

I sat thus, face to face with him, and again looked into those dark, lustrous, unfathomable eyes. They were black, but without the usual opaqueness of black eyes, shining, not with a surface light, but with a pure, serene, planetary flame. His brow, white and unwrinkled, was high and nobly arched, with great breadth at the temples, strongly resembling that of Poe. His nose had the Jewish prominence, without its usual coarseness: I remember, particularly, that the nostrils were as finely cut and as flexible as an Arab's. The lips were thin and rather long, but with an expression of indescribable sweetness in their delicate curves. His face was a long oval in form; and the complexion pale, but not pallid. As I looked upon him, I said to myself, 'The Prophet David!' and, since then, I have seen in the Hebrew families of Jerusalem, many of whom trace their descent from the princely houses of Israel, the same nobility of countenance.

'You are an American,' said he, after a pause. 'I have received an invitation to visit New York, and should like to go; but we Germans are afraid of the sea. But I may go yet: who knows? Music is making rapid advances in America; and I believe there is a real taste for the art among your people.' I assured him this was true, and hoped that he would still find it possible to visit us. 'Are you a musician?' he asked. 'No,' said I: 'I have devoted myself to literature. I have not achieved much, as yet; but I hope to succeed. I have ventured to bring with me a poem on Beethoven, whom, I know, you honour as a master.' – 'Ah!' said he; 'let me see it.' He then read it through carefully, partly aloud, with a very good English pronunciation; and, on concluding, asked, 'May I keep it? Here is a stanza which I like especially.' (Excuse me from quoting it.) 'Oh, you must per-severe! Let your art be all in all to you. You have your life still before you; and who knows what you may make of it?'

I rose to leave, fearful that I might be detaining him from some important labour. He again shook hands, and said, play-fully, 'Now we know one another, you must come and see me when-ever we happen to be in the same town. When you visit Leipzig or Berlin or Cologne, if you find I am there, come at once to my house; and we can have further talk, and become better acquainted.'

I was never able to take advantage of this kind invitation.

Bayard Taylor, quoted in Wilhelm Adolph Lampadius: *Felix Mendelssohn-Bartholdy: ein Denkmal für seine Freunde* (Leipzig, 1849; Eng. tr. W.L. Gage, New York, 1866), pp. 209–13 (with cuts)

JENNY LIND
(1820–1887)

Known as 'the Swedish nightingale', Jenny Lind made her public début as Agathe in *Der Freischütz* at the Stockholm Opera in 1838. She toured Austria and

Germany in 1844 and from 1847 sang frequently in London. In 1849 she abandoned the stage for the concert world and in 1852 married Mendelssohn's one-time pupil Otto Goldschmidt.

Letter of 22 October 1844

Last night I was invited to a very pleasant and elegantly furnished house, where I saw and spoke to Mendelssohn-Bartholdy, and he was incredibly friendly and polite, and spoke of my 'great talent.' I was a little surprised, and asked him on what ground he spoke in this way. 'Well!' he said, 'for this reason, that all who have heard you are of one opinion only, and that is so rare a thing that it is quite sufficient to prove to me what you are.'

Letter of 12 January 1846

Felix Mendelssohn comes sometimes to Berlin, and I have often been in his company. He is a *man*, and at the same time he has the most supreme talent. Thus should it be.

Jenny Lind, quoted in Henry Scott Holland and William Smith Rockstro, eds.: *Memoir of Mme Jenny Lind-Goldschmidt* (London, 1891), pp. 201, 323

XI

ST PAUL AND *ELIJAH*

JULIUS SCHUBRING

Subsequently to 1832, we frequently discussed the subject of oratorio texts. With regard to *St. Paul*, a considerable amount of preliminary labour had been got through before I knew anything about it: at Mendelssohn's request, I undertook a certain further amount of work of a subordinate kind, such as connecting and introducing certain suitable passages and songs. During this time, we were a great deal in communication with each other, sometimes orally and sometimes by letter. He always proved himself a thoughtful artist, and strove to obtain a clear appreciation of each separate point, such, for instance, as the admissibility of the chorale, of the narrative recitatives, etc. He rejected, also, much that was suggested, being so well acquainted with his Bible, that he obtained a great deal of valuable materials himself: for any assistance, he was, however, extremely grateful. That he would not accept my suggestions for the Paulinian doctrine of the justification by faith, but, at the appropriate place, substituted merely the general assertion: 'Wir glauben all an einen Gott [We all believe in one God]' was something that did not satisfy my theological conscience, though, perhaps, any extension of the work in this direction would have made it too long. We arranged *Elijah* together from beginning to end, and he was pleased that I should, without any further introduction, have commenced the oratorio with the passage of Elijah, and marked the overture with no. 2, with the addition of 'Muss drei Jahre dauern [Must last three years].' Regarding the oratorio of *Christus*,* he never exchanged a word with me; on the other hand, we had often previously talked about St. Peter and John the Baptist. What I told him of the account given in the gospel of Nicodemus concerning the descent of Christ into Hell, interested him in an extraordinary degree, and, from what escaped him, I am inclined to believe he intended turning it, sometime or other, to musical account.

Julius Schubring, 'Reminiscences of Felix Mendelssohn-Bartholdy', *Musical World*, 31 (12 and 19 May 1866); reprinted in *Mendelssohn and his World*, ed. R. Larry Todd (Princeton, 1991), pp. 230–31

* This was left unfinished at Mendelssohn's death. [RN]

HENRY PHILLIPS
(1801–1876)

English bass. In 1824 he sang the part of Caspar in the production of Weber's *Der Freischütz* at the English Opera House. In 1847 he sang a 'scena after Ossian', *On Lena's Gloomy Heath*, written for him by Mendelssohn the previous year.

I shall ever remember a conversation I had with Dr. Mendelssohn one evening, after the performance of his St. Paul. When I was complimenting him on the work he had written, he replied in his hasty, nervous way, 'Thank you! thank you! if I could once write a chorus equal to Handel's, I should be content.'

St Paul was first given in England in the autumn of 1836 in Liverpool:

In this first performance of 'St. Paul' I sang my part, which was rendered extremely difficult by being in manuscript, and in a very cramped, illegible hand, a few printed sheets only were interspersed with English words written over the German; altogether the part was anything but agreeable to take into an orchestra. The 'Walpurgis Night' was the next to arrest my attention, until his greatest work of all, 'The Elijah,' was first produced at the Birmingham Festival in the autumn of 1846. A strange circumstance occurred relative to his impression of my powers, for though I had sung and succeeded so well in 'St. Paul,' he had been led to believe that my register was not sufficiently extensive to execute the music of 'Elijah,' which, to use his own words, he considered too high for me, and that Staudigl was the only man who could sing it. I was consequently allotted the quartettes *only*, which we sang from manuscript parts in single lines; the task, therefore, became nervously difficult, and I confess it was with no very good grace that I sang in the oratorio. Having had much correspondence with him on the subject, rendered my surprise still greater about his hesitating when the 'Elijah' was produced. I never could account for it, unless

he was influenced by interested parties; and by his own feelings
towards his countryman Staudigl, who, despite his imperfect knowledge of our language, was a great and sterling artist, and as
unassuming as he was gifted and learned.

Mendelssohn [was] a small thin man, with sharp features, and
piercing eyes (Jew's eyes again) and a nervous, fidgetty manner. He
was so easily excited, that it sometimes threw us off our guard, and
frequently led us to think that we were singing wrongly. He was so
wrapped up in his art that he neglected all else. He never considered
dress – in fact, was so perfectly indifferent to appearances, that, on
one occasion, when conducting Elijah at Exeter Hall, he had a monstrous hole in his coat under the arm, that one might have put one's
hand through, which hole was displayed to great advantage when
wielding his baton. Of course, we did not distress him by pointing it
out, though it caused much amusement to those near him, both in
the orchestra and the room.

A circumstance of great annoyance occurred that evening, by the
admission into the orchestra of a huge Frenchman and his wife.
They were seated immediately behind the principal singers – that is,
the bass and contralto. We do now and then meet with very stout
people on our side of the channel – but there is a very great difference in the habits of fat individuals. In England, our great fat men
are generally of a lethargic turn, and slow in their movements, while
the Frenchman, heedless of his bulk, is all vigour and lightness,
nimble as a monkey, and often as mischievous. During the whole of
the first part, this man exhibited evident symptoms of extravagant
delight, first turning like a harlequin towards his wife, then
lifting up his eyes in admiration, and kissing his hand to poor
Mendelssohn, who seemed much annoyed.

At last, the Frenchman's feelings being excited to the highest
pitch, when Mendelssohn left the conductor's seat, our fat friend
made a rush at him, and, pushing us all aside, took the trembling
composer tight in his arms, and tried to kiss him. Mendelssohn
resisted him manfully, disentangled himself from him, rushed out of
the orchestra, the Frenchman hard after him, while we followed like
a pack of hounds at his heels. Again he caught the great musician,
and we made a charge to the rescue, by pulling his great coat-tails,
pinching his legs, knocking his hat off, and bestowing other little

attentions, that, at last, left him breathless, and disappointed in the passage. He stormed with rage, and was about to re-enter the orchestra, when a violent protest was raised, and he and his wife were packed off somewhere – I did not inquire where – and the field once more clear of the enemy.

We had now become so familiar with Mendelssohn, that we scarcely looked upon him as a visitor, and I believe he felt equally at home with us. He was not a man bigoted to his own ideas, or who would have them carried out, whether agreeable to the singer or not. An instance of this occurred with myself. The music of 'St. Paul' was too heavy and ponderous for my powers, and in that magnificent air, 'O God, have mercy,' there occurs at the end of the second movement these words, 'I will sing forth thy glorious praise.' I altered the passage, and took it an octave higher, which enabled me to impart much power and energy to it. Mendelssohn, when he first heard it, was much pleased, said it was an excellent thought, 'and, if I had known you before,' said he, 'I should have written it so.'

Henry Phillips, *Musical and Personal Recollections during Half a Century* (London, 1864), II, pp. 65, 230–36 (with cuts)

CHARLOTTE DOLBY
(1821–1885)

Miss Dolby, afterwards Madame Sainton-Dolby, made her first appearance at the Leipzig Gewandhaus Concerts, for which she had been engaged by Mendelssohn, on 25 October 1845.

We were dining at Dr. Härtel's, and were all seated at the table. The guests included Dr. and Madame Schumann; but Mendelssohn, who was also invited, came late. A vacant place had been left for him by my side. He arrived after the soup had been served, and excused himself by saying he had been very busy with his oratorio; and then turning to me he said, 'I have sketched the bass part, and now for the contralto.' 'Oh!' I exclaimed, 'do tell me what that will be like, because I am specially interested in that part.' 'Never fear,' he answered, 'it will suit you very well, for it is a true woman's part – half an angel, half a devil.' I did not know whether to take that as a compliment, but we had a good laugh over it.*

Charlotte Dolby, quoted in F.G. Edwards: *The History of Mendelssohn's Oratorio 'Elijah'* (London, 1896), p. 35

WILHELM ADOLPH LAMPADIUS

The London correspondent of the 'Signals for the Musical World' writes concerning the first impression of 'Elijah:' 'How shall I describe what to-day has been in the Music Hall? After such an intense enjoyment, it is a hard task to express one's feelings in cold words. It was a great day for the festival, a great day for the performers, a great day for Mendelssohn, a great day for art. Four da capos in the first part, four in the second, making eight encores, and at the close the calling-out of the composer, are significant facts, when one considers that it was the rigid injunction of the committee that the public should not testify its approval by applause. But the enthusiasm would be checked by no rules: when the heart is full, regulations must stand aside. It was a noble scene, the hall filled with men, the galleries gay with ladies, like so many tulip-beds, added to the princely music, and these thundering bravos.'

Wilhelm Adolph Lampadius: *Felix Mendelssohn-Bartholdy: ein Denkmal fur seine Freunde* (Leipzig, 1849; Eng. tr. W.L. Gage, New York, 1866), p. 130

WILLIAM POUNTNEY

A House in the Crescent
Mendelssohn, who was paying his ninth visit to England for the purpose – and, I think, his third to Birmingham – reached London on August 18, conducted two orchestral rehearsals at the Hanover Square Rooms, and arrived in Birmingham on Sunday, August 23. He seems to have stayed, as before, with his friend Joseph Moore, who 'managed the music in Birmingham,' and who had a

---

* In case the point of Mendelssohn's joke should be missed by anyone, it must be remembered that the contralto singer in 'Elijah' takes the parts of both the Angel and Jezebel, the Queen.

house in The Crescent – where he died, by the way, in 1851. Two full rehearsals of chorus and orchestra took up the eve of the production.

As Mendelssohn took his place at the conductor's desk, baton in hand, the whole chorus broke into hearty and spontaneous cheers. His method of conducting was entirely free of affectations, vigorous and vigilant, and only occasionally would he interject, with a whimsical expression on his almost swarthy face, 'Gentlemen, that won't do. No, no, I must have piano. When you come to fortissimo you may do as you like!'

For the role of the Prophet Mendelssohn brought with him the Austrian basso, Joseph Staudigl, famous on the Continent as a singer of Schubert's Lieder, for which he was reputed to be unrivalled. It is a tradition of the 1846 production that Staudigl at the final rehearsal sang the music of the part at sight. He was certainly a 'character.' He entered the Town Hall wearing a light brown 'stove-pipe' hat, and as he removed it a roll of papers, including his vocal score, fell out. This was only one of several little incidents which, according to my old friend Pountney, created a happy atmosphere at the grand rehearsal and went far to ensuring the smoothness and success of the first performance.

William Pountney, reminiscences recalled in *The Birmingham Mail*, 2 September 1946

J. SUTCLIFFE SMITH

At the 1846 Festival came *Elijah*. The various critics from all parts of England and elsewhere seem to have all held the opinion that a great musical work had come to bless the world, and they were not afraid of letting themselves go in their expression of admiration. Locally, there was naturally much pride and excitement; as the following account amply shows; 'From an early hour crowds of eager expectants marshalled themselves as near the building as the police arrangements would permit, and as soon as the doors were opened every reserved seat was filled, and even the far-off corners where there was standing room were packed ... When the composer mounted the rostrum, and was greeted with a breath of subdued applause, the scene was exceedingly animated. Every breath was now hushed – the birth of a new work of genius – the addition of a fresh pleasure to the circumscribed amount of human happiness – was at hand; and never was there a more eager auditory, nor one more fitting.

'At the close of the performance, the long pent-up excitement which had been gathering strength with every new feature of the oratorio, burst forth in a torrent of applause, renewed again and again ... By the universal fiat of the vast assembly, the composer was placed high in the roll of fame, with the hallowed glories of Handel, Beethoven, and Haydn. The illustrious composer bowed his acknowledgements, and his agitation was visible. He descended, and tried to escape the torrent of approbation; but another roar in which the audience and orchestra joined, called him back again before them; and with a modest air, he responded to the greeting of the assembly.'

The *Times*, in terms almost as picturesque, had the following notice of this historic event:

'Never was there a more complete triumph; never a more thorough and speedy recognition of a great work of art. *Elijah* is not only the *Chef d'œuvre* of Mendelssohn, but also one of the most extraordinary achievements of human intelligence. The greatest credit is due to the Band and Chorus. Unapproachable as is Mendelssohn as a conductor, unrivalled as is his experience of the orchestra and its resources, his work would never have won such instantaneous appreciation but for the zeal and artist-like unanimity of his forces. Mendelssohn, after thanking them, expressed his particular obligations to Mr. Stimpson, the Birmingham professor, who had for two months previously, so well and effectively trained the local choir.'

The accounts of this central event of the Birmingham Festivals would be incomplete if I were to omit what might be called an inside view of this first performance of the *Elijah*, and to the records of William Pountney, a bass singer at the 1846 Festival, I am indebted for many interesting points of information. He says: 'We sang from manuscript copies of the music that had been sent down from London. Mr. Stimpson, chorus-master, was then a vigorous young man; he was a smart choir trainer, and very little escaped his notice.'

Next comes a picture of Mendelssohn: 'I remember the rehearsal in the Town Hall . . . Mendelssohn himself conducted: it would be difficult to convey in writing the effect of his conducting. His face seemed to be lighted up with an expression hard to describe . . . He not only seemed full of his work but the same feeling seemed to be imparted to every member of the chorus, and we all felt resolved to do our very, very best.'

And certain other details are not without interest. These recount how Mr. Stevens – father of C.J. Stevens, sometime accompanist of the Festival rehearsals – was the choral secretary; how one of the tests for music reading was the bass of an old madrigal . . . how Pountney himself succeeded in this trial and received £1 as an engagement fee; how the rehearsals were held in the Old King Street Chapel; how something of a strike took place among the singers, owing to the older men receiving what was considered undue preference; how Mendelssohn saw a joke quickly, and laughed heartily; how Staudigl made a great impression with his mighty bass voice; and how Braham, at the age of between 70 and 80, sang tenor solos in the *Messiah* in this Festival.

J. Sutcliffe Smith: *The Story of Music in Birmingham*, (Birmingham, 1945), pp. 31–5 (with cuts)

F.G. EDWARDS

Mendelssohn commenced the rehearsal by playing the Overture from memory, to the delight and admiration of those who heard it. The lady vocalists gave the composer some trouble. The soprano requested him to transpose 'Hear ye, Israel,' a whole tone down, and to make certain changes to suit her particular style! 'It was not a lady's song,' she said. Mendelssohn resisted with studied politeness, and said, 'I intended this song for the principal soprano; if you do not like it I will ask the Committee to give it to some other vocalist.' Afterwards, when alone with Moscheles, he most unreservedly expressed himself as to the 'coolness of such suggestions.'

When 'O rest in the Lord' was tried over, the singer was anxious to introduce a long shake (on D) at the close! 'No,' said the composer, 'I have kept that for my orchestra,' and he then archly played the familiar shake, which is given to the flute in the orchestral accompaniment. He was still doubtful, even at the eleventh hour, whether he should not withdraw 'O rest in the Lord.' 'It is too sweet,' he said. His friends urged him at least to try its effect, and ultimately their advice was accepted.

The orchestral parts had been previously tried over and corrected at Leipzig; the way was therefore made smooth for the band rehearsals in London. These rehearsals took place at the Hanover Square Rooms on the Thursday and Friday preceding the Festival. 'Mendelssohn,' records the late Mr. Rockstro, 'looked very worn and nervous; yet he would suffer no one to relieve him, even in the scrutiny of the orchestral parts, which he himself spread out on some benches beneath the windows on the left-hand side of the room, and insisted upon sorting out and examining for himself.' The late Henry Lazarus, the eminent clarinettist, related to me a personal incident in connection with this first London rehearsal. Near the end of the chorus 'He, watching over Israel,' occurs the following instrumental phrase in the clarinets and flutes – a phrase which is not fully discernible in the pianoforte arrangement of the score, and which is practically inaudible at a performance:

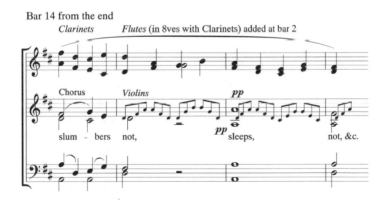

'Mr. Lazarus,' said Mendelssohn, 'will you kindly make that phrase a little stronger, as I wish it to stand out more prominently? I know I have marked it *piano*.' 'Of course,' adds Mr. Lazarus, 'I was playing it religiously as marked.'

Before going into the [Birmingham Town] Hall, Mendelssohn said to Chorley, the musical critic of the *Athenæum*: 'Now stick your claws into my book. Don't tell me what you like, but tell me what you *don't* like.' After the performance, he said in his merriest manner to Chorley: 'Come, and I will show you the prettiest walk in Birmingham.' He then led the critic and other friends to the banks of the canal, bordered by coal and cinder heaps. There, on the towing-path between the bridges, they walked for more than an hour discussing the new oratorio. According to the late Mr. Moore, it was then and there, amidst the scenery of the cinder heaps, that a sudden thought struck Mendelssohn to change 'Lift thine eyes' from a duet into a trio.

> He then quotes from a letter written by a Mrs Samuel
> Bache of Birmingham to her sister, Mrs Martineau:

To see him conducting was worth anything. He seemed inspired, and might well be forgiven for something of self-reverence, though he looked all humility; and when he came down from his chair when it was all over, he seemed all unstrung as if he could no more.

F.G. Edwards: *The History of Mendelssohn's Oratorio 'Elijah'* (London, 1896), pp. 76–8, 84–5, 91 (with cuts)

IGNAZ MOSCHELES

Diary entry, 28 August 1846 (the last day of the Birmingham Festival)

We had a miscellaneous selection; the chief feature consisting of pieces from Beethoven and Spohr. The orchestral parts of a short recitative, the words of which had been printed in the books for the audience, were not forthcoming; we were all in a difficulty, but Mendelssohn came to the rescue. He quietly betook himself to an adjoining room, and there, whilst the preceding pieces of the programme were being played, he composed the recitative, scored it, and copied the parts, and these were admirably played, with the ink scarcely dry, at first sight, by the band – the public knew nothing of what had happened – that's the way a Mendelssohn manages.

Ignaz Moscheles, quoted in Charlotte Moscheles: *Aus Moscheles Leben* (Leipzig, 1872; Eng. tr. A.D. Coleridge, London, 1873), II, p. 158

F. MAX MÜLLER

It was in the last year of his life that Mendelssohn paid his last visit to England to conduct his last oratorio, the 'Elijah.' It had to be performed at Exeter Hall, then the best place for sacred music. Most of the musicians, however, were not professionals, and they had only bound themselves to attend a certain number of rehearsals. Excellent as they were in such oratorios as the 'Messiah,' which they knew by heart, a new oratorio, such as the 'Elijah,' was too much for them; and I well remember Mendelssohn, in the afternoon before the performance, declaring he would not conduct.

'Oh, these tailors and shoemakers,' he said, 'they cannot do it, and they will not practise! I shall not go.' However, a message arrived that the Queen and Prince Albert were to be present, so nothing remained but to go. I was present, the place was crowded. Mendelssohn conducted, and now and then made a face, but no one else detected what was wrong. It was a great success and a great triumph for Mendelssohn. If he could have heard it performed as it was performed at Exeter Hall in later years, when his tailors and shoemakers knew it by heart, he would not have made a face.

F. Max Müller: *Auld Lang Syne* (New York, 1898), pp. 1–33; reprinted in *Mendelssohn and his World*, ed. R. Larry Todd (Princeton, 1991), pp. 256–7

XII

LAST YEARS

FERDINAND HILLER

In the midst of the manifold occupations and social meetings in which he gladly took part, and which he graced by his talent and brilliant conversation, there would come days of exhaustion, even of depression. At such times, visits from his friends, foremost among whom were David and Dr. Schleinitz, would always do him good. Sometimes he would amuse himself with doing little water-colour sketches – or he would read some poem of Goethe's, such as 'Hermann and Dorothea' or 'Iphigenie.' The first of these he was especially fond of, and he would go into raptures over the deep feeling which penetrates the most insignificant things in that wonderful work. He said one day that the line,

Und es lobte darauf der Apotheker den Knaster,*

was enough to bring tears into one's eyes. He would also get out Jean Paul sometimes, and revel in his humour; one evening he read aloud to me out of Siebenkäs† for at least an hour. But sleep was always his best resource. Several times I found him lying on the sofa before dinner, ready dressed, having been asleep for hours, after which he would awake with a capital appetite. A quarter of an hour after he would say with the air of a spoiled child, 'I am still quite tired;' would lie down again, saying how delicious it was, stretch himself out, and in a few minutes be fast asleep again. 'He can go on in that way for two days,' Cécile said to me, 'and then he is fresher than ever.' Nature supplied him with the best cure – but unhappily it could not remain so always.

Ferdinand Hiller: *Felix Mendelssohn-Bartholdy* (Cologne, 1874; Eng. tr. M.E. von Glehn, London, 1874), pp. 171-2

---

* 'And thereupon the apothecary praised the tobacco'; the book is full of the minutiae of bourgeois life. [RN]
† A book by Jean Paul [RN]

EDUARD DEVRIENT

February 1846

During these two days that I passed with Felix, I became clearly conscious of the change that had come over the sources of his inner life. His blooming youthful joyousness had given place to a fretfulness, a satiety of all earthly things, which reflected everything back differently from the spirit of former days.

His conducting of the concerts, everything that savoured of business, was an intolerable annoyance to him; the following winter he intended to let Gade conduct the concerts entirely. He took no longer any pleasure in the Conservatorium, he gave over the pianoforte pupils to Moscheles; not one of the young people studying compositions inspired him with any sympathy; he crossly declared them all to be without talent, and told me that he could not bear to see any more of their compositions, that none of them gave any hopes for the next generation of German musicians.

The increasing industry, which had become his second nature, incited him to be constantly composing. He called it 'doing his duty;' but it appeared to me, quite apart from considerations of health, that he would have better fulfilled his duty had he written less and waited for the happy moments when his creative power was spontaneous, which did not come so often now as formerly. I had remarked lately that he began to repeat himself in his composition; that he began, unconsciously, to copy older masters, especially Sebastian Bach, and that his writings exhibited certain mannerisms. I told him these things, and he received what I said without any irascibility, because he believed me to be completely in error. He spoke disparagingly of ideas that had been waited for and contrived, and said that when one had at heart to compose music, the first involuntary thought would be the right one, even though it might not be so new or so striking, or though it might recall Sebastian Bach; if it did, it was a sign that so it was to have been.

It did not seem to me that the severe criticism he applied to his finished works, and his proneness to alter them, fitted in with these views; I thought he did not discriminate between his impulse to work and to create.

Eduard Devrient: *Meine Erinnerungen an Felix Mendelssohn-Bartholdy* (Leipzig, 1869; Eng. tr. Natalia Macfarren, London, 1869), pp. 273-5

WILHELM ADOLPH LAMPADIUS

(June 1846)
From Liège he went to Cologne to take the direction of a great musical festival there. For this occasion he had set Schiller's 'Festival Song to Artists' to music, from the words, 'O sons of art, man's dignity to you is given: preserve it, man:' a noble text, which, with Mendelssohn's music, and sung by more than three thousand voices, must have produced a profound impression. Besides this, he directed other pieces, – his 'Bacchus Chorus,' from the 'Antigone;' a Te Deum by Bernhard Klein; and the chorus, 'O Isis and Osiris,' from the 'Magic Flute.' From this festival he turned his steps back to Leipzig. I spoke with him about the Cologne Festival. He seemed, on the whole, well satisfied with it. The material annoyances of the festival, the monstrous extortions of the Cologne landlords, &c., could not, of course, affect *him*; the gigantic massing of vocal material had amused him; and the patriotic element, the sympathetic blending of nationalities, Flemish and German, had pleased him. Musically, the chorus 'O Isis and Osiris,' had been the most satisfactory to him. On the whole, he was in the best of humours; praised the Düsseldorf Festival, soon to occur; and promised to let us know if anything very remarkable would be produced there.

Can it be wondered at, that, after a life so full of labours, and the incredible excitement and strain of this summer, on his return to Leipzig, Mendelssohn was taken sick? Yet he undertook to lead the subscription concerts, in connection with Gade, and worked hard to bring out in the best manner Beethoven's symphonies; as, for example, those in B flat, and in F major, which we had never heard so finely rendered. He also assisted in bringing before the world a new symphony in C major by Robert Schumann. But he brought out nothing new of his own; nor indeed did he give much of what he had written before. We heard nothing of his, excepting the scena and aria, the overture 'Meeresstille,' and the 'A-minor Symphony.' Besides this, Madame Dulcken played his concerto in D minor, and Clara Schumann that in G minor. Yet the whole course of concerts was excellent, and the programmes selected mostly from classical music. The historical concerts, which were continued after the manner of former seasons, Mendelssohn was not well enough to attend. Playing in public was forbidden him by his physician. He often complained much of headache. He was hardly prevailed upon to undertake to direct the performance of 'St Paul,' which took place in St Paul's Church, on Good Friday, 1847. He accounted for his great reserve as to appearing in public by pleading that he needed time for composition. He must labour till he was forty; then he would rest, he said.

Wilhelm Adolph Lampadius: *Felix Mendelssohn-Bartholdy: ein Denkmal für seine Freunde* (Leipzig, 1849; Eng. tr. W.L. Gage, New York, 1866), pp. 128–9, 132–3

HENRY FOTHERGILL CHORLEY

I passed the three last days of August, 1847, beside him at Interlaken in Switzerland, very shortly before his return to Leipzig, and that fatal attack of illness which ended in his death there on the fourth of November. He looked aged and sad; – and stooped more than I had ever before seen him do; but his smile had never been brighter, nor his welcome more cordial. It was early in the morning of as sunny and exhilarating a day as ever shone on Switzerland, that we got to Interlaken; and then and there I must see the place and its beauties. – 'We can talk about our business better out of the house:' – and forth we went, – at first up and down under the walnut trees, in sight of the *Jungfrau*, until, by degrees, the boarding-houses began to turn out their inhabitants. Then we struck off through the wood to a height called, I think, the *Hohenbühl*, commanding the lake of Thun and the plain with Neuhaus and Unterseen, – with the snow mountains all around us. It was while we were climbing up to this nook that the tinkling of the cowbells, which adds to, rather than takes away from, the solitude of mountain scenery, came up from some pastureland not far off. My companion stopped immediately, listened, smiled, – and began to sing

from the *overture* to 'Guillaume Tell.' 'How beautifully Rossini has found that!' he exclaimed. 'All the introduction, too, is truly Swiss. – I wish I could make some Swiss music. – But the storm in his *overture* is very bad!' And he went off again into the pastoral movement: speaking afterwards of Swiss scenery with a strength of affection that almost amounted to passion. 'I like the pine-trees, and the very smell of the old stones with the moss upon them.' Then he told, with almost a boyish pleasure, of excursions that he had taken with his happy party of wife and children. 'We will come here every year, I am resolved. How pleasant it is to sit talking on this bench, with the glorious *Jungfrau* over there, after your Hanover-square Rooms in London!'

But Mendelssohn must needs be drawn back into the concert-room, even at Interlaken. A new composition for the opening of the magnificent Concert Hall in Liverpool had been proposed to him; and this was to be talked over. He had already a new *Cantata* in view, I think, for Frankfurt; and mentioned some text from 'Die Herrmannschlacht' of Klopstock, as the subject which he had selected. 'But that,' he said, with his own merry laugh, 'would never do for Liverpool. No: we must find something else.' He spoke of Napoleon's passage of the Alps as an event he wanted to see arranged for music – again repeating, 'I must write something about this country – but that, again, will not do for England!' – I mentioned Wordsworth's ode on 'The Power of Sound,' as a noble poem full of pictures, from which, perhaps, portions might be detached fit for a composer's purposes; but he seemed to treat the idea of describing the various effects of music in music as too vague and hackneyed; and moreover objectionable, as having been done completely by Handel, in his 'Alexander's Feast.' Then he began to fear that he could get nothing ready by the time mentioned – 'for you know,' he went on, 'something of mine is to be sung in the *Dom* at Cologne, when the nave is thrown open – That will be an opportunity! – But I shall not live to see it!' and he paused, and put his hand to his head, with a sudden expression of weariness and suffering.

He had composed much music, he said, since he had been at Interlaken; and mentioned that stupendous *quartett* in F minor which we have since known as one of the most impassioned outpourings of sadness existing in instrumental music – besides some English service-music for the Protestant church. 'It has been very good for me to work,' he went on, glancing for the first time at the great domestic calamity (the death of Madame Hensel), which had struck him down, immediately on his return from England; 'and I wanted to make something sharp and close and strict' (interlacing his fingers as he spoke) – 'so that church-music has quite suited me. Yes: I have written a good deal since I have been here – but I must have quiet, or I shall die!'

I will not swear to the very order of words which Mendelssohn spoke,* but that day is too brightly printed in my memory, for a topic, or a trait, or a characteristic expression, to be forgotten. Life has too few such.

In answer to my inquiries concerning the opera on which he was understood to be engaged, he spoke long and freely concerning the theatre, and his own plans and purposes with respect to it. 'The time has come when I must try what I can do,' was his language, 'and after I have written four or five operas, perhaps I shall make something good. But it is so difficult to find a subject.' – Then he discussed many which had been proposed to him; speaking in the strongest manner of the unauthorised use of his name, which had been made in London by announcing 'The Tempest' as having been

---

* I may be permitted, however, to say that his use of English was much after the manner described. He understood and wrote our language thoroughly well; the slight touch of the foreigner in his speaking made it all the more racy. Sometimes his epithets were most precious. I remember once his venting his displeasure against a songstress whose behaviour had offended him, by declaring that 'she was like an arrogant cook.'

commenced by him with a view to its performance at a given period. 'The book is too French,' he said, 'and the third act is thoroughly bad. I would not have touched the opera till all that had been entirely altered. – And I never would tie myself to time in such a hasty manner! No; when I have finished something, I dare say that I shall get it produced some where.' He then went on to talk over other Shakspearian subjects; in particular 'The Winter's Tale;' a sketch from which had been laid before him: – this seemed in some degree to have engaged his liking. 'Something very merry,' said he, 'could be made with *Autolycus*.' How merry he could have made it, the world has since learned by the publication of his *operetta*, in which the knavish *Pedlar Kauz* plays so notable a part. Truer comedy does not exist in German music – not even in the most comical portions of Mozart's 'Die Entführung,' – than the dancing song of this precious knave, or the part taken by him in the serenade of the village girl, with its sentimental caricature of the German watchman's droning call.

'We have no one in Germany who can write opera books,' Mendelssohn continued. 'If Kotzebue had been alive . . . *he* had ideas!' and he warmed himself up as he talked, by recalling how a prosaic occasion of mere parade – the opening of the new theatre at Pesth – could inspire Kotzebue with such a characteristic invention as his 'Ruins of Athens,' so good for Beethoven to set. 'Well; I must do my best with "Loreley," for Geibel has taken great trouble with the poem. We shall see.' And then, again, he broke off suddenly, and put his hand to his head. 'But what is the use of planning anything? I shall not live.'

Who could attend to such a foreboding in one apparently so full of energy, and forecast, and enterprise? I confess that I ascribed it mainly to the impression left by the fearful trial which Mendelssohn had recently sustained in the loss of the sister to whom he was so tenderly attached. – Other painful ideas seemed to rise before him. He spoke with more fear than hope of the fermenting state of opinion in Germany, and its disastrous influences upon morals, education, good citizenship – on all that keeps society sound and makes home happy. He dwelt on the impatience of duty – on the sympathy shown to error and license – on the disregard of obligation – on the difficulties preparing for Germany by such perverse and preferred lawlessness among the middle classes – with tears in his eyes: for never was man of any country more sincerely, affectionately national. He spoke, too, and bitterly, of the folly and falsehood of those in high places, who had alienated the hearts which they might so easily have attached, and who had demoralized under pretext of educating a great people; giving illustrations, instances, anecdotes (which I need not say are sacred), with a nervous earnestness which showed how seriously and apprehensively his bright and quick mind had been at work on these subjects. – Then he turned to his own future plans. I had often before heard him discuss that point in every artist's career, at which retirement from close personal inter-course with the public is desirable, but never so emphatically as that day. He was determined to give up presenting himself to the public so freely as he had done. 'When one is no longer young, one should not go about playing and concert giving,' – and he expressed his strong wish, almost amounting to an intention, of settling down somewhere in the Rhine Land, not in any town, there to devote himself more eagerly than ever to composition. 'I shall be near England,' he added, 'and can come over as often as you wish; and I shall be within reach of our towns with all these new railroads; but I must live quietly, and get rid of all that noise and interruption, if I *am* to live.' And again was repeated the mournful presage; and the glow faded from his face, and the sad, worn look came back which it pained the very heart to see.

Later in the day, I was shown, with eager pleasure, the drawings made by him at Interlaken; for he drew landscapes faithfully, if not altogether gracefully, though in colour *'that green'* was owned by him to be a stumbling-block. I was shown, too, his piano – 'a shock-ing thing,' as he called it; 'but I am so glad that there was no decent piano in Interlaken! This will do to try a chord when I want it; but I do not wish to make finger-music.' – And he touched it – the last time that I heard him touch a piano – that I might hear what an old kettle it was!

We were bound for Fribourg; and I asked him much about Mooser's famous organ. He said that he had heard wonders concerning its *vox humana* stop. 'How odd,' he continued, 'that such an expressive thing, which can almost talk, should be made merely of two bits of wood.' I pressed him earnestly to go on with us, and try this marvel for himself. 'No,' he said, laughingly, 'those organists always like no one to play but themselves. There is always some difficulty: – and then there is the noise! I must give up organ-playing – and besides Winter is coming, and we had better draw quietly homewards.' There was some talk, too, of his being obliged soon to make a professional journey to Vienna, which further limited his time. In short, never had I seen him so full of plans; and surely never, in the annals of any art, had artist more honourably arrived at well merited and universal fame. – Vanity of vanities!

The second day of our stay at Interlaken was cloudy, with occasional torrents of rain: all the mountains were 'straitly shut up.' Mendelssohn spent nearly the whole day with us; indeed, I never was near him without being reminded of what we are told of Sir Walter Scott, that he was as lavish of goodwill and time in the entertainment of his friends as if he had had no earthly other thing to do. When and how he managed to write, were not easy to discover.

In the evening, chance brought the conversation on the ground of Italian music. He spoke again, in warm terms of admiration, of Rossini's 'Guillaume Tell' – and, to my surprise, with a good-natured cordiality, of Donizetti's 'Fille du Régiment.' 'It is so merry,' he said, 'with so much of the real soldier's life in it. They call it bad; and to be sure,' he continued, with a half humorous tone of self-correction, 'it is surprising how easily one can become used to bad music.' Then he began to ask about Verdi – having heard that there was something like a new effect in some of his *finales*; and he would have this described, and shown to him, as well as could be done. He expressed a wish, too, to hear Handel's organ *Concertos* properly played – speaking about them doubtfully, and with hesitation, because of the frivolous and old-fashioned passages for *solo* stops, with which they were full – talked eagerly of the *Grand Opera* at Paris, as of a theatre for which one day he might be asked to write (I almost think that some negotiations had passed on the subject) – and referred to his sojourn in Rome, as one which had been full of the highest and most important influences upon his career. It was *apropos* of Rome, that some one mentioned Shelley's 'Cenci,' which had been given to him by one of his English friends.

He spoke of it with almost angry dislike. 'No; it is too horrible! it is abominable. I cannot admire such a poem!'

The next morning, Mendelssohn drove with us to Lauterbrunnen. The view of the *Jungfrau* and the *Silberhorn* was superb as we went up the valley. Nor can ever have the fall of the *Staubbach* looked more magical than it did in the bright light of that late summer day, – its waters gleaming like a shower of rockets launched over the edge of the high cliff, their expended fires spreading and mingling as they fell and faded. Almost my last distinct remembrance of Mendelssohn is seeing him standing within the arch of the rainbow – which, as every reader of 'Manfred' knows, the *Witch of the Alps* flings round the feet of the cascade – looking upward, rapt and serious, thoroughly enjoying the scene. My very last is the sight of him turning down the road to wend back to Interlaken alone, while we turned up to cross the Wengern Alp to Grindewald. I thought even then, as I followed his figure, looking none the younger for the loose dark coat and the wide-brimmed straw hat bound with black crape which he wore, that he was too much depressed and worn, and walked too heavily! But who could have dreamed that his days on earth were so rapidly drawing to a close?

Henry Fothergill Chorley: 'The last days of Mendelssohn', *Modern German Music* (London, 1854; R/1973), II, pp. 384–400 (with cuts)

SIR JULIUS BENEDICT

The last performance he directed in Leipzig was that of 'St. Paul,' on Good-Friday, 1847, immediately after which he repaired to London, where the Committee of the Sacred Harmonic Society had offered him an engagement to direct the production of 'Elijah;' arriving on the 12th of April, 1847.

To describe how he overtasked his powers at the rehearsals at Exeter Hall, with a then most unruly and inefficient chorus; how his already excitable temper was painfully tried by the incredible difficulty and trouble he had in impressing and carrying with him the inert intelligence of his sluggish interpreters, would be impossible. But when he returned home after his labours, depressed – nay, almost subdued – by this dreadful fatigue, the change that had already manifested itself within him became only too perceptible in his outward appearance.

Sir Julius Benedict: *A Sketch of the Life and Works of the Late Felix Mendelssohn Bartholdy* (London, 1850), pp. 52–3

IGNAZ MOSCHELES
& LIVIA FREGE

The Mendelssohn family returned from a holiday in Switzerland in September 1847. Moscheles describes Felix's mental and physical state:

Diary entry, 17 September 1847
In mind dear Felix is the same as ever, but physically he seems altered; he is aged, weakened, and his walk is less elastic than before, but to see him at the piano, or hear him talk about art and artists, he is all life and fire. My new piece for eight hands, written for Benedict's Concert, gave rise to an animated discussion; it was to bear the title of 'Jadis et Aujourd'hui;' Mendelssohn opposed this, and I affirmed 'that the introductory fugues were meant to illustrate the good old times, the lighter movements the music of our own day.' 'But why so?; argued Mendelssohn; 'are not interesting fugues written now-a-days? Surely our time produces still some good things.' 'But the fashionable taste is a vitiated one,' I replied, 'people will only listen to light music and easy rhythms.' 'Yes, they will,' Mendelssohn broke in, eagerly; 'but they shall not. Don't you and I live? Don't we intend to write good music? We will prove that our time is capable of good; so please give up this title.' This request was not to be withstood, and therefore for 'Jadis et Aujourd'hui,' we substituted 'Les Contrastes,' with which my friend declared he was satisfied.

Diary entry, 3 October
After the Mendelssohns had dined with us, Felix and I amused ourselves at the piano with fugues and gigues by Bach; he then gave us an admirable imitation of the town musicians at Frankfurt, whose Polkas he had been condemned to listen to hundreds of times.

Diary entry, 5 October
Delightful afternoon at Mendelssohn's, and had much friendly talk about art-matters. He played me his last quartet, all four movements in F minor; the passionate character of the whole, and the mournful key, seem to me an expression of his deeply agitated state of mind; he is still suffering and in sorrow for the loss of his sister. He also showed me some of her manuscript Lieder – everything deeply felt, but not always original.

Diary entry, 9 October
We parted about one o'clock in the most cheerful mood. That very afternoon, however, Felix was taken very ill in Frau Frege's house; he had gone thither to persuade her to sing in the next performance of his 'Elijah.' 'She is afraid of appearing in public,' Mendelssohn had said some days before, 'and of not being in good voice; but no one can sing at all like her; I must go and encourage her.'

We are indebted to Frau Frege for the following account of what occurred in her house on the 9th of October: 'These were his words when he entered the room, "I come to-day, and intend coming every day, until you give me your consent, and I now bring with me again the altered pieces (of the 'Elijah'); but I really feel miserable, so much so that lately I actually cried over my Trio. To-day, however, before we talk of 'Elijah,' you must help me to put together a book of songs; the Härtels are pressing me so to publish it." He brought the book, Op. 71, and as a seventh Lied, the old German Spring Song, "Der trübe Winter ist vorbei," which he had composed in the summer of this year, but had not written out until the 7th of October. I knew pretty well,' said Frau Frege, 'how he would wish the songs to follow, and arranged them in order, one by one, upon the piano. After I had sung the first, he was very much moved, and asked for it again, adding, "That was a somewhat serious birthday present for Schleinitz on the 1st of October, but it is quite in accordance with my state of mind, and I can't tell you how melancholy Fanny's still unchanged rooms in Berlin made me. But I have indeed so much to be thankful to God for – Cécile is so well, and little Felix, too" (his youngest son, who was often out of health). He then made me repeat all the Lieder several times, and I still clung to my opinion that the "Spring Song" was a little out of place in the book. He then said, 'Be it so; the whole book is serious, and serious it must go into the world.' Although he looked very pale, I had to sing him the first song for the third time over, and he thanked me most kindly and amiably. He continued: "If you are not tired, let us try the last quartet out of the 'Elijah.'" I left the room to order lamps, and on my return found him in the next room on the sofa; his hands, he said, were cold and stiff, and it would be better and wiser to take a turn out of doors, he really felt too ill to make music. I wanted to send for a carriage, but he would not allow me, and after I had given him a saline draught, he left about 5.30. When he got into the air, he felt it would be better to go home instantly; once at home, he sat down in the corner of the sofa, where Cécile found him at 7 o'clock; his hands were cold and stiff as before. On the following day he suffered from such violent pain in the head, that leeches were applied; the doctor thought the digestive organs were attacked, and only at a later period pronounced the disease to be the result of an overwrought nervous system. Ever since Fanny's death I had been struck with his paleness when he conducted or played; everything seemed to affect him more intensely than before.'

Moscheles describes Mendelssohn's final hours:

Diary entry, 4 November 1847
Evening. – From two o'clock in the afternoon, at the hour when another paralytic stroke was dreaded, he gradually began to sink; he lay perfectly quiet, breathing heavily. In the evening we were all by turns assembled around his bed, contemplating the peaceful, seraphic expression on his countenance. The memory of that scene sunk deeply into our hearts. Cécile bore up with fortitude under the crushing weight of her sorrow; she never wavered, never betrayed her struggle by a word. The children had been sent to bed at nine o'clock. Paul Mendelssohn stood, transfixed with grief, at the bed-side of his dying brother. Madame Dirichlet and the Schuncks were expected in vain; Dr. Härtel had travelled to Berlin to fetch them and Dr. Schönlein, but they could not arrive in time to witness the closing scene.

From nine o'clock in the evening we expected every moment would be the last; a light seemed to hover over his features, but the struggle for life became feebler and fainter. Cécile, in floods of tears, kneeled at his pillow; Paul Mendelssohn, David, Schleinitz, and I, in deep and silent prayer, surrounded the deathbed. As his breathing gradually became slower and slower, my mind involuntarily recurred to Beethoven's Funeral March, 'Sulla Morte d'un' Eroe,' to that passage where he seems to depict the hero as he lies breathing his last, the sands of life gradually running out. The suppressed sobs of the bystanders, and my own hot tears, recalled me to the dread reality.

At twenty-four minutes past nine he expired with a deep sigh. The doctor persuaded the widowed Cécile to leave the room. I knelt down at the bedside, my prayers followed heavenwards the soul of the departed, and I pressed one last kiss on that noble forehead before it grew cold in the damp dew of death. For several hours we bewailed together our irreparable loss; then each one withdrew, to sorrow in silence.

What poor consolations are funeral honours, however grand and impressive, how miserably inadequate as expressions of grief for the loss of my beloved friend, whose memory will be sacred to me for the rest of my days.

Ignaz Moscheles, Livia Frege, quoted in Charlotte Moscheles: *Aus Moscheles Leben* (Leipzig, 1872; Eng. tr. A.D. Coleridge, London, 1873), II, pp. 177–8, 180–82, 185–6 (with cuts)

EDUARD DEVRIENT

6 November 1847
The following morning I went with the Dresden friends to Leipzig, to accompany Felix on his last journey. His brother, who had been called from Berlin when he was struck the second time, on the 30th October, recounted to me what happened during the last days.

On the 3rd Felix had spoken cheerfully with him for hours, until midday, then he became restless, and Paul and Cecilia were in alternate attendance at his bedside. Towards two o'clock Cecilia came in terror to call Paul, as she could not soothe the patient. Paul went in to him, scolded him in jest, which Felix was yet able to understand and respond to. But suddenly he started up, as though seized with a frightful pain in his head, his mouth open with an agonizing expression; he gave one piercing cry and sank back upon his pillow. Now all was over; from this time he lay in a dull half-sleep, answered only 'Yes,' and 'No;' and only once to Cecilia's tender inquiry, how he felt? answered 'Tired, very tired!' Thus he dozed quietly until twenty-four minutes past nine, when his breathing ceased and life was extinct.

Hensel, whom I met again now, and who was still quite crushed by the death of his wife, led me to the corpse, which he had thoughtfully decorated. There lay my beloved friend, in a costly coffin, upon cushions of satin, embowered in tall growing shrubs, and covered with wreaths of flowers and laurels. He looked much aged, but recalled to me the expression of the boy as I had first seen him; – where my hand had so often stroked the long brown locks and the burning brow, I now touched the marble forehead of the man. This span of time in my remembrance encloses the whole of happy youth, in one perfect and indelible thought.

Cecilia sent for me the following morning; she received me with the tenderness of a sister, wept in silence, and was calm and composed as ever.

She thanked me for all the love and devotion I had shown to her Felix, grieved for me that I should have to mourn so faithful a friend, and spoke of the love with which Felix had always regarded me. Long we spoke of him, it comforted her, and she was loth for me to depart. She was most unpretending in her sorrow, gentle, and resigned to live for the care and education of her children. She said, 'God would help her, and surely her boys would have the inheritance of some of their father's goodness.'

There could not be a more worthy memorial of him than the well-balanced, strong and tender heart of his mourning widow.

In the afternoon the immense throng of the funeral procession began to gather in front of the house, and was put in motion about four o'clock. The coffin was covered with a rich funeral pall of velvet embroidered in silver, and thickly set round with the customary offering in Leipzig of palm branches, of which there was a gigantic array round the sarcophagus, that gave it the aspect of an isle of peace in the midst of the surging crowd. Streets and open places were all filled with people; all the windows were crowded on the long and circuitous road that the procession was to pass, through the town and by the Gewandhaus, the scene of Mendelssohn's labours. The musicians led the way, playing a hastily-instrumented song without words by Mendelssohn;* six clergymen in full robes followed the bier, then came the relatives, the heads of the musical societies, then his friends, of whom many had arrived in the course of the day from a distance, led by Schubring and myself. A second division followed, preceded by clergymen; night was closing in when we arrived at the church of the University. The coffin was put down, by accident, close to where I stood; the palm branches rustled in my face; it seemed to me as though the departed whispered to me, 'I leave my peace with you!'

The procession was received at the church with the music in 'Antigone' that accompanies the corpse of Hœmon. The acute shake in it reminded me of a word Felix said to me when he was a boy, how he had met a military funeral procession, and that the music had begun with a high shake, which had appeared to him to convey an expression of sharp anguish. And thus he had applied it long years afterwards in 'Antigone,' and thus it did express the sharpness of anguish to those who accompanied his last earthly journey.

During the choral, 'Jesus meine Zuversicht,' the bier was placed upon a raised platform in the choir, with six high candelabra beside it, and at the end of the lighted church, below the organ, there loomed the orchestra, densely filled with musicians and singers. We heard choruses from 'St. Paul,' a discourse of Pastor Howard, then the final chorus of Bach's 'Passion,' 'Wir setzten uns mit Thränen nieder,' &c., 'Ruhe, sanfte Ruhe,'† and thus our mourning rites were brought to a close.

When the church was almost deserted, a female form, in deep mourning, was led to the bier; she sank down beside it, and remained long in prayer. It was Cecilia, taking her last farewell of the earthly remains of Felix; she knew that she would not long survive him.

The corpse was taken the same night by special train to Berlin,

---

* The one in E minor, Book 5
† 'We sat down in tears' and 'Rest, gentle rest'.

being received on its road with a pious tribute of song, by the vocal societies, at Cöthen and at Dessau. Arrived at Berlin, it was placed in the family vault, side by side with Fanny's remains, during a performance of Beethoven's 'Funeral March,' under Taubert's direction, singing of the Domchor and of the Singakademie, and a discourse by Pastor Berduschek.

Eduard Devrient: *Meine Erinnerungen an Felix Mendelssohn-Bartholdy* (Leipzig, 1869; Eng. tr. Natalia Macfarren, London, 1869), pp. 296–301

CLARA SCHUMANN

He died from the effects of three strokes which came one after another in the course of a fortnight, just as happened with his sister Fanny – it is as if his sister had drawn him after her, for he himself said to his family, 'I shall die like Fanny', and this seems to have become a fixed idea with him . . . Our grief is great, for he was dear to us, not only as an artist, but as a man and a friend! His death is an irreparable loss for all those who knew and loved him . . . A thousand cherished memories rise, and one feels tempted to exclaim, 'Why has heaven done this?' But it has taken him from earth in the full splendour of his powers, in the flower of his age . . . as an artist he stands at the highest summit of his fame – is it not happiness to die thus? If only we could have seen him once more! We saw him last on March 25th, and the last time he conducted in the hall of the *Gewandhaus* was at my concert on Nov. 16th last year, when I played his G minor concerto. If I tried to put into words everything that one loved in him, and of his, I should never make an end. I feel that our grief for him will last all our lives.

Clara Schumann, excerpts from her diaries, in B. Litzmann: *Clara Schumann, an Artist's Life* (London, 1913), pp. 436–7

INDEX

Albert, Prince, 204
Anderson, Mr., 142–3
Attwood, Thomas, 134

Bach, C. P. E., 158
Bach's music (J. S.), 88, 96, 109, 133–5,
    182
    A minor Fugue, 94
    B minor Mass, 163
    E flat chorale prelude, 159
    manuscripts given to Zelter, 211
    St Matthew Passion, 12–19, 133
Bartholdy, Jacob, 30–1
Beatty Kingston, Mr., 92–3
Beer, Michael, 175
Beethoven's music, 96, 102–3, 104,
    180
    7th symphony, 158
    8th symphony, 62, 64, 65, 159
    9th symphony, 29, 64, 103, 159,
        162
    Egmont Overture, 94, 138
    Moonlight Sonata, 197
    original piano manuscript, 84–5
    Piano Concerto in G major, 86, 138
    Piano Sonata (Op. 57), 167
    Piano Sonata (Op. 111), 93
Benecke, Mrs., 52–3
Benedict, Julius, 5–7, 56–7, 62–3, 246–7
Bennett, William Sterndale, 51, 132–3,
    147, 164, 202–6
Berlioz, Hector, 171–5, 181, 186
Beyer, Rudolf von, 8–9
Billing, Dr., 141
Bunsen, Christian von, 197

Camacho's Wedding (opera), 110–11
Cenci, The (play by Shelley), 245–6
Cherubini, Luigi, 163, 175, 177–8, 186
Chopin, Frédéric, 96, 158, 163, 176–7
Chorley, Henry Fothergill, 20–1, 86–7,
    191–2, 232, 240–6

Dando, J. H. B., 141, 204
David, Ferdinand, 201, 214, 237, 250
Davison, James William, 206–7
Day, Alfred, 118–19
Devrient, Eduard, 3, 33, 42–3, 199
    on M's early years, 3–5, 12–16
    on Cécile Jeanrenaud, 49
    on M's musical tastes/attitudes,
        110–12, 113–17
    on M's personality/appearance,
        193–6, 202, 211–12
    on M's last years, 238–9
    on M's funeral, 250–3
Dickens, Charles, 141
Dirichlet, Gustav Peter, 45
Dolby, Charlotte, 226–7
Dorn, Heinrich, 197–202

Edwards, Frederick George, 133–5,
    230–2
Ense, Karl August Varnhagen von, 9

Fille du régiment, La (opera by
    Donizetti), 245
Franck, Herman, 176
Frege, Livia, 248–9
Friedländer, Abraham, 198

Gade, Niels Wilhelm, 73, 163–4
    First Symphony, 63, 181
Gauntlett, Dr., 133–4, 136
Gerhardt, Livia, 201
Goethe, Johann Wolfgang, 8, 19, 20,
    81–5
Goldschmidt, Otto, 93, 220
Gounod, Charles, 181–2
Grove, George, 87, 93–5, 185–6
Grüneisen, Mr., 144–5
Gustedt, Jenny von, 19–20

Handel's music, 114, 205
Hans Heiling (opera by Marschner),
    111–12

Hauptmann, Herr, 73
Haydn's music, 61, 136
Hegel, Georg Wilhelm Friedrich, 12
Heinke, Henry, 123–4
Hensel, Wilhelm, 16, 251
Hiller, Ferdinand, 85–6, 96, 167
    on M's courtship, 48–9
    on M's time in Paris (1831/2), 85–
        6, 175–9
    on M's musical tastes, 114–15, 116
    on M's Leipzig visit (1839), 179–
        80, 207–11
    on Midsummer Night's Dream, 215
    on M's last years, 237
Hogarth, George, 142–3
Holland, Henry Scott, 166–7
Holstein, Hedwig von, 63
Horsley, Fanny & Sophy, 127–32
Horsley, William, 127, 144
Hummel's Septett in D Minor, 71, 72

Jeanrenaud, Cécile see Mendelssohn,
    Cécile
Jeanrenaud, Julie, 43
Joachim, Joseph, 88–9

Kalkbrenner, Friedrich, 176–7
Klein, Bernhard, 194
Klingemann, Karl, 5, 130, 132, 143–4

Lampadius, Wilhelm Adolph, 66–7, 91–
    2, 186–8, 227, 239–40
Lazarus, Henry, 231
Lind, Jenny, 5, 94, 166, 167, 219–20
Liszt, Franz, 177, 179–81
Lobe, Johann Christian, 99–108
Lumley, Benjamin, 117–18

Macfarren, George, 118–19, 144
'Maestro' (Mr Grüneisen), 144–5
Marschner, Heinrich, 112n
Marx, Adolf Bernhard, 26–9, 33–5,
    109–10
Massow, Herr von, 212
Mendelssohn, Abraham (father), 4–5,
    25, 26–7, 36–40
Mendelssohn, Cécile (wife), 44, 214
    descriptions of, 43, 48–51, 132,
        192, 203

engagement, 48–51
M's death, 249, 250, 251, 252
Mendelssohn, Fanny (sister), 16, 31–3,
    42, 45, 53–5, 181
    on M's revival of St Matthew
        Passion, 16–19
    descriptions of, 50, 193
    death, 253
Mendelssohn, Felix
    life & works (chronology), xi–xix
    early years, 3–21
    Jewish heritage, 9, 16, 185, 218–19
    family, 25–57
    Düsseldorf (1833), 36–40
    death of father (1835), 41–2
    engagement/marriage, 43–50
    as conductor, 61–7
    languages/lisp, 62, 126, 141–2,
        242n.
    as teacher, 71–7
    as performer and improviser, 81–
        96, 133
    musical tastes/attitudes, 99–119
    in Britain (1829–1844), 123–53
    friendship with Schumanns, 157–67
    and other composers, 171–82
    personality/appearance, 185–220
    last years, 237–49
    death/funeral, 249–53
    works:
        C major Overture, 112–13
        C minor symphony, 110
        C minor Trio, 214
        choruses from Antigone, 115–16
        D minor Trio, 89, 208–9
        Fingal's Cave overture, 173
        First Symphony, 61, 171–2
        Hebrides Overture, 85
        Midsummer Night's Dream
            Overture, 103–4, 106, 109–
            10, 189–90, 215
        operas, 10, 110–12, 116–18, 140
        oratorios (St. Paul/Elijah), 223–
            33
        Piano Concerto in D minor, 86–7
        Quartet in C minor (Opus 1), 6
        Quartet in F minor, 242
        Reformation Symphony, 86,
            113–14

Ruy Blas Overture, 142–3
Scottish Symphony in A minor,
 182
songs, 210
Songs without Words, 157–8,
 201
Mendelssohn, Karl (son), 213, 214
Mendelssohn, Lea (mother), 7–8, 35–6,
 41–2, 44–5
 descriptions of, 4, 16n., 27
Mendelssohn, Marie (daughter), 213
Mendelssohn, Moses (grandfather), 4
Mendelssohn, Paul (brother), 27–8,
 249, 250
Mendelssohn, Paul (son), 213, 214
Mendelssohn, Rebecka (sister), 45–7,
 27, 50, 193
Meyerbeer, Giacomo, 159, 162, 176
Moore, Joseph, 227, 232
Moscheles, Felix, 49–50, 56, 89–91,
 128, 196
Moscheles, Ignaz, 25, 81, 123, 135–6,
 140
 on M's family/marriage, 26, 42,
 50–1, 55
 on Birmingham Festival (1846),
 232
 plays duets with M, 127
 on M's last days, 247–50
Moscheles, Mrs., 123
Mounsey, Elizabeth, 134, 136
Mozart, Wolfgang Amadeus, 186
 Mozart's music, 83–4, 96, 102,
 115, 127, 145, 164
Müller, F. Max, 30, 180–1, 197, 233

Novello, Clara, 147
Novello, Sabilla, 141
Novello, Vincent, 134–5, 137

O'Leary, Arthur, 141

Paganini, Niccolo, 141
Philharmonic Society orchestra, 64–5,
 145–53
Phillips, Henry, 224–6
Plaidy, Herr, 73
Polko, Elise, 87–8
Pountney, William, 227–8, 229, 230

Reinecke, Carl, 76–7
Rellstab, H. F. Ludwig, 81–5
Richter, F., 73
Rietz, Edward, 199
Rockstro, William Smith, 71–6, 136–8,
 166–7, 213–15, 231
Rosen, Friedrich, 129, 197
Rossini, Gioacchino Antonio, 46, 178–
 9, 241, 245

Sainton-Dolby, Charlotte, 226–7
Schleinitz, Dr., 208, 237, 250
Schlesinger, Therese, 199
Schubring, Julius, 7, 61, 112–13, 188–
 91, 223, 252
Schumann, Clara, 95, 164–7, 201,
 253
Schumann, Robert, 64, 89, 132–3, 157–
 66, 201, 239
Shakespeare's plays, 242–3
Shaw, Mrs Alfred, 147
Smart, G., 149
Society of British Musicians, 144
Souchay, Edouard, 43–4
Spohr, Ludwig, 163
Staudigl, Joseph, 225, 228, 230
Sterndale Bennett *see* Bennett
Stimpson, Mr., 229
Sutcliffe Smith, J., 228–30

Taylor, Bayard, 217–19
Taylor, John Edward, 126
Taylor, Miss, 124–6

Varnhagen, Rahel, 200
Veit, Philippe, 43
Verdi, 245
Victoria, Queen, 138–40

Wagner, Richard, 63–5, 215–17
Wasielewski, Josef von, 77
Weber, Carl Maria von, 6, 114, 186
 Concert-Stück, 72
 Gipsies' March, 127
Wenzel, Herr, 73
Wieck, Clara *see* Schumann, Clara
Willis, Richard Storrs, 192

Zelter, Carl Friedrich, 9–12

Beyer on, 8
Devrient on, 14–15
Dorn on, 199–200
Hiller on, 210–11

Mendelssohn on, 77
Rellstab on, 82, 84
Zimmerman, Johanna, 198, 199, 200, 201